Baedeker

Rome

Contents

Nature, Culture, History
Pages 7–33

Sights from A to Z
Pages 37–159

Practical Information from A to Z
Pages 161–209

The Principal Sights at a Glance

Preface

This Pocket Guide to Rome is one of the new generation of Baedeker city guides.

Baedeker pocket guides, illustrated throughout in colour, are designed to meet the needs of the modern traveller. They are quick and easy to consult, with the principal sights described in alphabetical order and practical details about times of opening, how to get there, etc., shown in the margin.

Each guide is divided into three parts. The first part gives a general account of the city, its history, prominent personalities and so on; in the second part the principal sights are described; and the third part contains a variety of practical information designed to help visitors to find their way about and make the most of their stay.

The new guides are abundantly illustrated and contain numbers of newly drawn plans. At the back of the book is a large city map, and each entry in the main part of the guide gives the co-ordinates of the square on the map in which the particular feature can be located. Users of this guide, therefore, will have no difficulty in finding what they want to see.

How to use this book

Following the tradition established by Karl Baedeker in 1844, sights of particular interest, and hotels and restaurants of particular quality are distinguished by either one ★ or two ★★ stars.

To make it easier to locate the various sights listed in the "A to Z" section of the Guide, their co-ordinates on the large city map are shown in red at the head of each entry, e.g. ★Colosseo E 7 .

Only a selection of hotels, restaurants and shops can be given; no reflection is implied, therefore, on establishments not included.

The symbol ⓘ on a town plan indicates the local tourist office from which further information can be obtained. The post-horn symbol indicates a post office.

In a time of rapid change it is difficult to ensure that all the information given is entirely accurate and up to date, and the possibility of error can never be completely eliminated. Although the publishers can accept no responsibility for in-accuracies and omissions, they are always grateful for corrections and suggestions for improvement.

Facts and Figures

Coat of Arms of Rome
SPQR
Senatus Populus Que Romanus
Senate and People of Rome

General

Rome is the capital of the Italian Republic, the seat of the President (official residence the Quirinal Palace), of the government and of the two houses of Parliament (the Senate in Palazzo Madama, the Chamber of Deputies in Palazzo Montecitorio). Within the territory of Rome is the state of Vatican City, the smallest state in the world (area 0.44sq.km/110 acres), ruled by the Pope, who is also head of the Roman Catholic Church.

Rome is situated in the region of Latium in central Italy, in latitude 41° 52′ north and 12° 30′ east on the River Tiber, some 20km/12 miles inland from the Tyrrhenian Sea in the Campagna di Roma.

Situation

The city of Rome (Comune di Roma), chief town of the province of the same name (c. 4 million inhabitants) and of the region of Latium (Lazio), has an area of 1507sq.km/582sq. miles and a population of 2,723,300 (1992).

Area and population

Traditionally Rome was built on seven hills – the Capitol (Campidoglio), Palatine (Palatino), Aventine (Aventino), Quirinal (Quirinale), Viminal (Viminale), Esquiline (Esquilino) and Caelian (Celio); the Janiculum (Gianicolo) and the Pincian (Pincio) are not included within the traditional seven. The historic centre of the "Eternal City" was bounded on the west by the Tiber and on the East by the Servian Walls (parts of which are still visible), built in the 4th c. B.C. Around this central core there grew up whole new districts, which the Emperor Aurelian surrounded with a protective ring of walls at the end of the 3rd c. A.D. In

Topography

◄ Oceanus, god of the sea on the Trevi Fountain

7

the course of centuries further districts developed, such as the Borgo Pio around the Vatican and Ostiense around the church of San Paolo fuori le Mura; and after Rome became capital of a united Italy in 1870 new quarters including Prati and Paroli developed. The suburbs of Greater Rome now extend far into the surrounding plain, the Roman Campagna, in the north and south.

Districts

The city is traditionally divided into 22 *rioni* or wards (the older parts of the town), 18 *quartieri* (the new districts), 11 *suburbi* (suburban districts) and the Agro Romano, by far the largest of the units in the area. In antiquity the Agro Romano served the city with agricultural produce and fresh meat until the construction of the Aurelian walls, when it reverted to fallow land and became a strategic defence against enemy invasion. Following the recent administrative reform Rome is now divided into 20 *circoscrizioni* (districts).

Administration

The Comune di Roma is governed by a Mayor and a Municipal Council, the headquarters of which are on the Capitol. Local government elections are held every five years. The organisation of the new *circoscrizioni* is still at an early stage.

Borgate

Since the 1930s numerous new suburbs (the "borgate") have been developed around Rome. Their residents are farm workers, those unskilled and without possessions, who left the south of Italy (Mezzogiorno) to seek a better life in Rome. The strict limitation imposed on the influx of people into the capital was counteracted by a government housing programme and the construction of settlements outside Rome. The first housing was primitive and overcrowded; at the end of the Second World War the housing shortage was acute. The next generation of Borgate houses were distributed haphazardly around the Roman countryside (e.g. in Torre Angela). Daily life in the Borgate nowadays is dominated by unemployment and increasing crime. These problems, as described by Pier Paolo Pasolini in his novel about the Borgate, have also affected the more modern settlements of Laurentina, Corviale, Spinaceto and Tor Bell Monaco.

Restoration

The huge increase of vehicles in use and the emission from oil-fired heating has led to excessive pollution in Rome. Centuries old buildings quickly fall victim to pollution. Since the early 1980s comprehensive restoration has been undertaken. The long-term plans are to restrict the amount of traffic in the inner city, e.g. on the Via dei Imperiali, and create archaeological "zones". In the meantime the extent of the restoration work necessary is still evident as numerous building are encased in scaffolding.

Population and Religion

Population

The rise of Rome to become the capital of a world empire was accompanied by a steady increase in population, so that by the beginning of the Christian era the city had a population of about a million. After the fall of the Western Empire the population dropped to 25,000, recovered during the golden centuries of the medieval period and then fell even lower, before beginning to increase again slowly after the Pope's return from exile in Avignon (15th c.). In 1870 the city's population was 200,000, in 1921 some 700,000. In the last sixty years the total has risen to about three million as a result of the drift of the rural population from the provinces and immigrants from southern Italy. In the inner city the population is decreasing. The principal cause of this is the laws governing rents; these were kept so low that no landlord would spend money on his property. Tenants were forced to move from rundown dwellings to the new areas in the suburbs. When houses are empty they are

View from Gianicolo over Trastevere to the inner city

lavishly renovated and let at many times the original figure to firms or foreigners to whom the regulations do not apply.

But the population which fills the streets of Rome is not made up solely of Italians. Apart from the hundreds of thousands of tourists there are very many priests and nuns from all over the world, and in recent years there have been increasing numbers of Africans from former Italian colonies such as Somalia as well as immigrants from other countries.

The overwhelming majority of the membership of the Catholic Church is, in the truest sense of the word, *Roman* Catholic. The Jewish synagogue, the churches of other Christian denominations and the mosque and Islamic cultural centre, now under construction on Monte Antenne, are a reminder of the fact that almost every other religious confession is represented in Rome. Many countries have their own national churches in the city, including the Anglican church in Via dei Babuino, the Church of Scotland in Via XX Settembre and the American church in Via Napoli.

Religion

Transport

Rome lies on both banks of the Tiber, some 20–30km/10–20 miles above its mouth. In ancient times seagoing ships could sail right up the river to the city, but in the course of centuries the Tiber has silted up and is now used only by small craft and houseboats. Ostia, which was one of the largest ports in the Mediterranean in Roman times, is now suitable only for fishing boats and pleasure craft. The Mediterranean port for Rome is now Civitavecchia, 85km/53 miles to the north-west of the city.

Port

9

Culture

Airports

Rome has two large international airports, the Leonardo da Vinci Airport in Fiumicino (scheduled services, both domestic and international), situated on the coast 25km/15 miles west of the city, and Ciampino Airport (mainly charter flights and military traffic), about 14km/9 miles from the city on the Via Appia Nuova. The Aeroporta dell'Urbe is used only by light aircraft (sightseeing flights for tourists).

Railway and Underground

Rome is an important railway junction for traffic between northern and southern Italy and services to the east of the country, but the railways play little part in transport within the city. Altogether Rome has only ten railway stations; the Vatican has its own station. The main station is Stazione Termini, at which most long-distance trains arrive, though some use the Tiburtina and Ostiense stations.

Most of the city's business and commuting traffic is carried by buses.

Rome has two underground railway lines in the Metropolitana system. The first (line B) runs from the Termini station to the EUR district and on to Ostia; the second (line A), completed in 1980, runs from Cinecittà (Film City), south-east of the city, by way of Termini to the district just north of St Peter's.

Visitors who are not pressed for time can have a leisurely trip around central Rome on the "Circolare", one of the last surviving tram routes.

Motorways and trunk roads

In ancient Rome nine great consular highways started from the Golden Milestone in the Forum Romanum – the Aurelia, Cassia, Flaminia, Salaria, Tiburtina, Prenestina, Casilina, Tuscolana and Appia. These main routes – now all represented by modern roads folllowing the same line – were supplemented by an excellent network of secondary and minor roads.

Modern traffic is served by a ring road of motorway standard round the city. The Grande Raccordo Annulare, and a number of motorways which replace or supplement the old trunk roads:

A1: north to Florence, Bologna, Milan and the Brenner Pass.
A2: south to Naples, Bari, Reggio di Calabria and Sicily.
A12: north-west to Civitavecchia, connecting to Leonardo da Vinci Airport.
A24: east to L'Aquila, the Gran Sasso andd Pescara.
There is also an expressway to Latina.

Inner city traffic

Rome's city traffic is generally chaotic. For many years no action was taken to alleviate the problem, and now radical recommendations have been made to bar traffic from certain parts of the city, e.g. from the Centro Storico, already operating a permit-only system. As this may prove an unpopular solution, the government is unlikely to support these plans, and traffic conditions will remain the same for some time to come.

Culture

General

Although Rome was capital of the Papal States for many centuries, it did not become capital of the whole of Italy until 1870, and accordingly its dominance in the fields of culture and scholarship is less firmly established than in other more centrally organised states, since the old capitals of the various republics, grand duchies and kingdoms into which Italy was formerly divided, still retain something of their former importance in these fields. However, with its universities, scientific institutes, its libraries, its opera house, theatres and orchestras, Rome has a rich cultural and intellectual life, and one that by no means looks back to its past greatness.

Universities and libraries

Rome's University City, home of the State University of Rome, was built between 1932 and 1935. For many centuries higher education was

Roman mosaics . . .   *. . . in St Clement's Church*

Jacob and Joseph Lünette in the Sistine Chapel

The elegant Via Condotti from the bottom of the Spanish Steps

in the hands of Papal academies and institutions run by religious orders, in particular the "Sapienza", and in addition to the University of Rome with its fourteen faculties and 130,000 students, an important part is still played by the Università Cattolica del Sacro Cuore (Catholic University of the Sacred Heart, a school of medicine), the Pro Deo International University of Social studies and the Papal universities, chief among them the Gregoriana (a Jesuit institution), which train candidates from all over the world for the priesthood.

Numerous libraries (state-run, Papal and private), with their stocks of manuscripts and incunabula, as well as later printed books down to the most recent literature, cater for the needs of scholarship.

Museums — Rome has 70 museums. The most popular, apart from the Vatican museums with one and a half million visitors a year, is the Museo Nazionale Etrusco in the Villa Giulia (*c.* 100,000 visitors annually); only half as many visitors go to the Museo Nazionale Romano, probably because of the lengthy restoration work which restricts viewing of the collections.

Academies and learned societies — With its wealth of ancient buildings, churches and museums, Rome offers unique scope for artistic, historical, archaeological and religious studies. There are numerous State-sponsored and Papal academies and institutes concerned with the study of the Roman past and with the promotion of culture and scholarship, including the Accademia Nazionale dei Lincei (founded 1603) and the Accademia Nazionale San Luca (with its own gallery). Many foreign countries maintain learned institutions of high standing in Rome, including the British, American and Swedish Schools, the French Academy and the German Archae- ological Institute.

Theatres and orchestras — Rome has some 40 theatres, with a new one being established every now and then or an old one closing down. Touring companies still give the majority of performances, though many companies have been formed in Rome in recent years. Plays by Pirandello, Goldini, Shakespeare, Brecht and Strindberg are particularly popular with Roman audiences.

Commerce and industry

As capital of the Roman Empire, Rome was also the leading economic and commercial centre in the Mediterranean, a role it has never recovered, either under the Popes, the kings of Italy or the present republic. In the industrial development of Europe and the commercial activity of modern times it has occupied a marginal position. Only in the fields of films and fashion has Rome a commercial function extending beyond Italy. Rome has established its international status in the spheres of art and religion, but it has rarely played a comparable part in the economic and social fields.

International status

The main centres of industry and commerce in Italy have long been in the north, in Piedmont and Lombardy, Liguria and Veneto. However, since much of the Italian economy has been nationalised in recent years, Rome has gained increased importance as the headquarters of state-run industries. Its situation in central Italy also gives it an important economic role as a bridge between the north and south of the country.

National position

Today, as in the past, Rome has little industry, and the majority of the working population is employed in administration and the service trades. The distortion of the employment pattern reflects the fact that Rome has never established an industrial tradition but has continued to acquire increased administrative functions, as well as being one of the great Meccas for tourists and pilgrims. In recent years, however, the number of small industrial establishments in the area around Rome has increased. Rome is becoming more and more important as a banking and insurance centre.

Industrial tradition

Prominent Figures in Roman History

Pope Alexander VI
(c. 1431–1503)

Posterity has branded Pope Alexander VI (1492–1503) as a nepotist and libertine. Though he brought no credit to the Church, his reign is commemorated by a small coat of arms on the walls of the Vatican Palace (at the end of the right-hand colonnade, near the post office). His main object was the aggrandisement of the Borgia family to which he belonged; using the Papacy as an instrument, he sought to establish himself as the ruler of a hereditary monarchy and for this purpose to secularise the States of the Church.

A cardinal at the age of 26, he learned in the world of the Italian Renaissance to forget all scruples. Although a man of driving energy and a great patron of the arts, he dishonoured his position as the "vicar of Christ" and successor to St Peter by his addiction to sexual pleasures. Savonarola, falling foul of the Borgias, died at the stake; the Papacy survived.

Augustus
(63 B.C.–A.D. 14)

Augustus, originally Gaius Octavianus, Caesar's grand-nephew and adoptive son, became the first Emperor (Imperator) of the Roman Empire. In 43 B.C. he allied himself with Mark Antony and Lepidus as a member of the Triumvirate established to conduct the war against Caesar's murderers. The three triumvirs divided the territories held by Rome between them, Augustus taking the west, Mark Antony the east, Lepidus Africa. After defeating Antony and Cleopatra at Actium in 31 B.C., Augustus became sole ruler. In the Augustan age which followed he pacified the Empire, strengthened its frontier defences and was a generous patron of art and learning. The poets of the period included Virgil, Horace and Ovid. His most notable monuments in Rome are his Mausoleum, with the Ara Pacis (Altar of Peace), and his house on the Palatine. A bust and a marble statue in the Vatican Museums depict him in a magnificent – if idealised – aspect.

Gian Lorenzo
Bernini
(1598–1680)

Baroque Rome would be unthinkable without Gian Lorenzo Bernini, son of the sculptor Pietro Bernini, who left his mark on the city, both as architect and as sculptor. Popes and cardinals commissioned countless buildings and works of sculpture from him, and his patrons can often be identified by the heraldic devices which he incorporated into the decoration of a building. Under the 17th c. Popes, Urban VIII (1623–44: the three bees of the Barberini family), Innocent X Pamphili (1644–55: a dove holding a branch surmounted by lilies) and Alexander VII Chigi (1655-67: a tree and a star over a hill), Bernini created a whole series of masterpieces, spurred on by his bitter rivalry with his great contemporary Borromini: the bronze baldacchino and the tomb of Urban VIII in St Peter's, the figure of St Theresa in ecstasy in Santa Maria della Vittoria, the Fountain of the Four Rivers in the Piazza Navona, St Peter's Square with its colonnades, the Church of Sant'Andrea al Quirinale, the Scala Regia in the Vatican and the statues now to be seen in the Villa Borghese Museum, to name only a few.

Julius Caesar
(100–44 B.C.)

Gaius Julius Caesar, a talented general, ambitious politician, generous victor and historian, who prided himself on his literary skill, was the outstanding figure of the closing years of the republican period, of such commanding historical stature that his name was given to the holder of supreme political power, the Caesar (which later gave the German "Kaiser").

Originally destined for the priesthood, he began his military career in 81 B.C., studied in Rhodes from 76 to 73 and was elected to the post of

Julius Caesar

Bernini

Emperor Hadrian

Pontifex Maximus in 63. He allied himself with Pompey and later with Crassus, and thereafter, as a member of the first Triumvirate, was able to put his political and social ideas into effect against the will of the Senate. From 58 to 51 he was engaged in the Gallic War, first dealing with the Helvetii and then subduing Gaul (53 B.C.); in 55 he crossed the Rhine into Germany, and in that and the following year launched two brief invasions of Britain. In 49 he crossed the River Rubicon in northern Italy, thus bringing his army, without permission, into territory under the authority of the Senate. After fighting in Spain and Greece, spending half a year in the Egyptian city of Alexandria (where the Egyptian queen Cleopatra bore him a son) and waging further wars in Africa and Spain, he was appointed Dictator in 48 B.C. and confirmed in that office with a ten-year tenure in 46. As Dictator he ruled like an absolute monarch, lived in regal state and claimed quasi-divine veneration (in the Forum of Caesar which he built below the Capitol). All this increased the number of his enemies, and on the Ides of March he was murdered by a group of conspirators, including his "son" Brutus.

Giorgio de Chirico was born in 1888 in Volos, capital of Thessaly, Greece, of Italian parents. He studied at the Academy of Art in Munich from 1906 to 1909, where he was introduced to the paintings of Arnold Böcklin and Max Klinger, and to the writings of Schopenhauer and Nietzsche. The artist moved constantly, but after the Second World War he settled in Rome, where he died in 1978.

Giorgio de Chirico (1888–1978)

De Chirico, with Carlo Carrà, is considered to be the founder of the "Pittura Metafisica" movement of modern Italian painting. His pictures, harsh and three-dimensional, portray mundane objects and townscapes, which are made to appear alien and mysterious through the unusual combination with other objects, particularly mannequins. There is an emptiness in the restrained use of colour which is infused with a sense of metaphysical dread. From 1919/20 onwards de Chirico abandoned the Pittura Metafisica. Of his earlier works, forerunners of Surrealism, the most important are: "The Soothsayer's Reward" (1913), "Secret and Melancholy of a Street" (1914), "The Great Metaphysician" (1917) and "Large Metaphysical Interior" (1917).

Constantine (Flavius Valerius Constantinus) lived as a young man at Diocletian's court, and thus gained at an early age some understanding of the conduct of public business, as well as witnessing the Diocletianic persecution of Christians. In 306 he became joint Caesar with Maxentius, whom he defeated at the Milvian Bridge (still standing) in 312. In 324 he defeated his other rival Lucinius. With the Edict of Milan (313), which allowed Christians freedom of worship, he prepared the way for

Constantine I, the Great (c. 285–337)

Christianity to become the state religion. In 330 he transferred the imperial capital from Rome to the newly founded city of Constantinople (later Byzantium, and still later Istanbul). He was baptised shortly before his death in 337, and is venerated as a saint by the Greek, Armenian and Russian churches.

Remains in Rome dating from his reign include the Basilica of Maxentius in the Forum (which he completed), Santa Costanza (built to house the tomb of his daughter), parts of a colossal statue of the Emperor in the Palazzo dei Conservatori on the Capitol and the early Christian basilicas which were begun while he was in power.

Enrico Fermi
(1901–1954)

The physicist Enrico Fermi was born in Rome; he was chiefly concerned with the theories of quantum mechanics (of Werner Heisenberg, 1925, and others). His research led to the discovery of the production of new artificial radioactive elements, and he was awarded the Nobel Prize for Physics in 1938.

In 1942 Fermi succeeeded in producing the first controlled nuclear reaction at the University of Chicago, in a purpose-built uranium reactor which he had developed. The first commercial breeder reactor (Detroit, USA) was named after him, as was the US Atomic Energy Commission's Enrico Fermi Prize, awarded annually since 1954. Fermi died in Chicago.

Pope Gregory I,
the Great
(c. 540–604)

Gregory was a scion of the Roman senatorial aristocracy. The judgements of his contemporaries and of ecclesiastical historians range from admiration to condemnation, for he was a man of contrasts, with good qualities and bad. He is perhaps best known nowadays for sending the first missionaries to England. Extremely wealthy, he himself founded the monasteries in which he lived as a Benedictine monk. He had voluntarily chosen a lowly manner of life, but there was no true humility in this, for he strove too hard and too blatantly to gain the favour of the Romans. In the style "servant of the servants of God", which he assumed for himself and his successors, there is an element of the false modesty which counts itself as a merit. Gregory was a monk, a vocation which in him seemed to carry with it a certain narrowness and pettiness, but this nevertheless had the result of enhancing the religious dimension of the Papacy. When old and ailing, tortured by gout, he wrote edifying literature, including a "Pastoral Rule", which was diligently studied by the churchmen of the Middle Ages.

Pope Gregory VII
(c. 1019/1030–
1085)

Gregory VII (Pope 1073–85), "a monk from his mother's womb" – fanatically devoted to the spiritual life and despising all things terrestrial, uncompromising to the point of self-forgetfulness – restored the standing of the Papacy after centuries of decadence. The "monk Hildebrand", feared and cursed by emperors and kings but canonised by the Church, sought to bring the Church back to purity. Small in stature and physically unimpressive but filled with inflexible determination, with a manner that was seldom winning and usually harsh and challenging, he had only one objective – to raise the status of the Papacy and renew the spirit of the Church – and he was strengthened in his endeavours by the assurance of his transcendental mission. He employed a variety of means to help towards achieving his aims – the prohibition of simony (the sale of ecclesiastical offices) and the marriage of priests, the excommunication of King Henry IV of Germany, crusades against the infidel. He did not scruple to enforce the Church's claims by the sword. Nor did he conceal his urge to dominate and command; he demanded only one thing – obedience. Showing little love for any man and inspiring little love in return, a bitter hater and bitterly hated, he drove the course of history on, and the German king was compelled to do penance at Canossa. Gregory had no sense of moderation, but had he not set himself such far-reaching goals, the Papacy would have sunk into mediocrity.

Hadrian (Publius Aelius Hadrianus), Trajan's successor and, like him, born in Spain, was Emperor from 117 to 138. One of the first concerns of his long reign was to strengthen the defences of the Empire, and he was responsible for the construction of two fortified frontier lines, Hadrian's Wall in England and the Limes in Germany, of which substantial remains survive. He liked to travel widely and is said to have visited every province in the Empire; as far away as Luxor in Egypt there is an inscription in his name on the Colossi of Memnon. This emperor, with the beard of a philosopher, whose favourite city was Athens, was a great admirer of Greek culture and promoted the diffusion of Hellenistic thought in the Roman world. He was a great builder, and there is much evidence of this still to be seen in Rome – the Mausoleum of Hadrian (Castel Sant'Angelo), the Pantheon and Hadrian's villa at nearby Tivoli.

Hadrian
(76–138)

The desperate rising of the Jews under Bar Kochba in Judaea (132–135) took place during Hadrian's reign.

A member of the Lombard nobility who became Pope at the age of 37, Innocent III was a man of commanding personality. Imperious and a born ruler, he nevertheless sought conciliation. There were many sides to his nature; he could be haughty and commanding or mild and sympathetic, winning and humorous or majestic and unapproachable. He saw the kingdoms and peoples of the world as fit subjects for his rule. Innocent was a shrewd politician, but not wise enough to leave politics alone on occasion, and too much of a politician to be always wise. He was the most fully rounded man to occupy the Papal throne, and during his reign the Papacy was seen in its most powerful form.

Pope Innocent III
(c. 1160/1–1216)

Two Popes are generally granted the style of "the Great", Leo I and Gregory I. Leo (Pope 440–461), a Tuscan, was determined to assert his rule and extend the powers of the Papacy and use them to the full. He was the first Pope to realise clearly the potentialities of his office, and the pride of the aristocrat whose secular power had been destroyed by the fall of the Western Empire was now projected into the spiritual field. The primacy of the Church in Rome was established and consolidated through Leo's skill in formulating its doctrine and its bold conception of the role of the Pope; it was reflected in the practical administration of the Church and given expression in the orthodox creed. Leo's courage was demonstrated during the troubled period of the great migrations. Raphael did him honour in the Stanze in the Vatican, Leo XII in a marble relief in St Peter's (far end of the left-hand aisle).

Pope Leo I, the
Great
(d. 461)

Marcus Aurelius Antoninus was Emperor from 161 to 180. Born in 121 he attracted the interest of Hadrian at an early age and by his desire was adopted by Hadrian's successor Antoninus Pius and initiated into the business of government. Marcus Aurelius was faced throughout his reign with ever increasing external dangers – the Chatti in Germany, the Caledonians in Britain – while in Syria the Parthians shook off the Roman yoke. The security of the Empire was threatened by risings of the Quadi, the Marcomanni, the Jazyges, a people of herdsmen in the Nile delta, and the Moors in Spain. Marcus Aurelius died in Vindobona (Vienna) in 180. In spite of his numerous wars he is thought of as the philosopher on the Roman Imperial throne.

Marcus Aurelius
(121–180)

Michelangelo Buonarotti, a Renaissance genius who was sculptor, painter, architect and poet, and perhaps the greatest artist of all time, was born in Caprese (Casentino, Tuscany) and spent his youth and period of apprenticeship in Florence, to which he constantly returned after a year spent working in Bologna (1494–5) and several long stays in Rome. Florence was then ruled by the Medici, those great patrons of the arts, for whom Michelangelo produced numerous works.

Michelangelo
(1475–1564)

Marcus Aurelius

Michelangelo

Raffael

His first stay in Rome, during which he created the "Pietà" in St Peter's, began in 1496. In 1505 Pope Julius II della Rovere summoned him back to the Vatican and invited him to design his tomb. (This commission was a burden to Michelangelo for most of his life; even after the Pope's death there were still disputes with his heirs.) Between 1508 and 1512 Michelangelo laboured on the frescoes of the Creation on the ceiling of the Sistine Chapel; in 1513–14 he carved two figures of slaves (now in the Louvre) for Julius' monument, and thereafter until 1516 worked on his famous figure of Moses, now in San Pietro in Vincoli in Rome. The completion of the Pope's tomb continued to be delayed, with repeated alterations in the design.

In Florence (1520–34) Michelangelo was responsible for the building of the Medici chapel of San Lorenzo and the sculpture for the Medici tombs.

Between 1536 and 1541 he created the famous fresco of the Last Judgment on the altar wall of the Sistine Chapel, perhaps the most magnificent painting in the world. In 1545 Julius II's tomb was finally set up in San Pietro in Vincoli. Michelangelo now increasingly occupied himself with architecture, working on the Palazzo Farnese, the Piazza del Campidoglio and St Peter's, whose gigantic dome is his greatest architectural achievement.

After a richly creative life, during which he had known difficulties but could look back on tremendous achievements, Michelangelo died in Rome in 1564. His tomb is in the Church of Santa Croce in Florence.

Alberto Moravia
(1907–90)

Alberto Moravia was born A. Pincherle in Rome, the son of Moravian immigrants. He is considered one of the leading exponents of psychological realism in Italy. He was president of the International PEN Club from 1959 to 1962. The author deals mainly with the inter-relationship between the sexes and family psychology. As a keen, though ironic and distanced observer, he relates episodes from the lives of the middle classes and from the prostitute's environment. Moravia mercilessly criticises the middle classes and their moral indifference; alienation and boredom are constant themes in all his works. As well as many novels and short stories, Alberto Moravia has written plays, essays and travel guides.

Nero
(A.D. 37–68)

Claudius Drusus Germanicus Nero, who liked to see himself as a poet, musician and painter rather than as a ruler required to take political decisions, was Emperor from A.D. 58 to 68. Coming to power as a mere youth, he was only 31 when he died. In his early years of rule he behaved with moderation, but later instituted a reign of terror, in the course of which he murdered both his mother (A.D. 59) and his wife

Octavia (A.D. 62). He was believed to have been responsible for the burning of Rome in 64, though he himself attributed the blame to the Christians, whom he accordingly persecuted. In the year 68 there was unrest in many provinces of the Empire, and Nero, outlawed by the Senate, committed suicide.

The name of the Colosseum comes from the colossal statue of Nero which stood there. His "Golden House", a gigantic palace on the Mons Oppidus, provided a stimulus for Renaissance painters and sculptors.

This Pope of the Baroque period can fairly be mentioned in the same breath as the great figures of antiquity; indeed he himself invited the comparison by setting up a statue of himself on the façade of St Peter's, with the inscription "Paulus Burghesius Romanus" and a crowned eagle in his coat of arms. During his reign he incurred the charge of nepotism, though in other respects his life style was modest.

Pope Paul V
(1552–1621)

It was long since the world had revolved round Rome (indeed it was now known to revolve round the sun; Galileo's first trial was held in Paul's reign), and the States of the Church were now only of marginal importance in European affairs. Although this was apparent to others, Paul – a cultivated but stubbornly contentious lawyer – did not fully appreciate it and overestimated his influence on the great powers. All the efforts of his diplomats could not prevent the outbreak of the Thirty Years' War, in which the whole of Europe was soon embroiled.

Luigi Pirandello, born in Sicily, studied philology in Palermo, Rome and Bonn. In 1925 he founded the "Teatro d'Arte" and received the Nobel Prize for Literature in 1934.

Luigi Pirandello
(1867–1936)

The author, one of the most important dramatists and novelists of this century, first wrote realistic novels and stories set in his native Sicily. He turned to stage plays when he was over 50 years old and liberated the Italian theatre from its mainly provincial traditions. Pirandello's principal theme is the constant reversal of appearance and reality; man can never be fixed as a natural or social being and is never sure of his own reality. Psychologically Pirandello anticipates existentialist thought which emerged after the Second World War, particularly in French literature. His plays, such as "The Fool's Cap" (1917) and "Henry IV" (1922) are more like sketches than complete stage plays. In "Six Characters in Search of an Author" (1921) Pirandello created an effective vehicle to portray the interaction of appearance and reality, when six people enter a play rehearsal, looking for an author to write the drama of their own lives.

Raphael – Raffaello Santi or Sanzio – was born in 1483 in Urbino (Marche region) and died in Rome in 1520. Like Michelangelo he was a painter, sculptor and architect, but it is mainly his paintings that have earned him his world renown. He began his career as assistant to his father, Giovanni Santi, who was also a painter, and thereafter he became a pupil of Perugino. In 1504 he went to Florence and in 1508 to Rome, where seven years later, at the age of 32, he was put in charge of the building of St Peter's and made conservator of ancient monuments. The young painter gained the favour of Roman society and was given many commissions, while he appealed to ordinary people with the fervent piety of his Madonnas, works of incomparable beauty. His greatest achievement is to be seen in the Stanze di Raffaello in the Vatican – the magnificent frescoes which represent the high point of Renaissance painting.

Raphael
(1483–1520)

Whether Romulus and Remus ever existed may be questioned, but at any rate legend ascribes the foundation of Rome to Romulus, who is said to have established the first settlement on the Palatine, to have laid down military and civil regulations for the new town and to have

Romulus and
Remus

formed the Romans on the Palatine and the Sabines on the Quirinal into a single community. His origins were also shrouded in legend. Romulus and Remus were said to have been the twin sons of the god Mars and Rhea Silvia, daughter of King Numitor of Alba Longa. Amulius, Numidor's brother, had driven him from the throne and made Rhea Silvia a vestal virgin (and accordingly subject to a vow of chastity), thus securing undisputed power for himself. He caused the twins, Romulus and Remus to be exposed soon after their birth, but they were suckled by a she-wolf (which became the heraldic animal of Rome) and later found by a shepherd named Faustulus. They then killed their uncle, founded Rome and carried out the rape of the Sabine women to provide wives for the men of Rome. During the battle with the Sabines Romulus killed his brother Remus.

The death of Romulus was also the subject of numerous legends. he was said to have been murdered, to have disappeared into the earth, together with his horse, on the site of the Forum and to have ascended to join the gods. However this may be, he was worshipped in Rome as a god.

Trajan
(A.D. 53–117)

Trajan (Marcus Ulpius Traianus) was the first native of Spain to become Emperor. Having been adopted by the Emperor Nerva by virtue of his outstanding military and political capacity, he came to the imperial throne in 98 and reigned until 117.

During Trajan's reign the Roman Empire reached its greatest extent. In the two Dacian wars he subdued Dacia, a country rich in gold (cf. the scenes on Trajan's Column), and in the Parthian war he advanced into Mesopotamia and Assyria. In 117, however, the oppressed Parthians and Jews rose against Roman rule. Trajan's frequent campaigns earned him the name of the "soldier Emperor". He died in the town of Selinus in Asia Minor on his way back from the Persian Gulf.

He left his monument in the form of the Forum of Trajan, with the famous column, originally crowned by a statue of the Emperor.

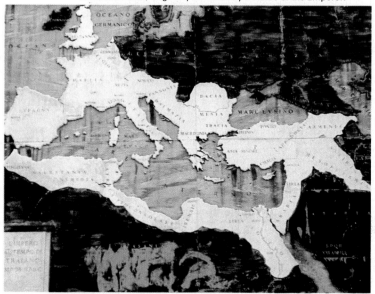

The Roman Empire reaches its greatest extent under Trajan

History of Rome

Chronology

Many explanations have been put forward to show why a group of small Etruscan, Latin and Sabine settlements in the lower Tiber valley developed into the great city of Rome, the "Eternal City", *caput mundi* ("head of the world"), capital of the Roman Empire, focal point of western Christendom and the Roman Catholic Church and one of the great artistic centres of the world. It is one of the enigmas of history, however, how great centres of political power and culture come into being.

The Romans dated the foundation of Rome to April 21st 753 B.C. and surrounded the event with a web of legend; the story of Romulus, who together with his twin brother was exposed and left to die by a wicked king, but who was found and brought up by a she-wolf (or by a shepherd) and established the settlement on the Palatine to which he gave his name. However this may be, there is evidence of the existence of a settlement at the beginning of the first millennium B.C.; this increased in size, had its religious, political and military centre on the Capitol, was ruled for a period by kings probably stemming from northern Etruria and then, in 510 B.C., threw off the Etruscan yoke and became a republic. Religious and political leadership lay in the hands of the better class of citizens, the patricians, but their position was continually threatened by the ordinary people, the plebeians. In spite of these internal conflicts and of external threats from the neighbouring peoples and the Gauls (387), the city grew in size and in the 4th c. B.C. extended its authority into Latium. By the 3rd c. the republic was militarily, economically and culturally so strong – having gained control of the whole of central and southern Italy in 270 B.C. – that it was ready to aim at becoming the dominant power in the Mediterranean. After the defeat of Carthage in the three Punic Wars (between 264 and 146) there was no rival power to prevent Rome from conquering the countries bordering the Mediterranean.

Origins to mastery of the Mediterranean

The more powerful Rome became – a rise which was reflected in the erection of ever larger and more handsome buildings – the more acute became the city's internal tensions and conflicts. Peasants, soldiers and officials, nobles and plebeians were all at odds with one another, and Rome suffered a succession of civil wars, under Spartacus and the Gracchi (133–121), Marius and Sulla (120–70), Pompey and Caesar (70–44). Conspiracies and the ambitions of individuals (Cataline) brought constant unrest, and the climax came with the murder of Caesar by Brutus on the Ides of March in the year 44.

Civil wars

Although the Republic, under the rule of the consuls, had seen great constructional enterprises – aqueducts, roads, temples, public buildings – the Emperors set new standards of scale and magnificence. Augustus (31 B.C.–A.D. 14) found a city of brick and left one of marble. Nero (54–68), whether or not he ordered the burning of Rome which destroyed its slums, used the space thus made available for the erection of splendid buildings such as his Domus Aurea ("Golden House"). Vespasian (69–79) began the construction of the Flavian Amphitheatre or Colosseum, which was inaugurated by his son Titus (79–81) with a series of splendid spectacles. In the reign of Trajan (98–117), a native of Spain, the Empire reached its greatest extent – from Scotland to Mesopotamia, from the Danube to Morocco.

The Empire

Each Emperor vied with his predecessors in altering and embellishing the city, each seeking to impose his indelible stamp on Rome, in the knowledge that his successors in turn would endeavour to outdo him.

Chronology

Temples and baths, victory columns and triumphal arches, theatres, palaces and mausoleums gave Rome imperial dignity and splendour, and many of them are still imposing landmarks in the modern city.

Constantine and Christianity

In the reign of Constantine (306–337) the power of Rome declined and took on a different aspect. The edict issued by the Emperor Galerius in 311, giving all religions equal rights, ended the persecution of Christians and enabled the Christian community to erect public buildings for the purposes of worship. Constantine's victory over his co-Caesar Maxentius at the battle of the Milvian Bridge paved the way for Christianity to become the predominant religion of the Empire (Edict of Milan, 313).

Rome now became the spiritual centre of Christendom. Evidence of this new status is given by the large basilicas which were founded in the 4th and 5th c. and which still exist – St John Lateran (San Giovanni in Laterano), St Peter's (San Pietro in Vaticano), St Paul without the Walls (San Paolo fuori le Mura), St Lawrence without the Walls (San Lorenzo fuori le Mura), St Sebastian (San Sebastiano), St Stephen (San Stefano Rotondo), SS Cosmas and Damian (Santi Cosma e Damiano), St Clement (San Clemente), Santa Maria Maggiore and Santa Croce in Gerusalemme. The Bishop of Rome, as successor to St Peter, now attained a position of predominance in the Western Empire and throughout western Europe.

The great migrations

The first flowering of Christian culture was blighted by the troubled period of the great migrations of barbarian peoples. Rome was captured and plundered by Alaric's Visigoths in 410, Genseric's Vandals in 455 (though without the destruction commonly associated with the name of the Vandals) and Totila's Ostrogoths in 546. The Western Empire came to an end when Odoacer deposed the Emperor Romulus Augustulus in 476, and thereafter the Germanic peoples and the Byzantines contended for the succession. Popes Leo the Great (440–461) and Gregory the Great (590–604) sought to protect the city, but without lasting success, and the population of Rome sank to no more than 25,000.

The city began to recover only when Pope Stephen II appealed to the Frankish king, Pippin or Pepin the Short, for help against the Lombards, and in return for legitimising the Carolingian line was presented by Pippin with territories which became the nucleus of the States of the Church, and when this alliance between the German kings and the Papacy in the "Holy Roman Empire" was confirmed by Charlemagne's coronation as Emperor by Pope Leo II in St Peter's on Christmas Day in the year 800.

Rome's recovery was promoted by the support which the secular power of the Emperor was able to give to the spiritual authority of the Pope. However, this help was not always available, and when it was not the great families of the city – the Frangipani, Pierleoni, Colonna and Orsini – and the nobles of the surrounding areas became involved in bloody feuds with one another and with the Pope.

The history of the Papacy in the 9th and 10th c. is wrapped in obscurity, but about the year 100 the Popes began to regain increased authority. Their new wealth was reflected in the building and embellishing of churches; the four churches dedicated to the Virgin, Santa Maria in Cosmedin, in Trastevere, in Aracoeli and sopra Minerva are perhaps the most notable among many more. Innocent III (1198–1216) master of emperors and kings, brought the Papacy to a peak of authority which it retained for a century.

Exile of the Popes in Avignon

Rome faced a further threat when, under pressure from the French king, the Popes were compelled to reside in Avignon in southern France. During this "Babylonian captivity" (1309–77) Rome declined once again. Churches and palaces fell into ruin, the streets and squares were deserted and the population sank to 20,000.

Things were no better when the Popes returned to Rome, for between 1378 and 1417 western Christendom was wracked by the Great Schism, with rival candidates competing for the Papal throne.

During the 15th c. a succession of shrewd and intelligent Popes, inspired by the ideas of humanism and the Renaissance which was just beginning, deployed the inherited resources of the Papacy and gradually restored Rome to is position as the centre of Christendom and of European art – though they must also bear their share of responsibility for the division of western Christendom into two by the Reformation. Over three centuries, from 1417 to the end of the 17th c., the Popes turned Rome into a stage for the display of their magnificence, creating the world's most splendid city, an enchanted garden of handsome streets and squares, churches and fountains which exploited to the full the artistic resources of the Renaissance and Baroque. The greatest artists of the day vied with one another in embellishing Rome. Without Bramante, Raphael, Bernini and Borromini the Popes would not have enjoyed the stature they do; but without such princely patrons – the demanding Julius II della Rovere, the art-loving Leo X Medici, Paul III Farnese, Gregory XIII Boncompagni, Paul V Borghese – these artists could not have achieved what they did. The three bees from the Barberini coat of arms, the heraldic trademark of the great builder Urban VIII (1623–44) are found all over Rome – on the baldacchino over the high altar in St Peter's, on the Chapel of the Sacrament (also in St Peter's), on churches and fountains; but so too are the flowers and animals, the stars and hills which are the emblems of other Popes.

Renaissance and Baroque

The sack of Rome by the Emperor Charles V's landsknechts in 1527 barely disturbed the great burst of building activity; indeed it rather provided a stimulus to fresh endeavour.

During these centuries the Popes devoted themselves almost entirely to the embellishment of their city, but their temporal power now began to decline, and with it the importance of Rome. While in earlier days they had set armies in motion to achieve their aims, they were now compelled to rely on the skill and intrigues of their diplomats

Decline of Papal power

The French Revolution and the Napoleonic whirlwind which upset the old order in Europe did not leave Rome unscathed. In 1798 it became the capital of the Roman Republic, and from 1809 to 1811 it was part of the French Republic and the residence of Napoleon's only son, who bore the title of Roi de Rome. In 1814 the Congress of Vienna restored the city's status as capital of the States of the Church, with the Pope as sovereign ruler, but in 1870 the position was changed again, when the French troops which supported Papal authority were withdrawn on account of the Franco-Prussian War and Italian forces moved into the city through the Porta Pia. In the same year Rome became capital of the new kingdom of Italy, and in protest against the loss of his territories the Pope withdrew behind the walls of the Vatican.

Rome's position as the capital of Italy was reflected in the construction of numbers of government offices and public buildings, mingling the styles of the 19th c. with the architecture of earlier periods. There was a further burst of building activity when Mussolini came to power in 1922, and Rome now grew to be the largest city in the Mediterranean area. The Lateran Treaties of 1929 re-established good relations between the Italian government and the Papacy, and the Pope became sovereign ruler of the Vatican State and its extra-territorial enclaves. 19th and 20th c. Italian governments and successive Popes have fostered art and research.

Kingdom and Republic of Italy

Notable recent events in Papal Rome are the Second Vatican Council (1962–65), in which more than 3000 bishops from all over the world took part, and the election of Karol Wojtyla, Archbishop of Cracow, as Pope John Paul II in 1978 – the first non-Italian Pope for 453 years. In 1981 the Pope was attacked and wounded in St Peter's Square.

In 1984 the USA resumed full diplomatic relations with the Vatican after more than 100 years. A new concordat was signed between Italy and the Holy See (this guarantees religious freedom, but Roman Catholicism ceases to be the state religion in Italy and Rome is no longer the "Holy City").

Emperors and Popes

Not all usurpers and co-Caesars are listed.

The regnal dates for all Popes before Pontianus (230–235) are based on later reconstructions.

All Popes from Peter to Gelasius (d. 496) are venerated as saints; later Popes who have been canonised are indicated by the prefixed "St".

Year	Emperors	Popes
B.C.		
44	Murder of Caesar	
27	Octavian becomes Augustus	
A.D		
14	Tiberius	
37	Caligula	
41	Claudius	
54	Nero	
63/67		Martyrdom of Peter
64/67		Linus
68	Galba	
69	Otho	
69	Vitellius	
69	Vespasian	
79	Titus	Anencletus (Anacletus I, c. 79)
81	Domitian	Clement I (90/92)
96	Nerva	
98	Trajan	Evaristus (99/101)
		Alexander I (c. 107)
117	Hadrian	Xystus (Sixtus I, c. 116)
		Telesphorus (c. 125)
138	Antoninus Pius	Hyginus (136/138)
		Pius I (140/142)
		Anicetus (154/155)
161	Marcus Aurelius, with Lucius Verus (d. 169)	Soter (c. 166)
		Eleutherius (c. 174)
180	Commodus	Victor I (c. 189)
193	Pertinax	
193	Didius Julianus	
193	Septimius Severus	Zephrinus (198/199)
211	Caracalla, with Geta (d. 212)	
217	Macrinus	
218	Elagabalus	Calixtus I (c. 217)
222	Alexander Severus	Urban I (222)
230		Pontianus (230–235)
235	Maximinus I	Antherus (235–236)
236		Fabian (236–250)
238	Gordian I and II	
238	Pupienus	
238	Balbinus	
238	Gordian III	
244	Philip the Arab	
249	Decius	
251	Hostilianus	
253	Trebonianus Gallus	Cornelius (251–253)
253	Aemilianus	Lucius I (253–254)
254	Valerian	Stephen I (254–257)

Year	Emperors	Popes
257	Gallienus	Sixtus II (257–258)
268	Claudius II	Dionysius (*c.* 259–268)
270	Aurelian	Felix I (*c.* 269–274)
275	Tacitus	Eutychianus (*c.* 274–283)
276	Probus	
282	Carus	
283	Carinus and Numerian	Caius (*c.* 282–296)
284	Diocletian	
286	Maximian (co-Caesar until 305)	
296		Marcellinus (*c.* 296–304) Then a vacancy for three years during the Diocletianic persecutions
305	Constantius I (d. 306) and Galerius (d. 311)	
306	Constantine I (sole ruler 324–337)	
306	Severus (d. 307)	
308	Licinius (to 324, d. 325)	Marcellus (307/308)
309	Maximinus II (d. 313)	Eusebius (308/310) Miltiades Sylvester I Marcus
337	Constantine II (d. 340) Constantius II (sole ruler 350–360, d. 361) Constans (d. 350)	Julius I
352		Liberius (325–355, 358–366) Felix II (355–358)
361	Julian (the Apostate)	
363	Jovian	
364	Valentinian I (d. 375) and Valens (d. 376)	
366		Damasus I
375	Gratian (d. 383)	
375	Valentinian II (d. 392)	
379	Theodosius I (sole ruler 392–395)	
383	Arcadius	
384		Siricius
395	*Western Empire* Honorius (reigned in West 395–423)	
399		Anastasius I
401		Innocent I
417		Zosimus
418		Boniface I
422		Celestine I
425	Valentinian III	
432		Sixtus III
440		Leo I, the Great
455	Petronius Maximus	
455	Avitus	
457	Majorian	
461	Libius Severus	Hilary
467	Anthemius	
468		Simplicius
472	Olybrius	
473	Glycerius	

Emperors and Popes

Year	Emperors	Popes
474	Julius Nepos	
475	Romulus Augustulus	
476	*Fall of Western Empire*	
483		Felix III
492		Gelasius I
496		Anastasius II
498		Symmachus
514		Hormisdas
523		John I
526		Felix IV
530		Boniface II
533		John II
535		St Agapetus I
536		St Silverius
537		Vigilius
556		Pelagius I
561		John III
575		Benedict I
579		Pelagius II
590		St Gregory I, the Great
604		Sabinian
607		Boniface III
608		St Boniface IV
615		St Deusdedit (Adeodatus I)
619		Boniface V
625		Honorius I
640		Severinus
640		John IV
642		Theodore I
649		St Martin I
654		St Eugenius I
657		St Vitalian
672		Adeodatus II
676		Do(m)nus
678		St Agatho
682		St Leo II
684		St Benedict II
685		John V
686		Conon
687		St Sergius I
701		John VI
705		John VII
708		Sisinnius
708		Constantine I
715		St Gregory II
731		St Gregory III
741		St Zacharias
752		Stephen II
752		Stephen III
757		St Paul I
767		Constantine II
768		Philip
768		Stephen IV
772		Adrian I
795		St Leo III
	Revival of Western Empire	
800	Charlemagne	

Year	Emperors	Popes
814	Louis I, the Pious (813, d. 840)	
816		Stephen V
817		St Paschal I
824		Eugenius II
827		Valentine
827		Gregory IV
843	Lothair (823)	
844		Sergius II
847		St Leo IV
855	Louis II (852)	Benedict III
858		St Nicholas I
867		Adrian II
872		John VIII
875	Charles the Bald (d. 877)	
881	Charles the Fat (d. 888)	
882		Marinus I
884		Adrian III
885		Stephen VI
887	Arnulf (896, d. 899)	
891		Formosus
896		Stephen VII
897		Romanus
897		Theodore II
898		John IX
900	Ludwig the Child (German king)	Benedict IV
903		Leo V
903		Christopher
904		Sergius III
911	Conrad I (German king)	Anastasius III
913		Lando
914		John X
919	Henry I (German king)	
928		Leo VI
928		Stephen VIII
931		John XI
936	Otto I	Leo VII
	Holy Roman Empire (962)	
939		Stephen IX
942		Marinus II
946		Agapetus II
955		John XII
963		Leo VIII
964		Benedict V
965		John XIII
967	Otto II	
973		Benedict VI
974		Benedict VII
983	Otto III	John XIV
985		John XV
996		John XVI
999		Silvester II
1002	Henry II (1014)	
1003		John XVII
1003		John XVIII

Emperors and Popes

Year	Emperors	Popes
1009		Sergius IV
1012		Benedict VIII
1024	Conrad II (1027)	John XIX
1032		Benedict IX
1039	Henry III (1046)	
1045		Gregory VI
1046		Clement II
1048		Damasus II
1049		St Leo IX
1055		Victor II
1056	Henry IV (1084)	
1057		Stephen X
1059		Nicholas II
1061		Alexander II
1073–85		St Gregory VII (Hildebrand)
1086		Victor III
1088		Urban II
1099		Paschal II
1106	Henry V (1111)	
1118		Gelasius II
1119		Calixtus II
1124		Honorius II
1125	Lothair (1133)	
1130		Innocent II
1138	Conrad III of Hohenstaufen (German king)	
1143		Celestine II
1144		Lucius II
1145		Eugenius III
1152	Frederick I Barbarossa (1155)	
1153		Anastasius IV
1154		Adrian IV
1159		Alexander III
1181		Lucius III
1185		Urban III
1187		Gregory VIII
		Clement III
1190	Henry VI (1191)	
1191		Celestine III
1198	Philip of Swabia (German king) Otto IV (1209)	Innocent III
1212	Frederick II (1220)	
1216		Honorius III
1227		Gregory IX
1241		Celestine IV (d. 1241)
1243		Innocent IV
1250	Conrad IV (German king)	
1254	*Interregnum*	Alexander IV
1261–4		Urban IV
1265–8		Clement IV
1271		Gregory X
1273	Rudolf of Habsburg (German king)	
1276		Innocent V
		Adrian IV
		John XX or XXI
1277–80		Nicholas III
1281		Martin IV

Year	Emperors	Popes
1285–7		Honorius IV
1288–92		Nicholas IV
1292	Adolf of Nassau (German king)	
1294		St Celestine V
		Boniface VIII
1298	Albert I (German king)	
1303–4		Benedict XI
1305–14		Clement V (d. 1314)
1308	Henry VII of Luxembourg (1312)	
1314	Ludwig the Bavarian (1328)	
	(Frederick of Austria)	
1316		John XXII
1334		Benedict XII
1342		Clement VI
1346	Charles IV of Luxembourg (1355)	
1352		Innocent VI
1362		Urban V
1370		Gregory XI
1378	Wenceslas (German king)	Urban VI
1389		Boniface IX
1400	Rupert of the Palatinate (German king)	
1404		Innocent VII
1406		Gregory XII (abdicated 1415, d. 1417)
1409		Alexander V
1410	Sigismund (1433)	John XXIII (deposed 1415, d. 1419)
1417		Martin V
1431		Eugenius IV
1438	Albert II (German king)	
1440	Frederick III (1452)	
1447		Nicholas V
1455		Calixtus III
1458		Pius II (Aeneas Sylvius Piccolomini)
1464		Paul II (Pietro Barbo)
1471		Sixtus IV (Francesco della Rovere)
1484		Innocent VIII (Giovanni Battista Cybo)
1492		Alexander VI (Rodrigo Borgia)
1493	Maximilian I (1508: not crowned)	
1503		Pius III (Francesco Todeschini Piccolomini)
		Julius II (Giuliano della Rovere)
1513		Leo X (Giovanni de' Medici, d. 1521)
1519	Charles V (1530)	
	Last Emperor crowned in Italy	
1522		Adrian VI (Dedel of Utrecht)
1523		Clement VII (Giulio de' Medici)
1534		Paul III (Alessandro Farnese, d. 1549)
1550		Julius III (Giovanni Maria del Monte)
1555		Marcellus II (Marcello Cervino)

Emperors and Popes

Year	Emperors	Popes
		Paul IV (Giovanni Pietro Caraffa)
1556	Ferdinand I	
1559		Pius IV (Giovanni Angelo de' Medici, d. 1565)
1564	Maximilian II	
1566		St Pius V (Michele Ghislieri)
1572		Gregory XIII (Ugo Boncompagni)
1576	Rudolf II	
1586		Sixtus V (Felice Peretti)
1590		Urban VII (Giovanni Battista Castagna)
		Gregory XIV (Niccolò Sfondrati)
1591		Innocent IX (Giovanni Antonio Facchinetti)
1592		Clement VIII (Ippolito Aldobrandini)
1605		Leo XI (Alessandro de' Medici)
		Paul V (Camillo Borghese)
1612	Matthias	
1619	Ferdinand II	
1621		Gregory XV (Alessandro Ludovisi)
1623		Urban VIII (Maffeo Barberini)
1637	Ferdinand III	
1644		Innocent X (Giovanni Battista Pamphili)
1655		Alexander VII (Fabio Chigi)
1658	Leopold I	
1667		Clement IX (Giulio Rospigliosi, d. 1669)
1670		Clement X (Emilio Altieri)
1676		Innocent XI (Benedetto Odescalchi)
1689		Alexander VIII (Pietro Ottoboni)
1691		Innocent XII (Antonio Pignatelli)
1700		Clement XI (Giovanni Francesco Albani)
1705	Joseph I	
1711	Charles VI	
1721		Innocent XIII (Michelangelo Conti)
1724		Benedict XIII (Vincenzo Maria Orsini)
1730		Clement XII (Lorenzo Corsini)
1740		Benedict XIV (Prospero Lambertini)
1742	Charles VII	
1745	Francis I	
1758		Clement XIII (Carlo Rezzonico)
1765	Joseph II	
1769		Clement XIV (Giovanni Antonio Ganganelli, d. 1774)
1775		Pius VI (Giovanni Angelo Braschi, d. 1799)
1790	Leopold II	
1792	Francis II	
1800		Pius VII (Gregorio Chiaramonti)
1806	*Francis II gives up the Imperial crown: end of the Holy Roman Empire*	
1823		Leo XII (Annibale della Genga)

Year	Emperors	Popes
1829		Pius VIII (Francesco Saverio Castiglioni, d. 1830)
1831		Gregory XVI (Mauro Capellari)
1846		Pius IX (Giovanni Maria Mastai-Feretti)
	Kingdom of Italy	
1861	Victor Emmanuel II (King of Italy)	
1878	Umberto I	Leo XIII (Gioacchino Pecci)
1900	Victor Emmanuel III	
1903		Pius X (Giuseppe Sarto)
1914		Benedict XV (Giacomo della Chiesa)
1922		Pius XI (Achille Ratti)
1939		Pius XII (Eugenio Pacelli)
1946	Umberto II (leaves Italy on 13 June 1946)	
1958		John XXIII (Angelo Giuseppe Roncalli)
1963		Paul VI (Giovanni Battista Montini)
1978		John Paul I (Albino Luciani, d. 28 September 1978)
1978		John Paul II (Karol Wojtyla)

Statue of Camillo Cavour

Monument to King Victor Emmanuel II

Quotations

Ammianus
Marcellinus
(b. about A.D. 330)

(The Emperor Constantine visits Rome in the 4th c.)
"As the Emperor reviewed the vast city and its environs, spreading along the slopes, in the valleys and between the summits of the Seven Hills, he declared that the spectacle which first met his eyes surpassed everything he had yet beheld. Now his gaze rested on the Temple of Tarpeian Jupiter, now on baths so magnificent as to resemble entire provinces, now on the massive pile of the amphitheatre, massively compact, or Tivoli stone, the summit of which seems scarcely accessible to the human eye; now on the Pantheon, rising like a fairy dome, and its sublime columns, with their gently inclined staircases, adorned with statues of departed emperors; not to enumerate the Temple of the City, the Forum of Peace, the Theatre of Pompey, the Odeum, the Stadium and all the other architectural wonders of eternal Rome. When, however, he came to the Forum of Trajan, a structure unequalled by any other of its kind throughout the world, so exquisite, indeed, that the gods themselves would find it hard to refuse their admiration, he stood as if in a trance, surveying with a dazed air the stupendous fabric which neither words can picture nor mortal ever again attempt to rear."

François-René de
Chateaubriand
(1768–1848)

"Whoever has nothing else left in life should come to live in Rome; there he will find a land which will nourish his reflections, walks which will always tell him something new. The stone which crumbles under his feet will speak to him, and even the dust which the wind raises under his footsteps will seem to bear with it something of human grandeur."

Charles Dickens
(1812–1870)

"We entered on the Campagna Romana; an undulating flat . . . where few people can live; and where for miles and miles there is nothing to relieve the terrible monotony and gloom . . . We had to traverse thirty miles of this Campagna, and for two-and-twenty we went on and on, seeing nothing but now and then a lonely house, or a villainous-looking shepherd . . . tending his sheep. At the end of that distance, we stopped to refresh the horses, and to get some lunch, in a common malaria-shaken despondent little public-house . . . When we were fairly going off again, we began, in a perfect fever, to strain our eyes for Rome; and when, after another mile or two, the Eternal City appeared, at length, in the distance, it looked like – I am half afraid to write the word – like LONDON!!! There it lay, under a thick cloud, with innumerable towers, and steeples, and roofs of houses, rising up into the sky, and high above them all, one Dome. I swear, that keenly as I felt the seeming absurdity of the comparison, it was so like London, at that distance, that if you could have shown it me in a glass, I should have taken it for nothing else."

Edward Gibbon
(1737–94)

"It was at Rome on the 15th of October, 1764, as I sat musing amidst the ruins of the Capitol, while the barefooted friars were singing vespers in the Temple of Jupiter, that the idea of writing the decline and fall of the city first started to my mind."

Johann Wolfgang
von Goethe
(1749–1832)

"I have now been here for seven days, and am gradually getting some general idea of the city. We walk about Rome most diligently, and I familiarise myself with the layout of the ancient and the modern city, look at the ruins and the buildings, and visit this villa or that. I take the principal sights very slowly, look at them attentively, go away and come back again; for only in Rome can one prepare oneself for Rome.

I must confess, however, that it is a bitter and sorry business disentangling the old Rome from the new; but one has to do it, and must hope that one's efforts will be rewarded. One encounters traces of inconceivable magnificence and inconceivable destruction: what the barbarians left standing the builders of modern Rome have devastated.''

''Rome will give you so many pretty girls that you will say,'This city has everything that the world can offer.' As many fields of corn as has Gargara, as many grapes Methymna, as many fish the sea, as many birds the trees, as many stars the sky, so many girls has this Rome of yours.''

Ovid
(43 B.C.–A.D. 17)

I found that (Rome) flourisheth beyond all expectation, this new even emulous to exceed the old, the remnants of the old adding to the splendour of the new . . . A man may spend many months at Rome and yet have something of note to see every day.''
(''Il Mercurio Italico; an Itinerary contayning a Voyage made through Italy in the yeare 1646 & 1647'', 1648)

John Raymond
(17th c.)

''The society of Rome is excellent; and the circumstance of every man, whether foreigner or native, being permitted to live as he pleases, without exciting wonder, contributes essentially to general comfort. At Rome, too, every person may find amusement: for whether it be our wish to dive deep into classical knowledge, whether arts and sciences be our pursuit, or whether we merely seek for new ideas and new objects, the end cannot fail to be obtained in this most interesting of Cities, where every stone is an historian.''
(''Traveller's Guide'', 8th edition, 1832)

Mariana Starke

''The head and crown of all churches is without any doubt St Peter's; and if the ancients held it a misfortune not to have seen the Temple of Olympian Jupiter, this could be said even more aptly of St Peter's. For this building is larger than the temples of the Greeks and Romans and surpasses them all in architectural quality and magnificence. I never go there without praising God for granting me the happiness of seeing this wonder, of seeing it and learning to know it over many years.''

Johann Joachim
Winkelmann
(1717–68)

''All roads lead to Rome.''

Proverb

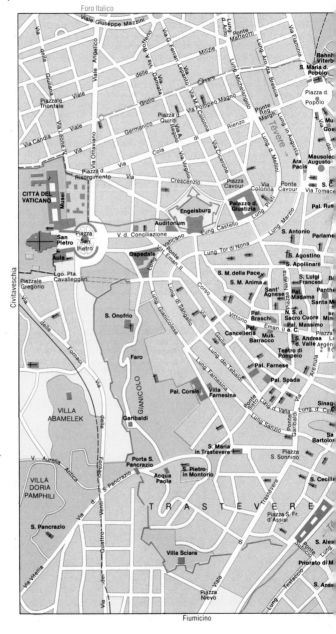

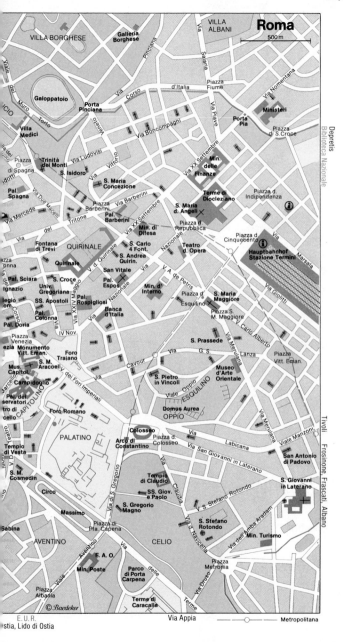

Rome from A to Z

Suggestions for planning a short stay in Rome will be found under "Sightseeing Programme" in the Practical Information Section.

★Ara Pacis (Altar of Peace)   D 5

Between the Mausoleo di Augusto (see entry) and the Tiber stands the Ara Pacis Augustae, Augustus' Altar of Peace. After the troubled period of civil war and his defeat of his opponents Augustus brought peace to the Roman Empire and made possible the glories of the Augustan age. Accordingly, we are told in *Res Gestae*, the inscription recording Augustus' career which is reproduced on the outside of the building housing the Altar of Peace, "the Senate resolved to erect the Altar of the Augustan Peace as a votive offering on the Field of Mars". The Altar, constructed between 13 and 9 B.C., was brought to light again in the 16th and 19th c. It gives consummate expression to the Imperium Romanum of Augustus, the Roman world empire with its assertion of Roman power, its religious ceremonies, its Imperial house and the institutions on which it was based.

The lower part of the screen enclosing the altar, of Carrera marble, is richly decorated with reliefs of foliage ornament (acanthus, ivy, laurel, vines), with birds and reptiles interspersed among the leaves. The upper part is occupied by a sculptured frieze, running round all four sides – mythological scenes on the ends, historical scenes on the long sides. A flight of ten steps leads up to the platform (11.62×10.60m/38×35ft), in the centre of which stands the altar.

The altar itself, guarded by lion-sphinxes, was decorated with reliefs (only about a third of which have survived) representing sacrificial ceremonies.

Situation
Via di Ripetta/
Piazza Augusto
Imperatore

Buses
2, 26, 81, 90, 115,
507, 911, 913

Opening times
Tues.–Sat.
9am–1.30pm,
Sun. 9am–1pm,
also in summer
Tues., Thur. and
Sat. 4–7pm

★Arco di Costantino (Arch of Constantine)   E 7

The triumphal arch erected by the Senate in honour of the Emperor Constantine, "liberator of the city and bringer of peace", after his victory over Maxentius in the battle of the Milvian Bridge A.D. 312 is the largest (21m/69ft high, 25.7m/84ft wide, 7.4m/24ft deep) and best preserved of Roman triumphal arches, in spite of the fact that it, like the Colosseum (see Colosseo), was incorporated in the castle of the Frangipane family and was not disengaged until the 16th (partly) and 19th c. (completely). Extensive restoration was completed in 1990. The arch, with three openings, is decorated with reliefs taken from earlier structures, which the sculptors of the early 4th c. were unable to equal. Some of the scenes, therefore, have little to do with Constantine and his military achievements – a boar hunt and a sacrifice to Apollo, taken from a monument of the time of Hadrian, scenes from the reigns of Trajan and Marcus Aurelius. The side facing the Colosseum bears the Latin inscription: "To the Emperor Caesar Flavius Constantinus Maximus, the pious and jubilant Augustus, the Senate and the peoples of Rome dedicate this arch as a token of his triumph as, by the inspiration of God and his magnanimity, he and his army liberated the state in rightful war from the tyrant and from all rebellion".

Situation
Piazza del
Colosseo/Via di San
Gregorio

**Underground
station**
Colosseo (line B)

Buses
11, 15, 27, 81, 85,
87, 88, 118, 673

Trams
13, 30, 30b

◀ *Inside the Pantheon*

Frieze in the Ara Pacis Augustae (altar of peace)

Arch of Constantine (Arco di Costantino)

★ Arco di Giano (Arch of Janus Quadrifrons)   D 7

This marble structure in the Via del Velabro, in front of the church of San Giorgio in Velabro (see entry), was long thought to be part of the temple of Janus. In fact is was a covered passage (*Janus*) with opening on four sides (*quadrifrons*) at a busy street intersection in the commercial quarter of Rome.

The arch was built in the Constantinian period, incorporating material from earlier buildings. During the Middle Ages it became a strong point of the Frangipane family.

Situation
Via del Velabro

Buses
15, 80, 90

★ Basilica di Massenzio (Basilica of Maxentius)   E 7

The ruins of the Basilica of Maxentius or of Constantine (begun in A.D. 306–312 by Maxentius and completed by Constantine), between the Via dei Fori Imperiali and the Forum (see Foro Romano), still give an imposing impression of this great building, which, like other Roman basilicas, served both as a law court and a place for doing business. The central aisle, with a vaulted roof, measured 60×25m/220×80ft, and rose to a height of 35m/115ft; the lateral aisles were 24.5m/80ft high. The basilica was modelled on the gigantic Baths erected by Caracalla and Diocletian. The main piers were fronted by massive Corinthian columns, one of which, bearing a statue of the Virgin, now stands in front of the church of Santa Maria Maggiore (see entry). This last great building of the Roman Imperial period – inaugurated in the year in which the capital was moved to Constantinople – provided the inspiration for later European architecture, including St Peter's (see San Pietro). The ruin of the basilica was hastened when Pope Honorius I removed the bronze roof-tiles and used them to roof Old St Peter's. An earthquake in the 9th c. caused further damage. The remains of a statue of Constantine, which once stood in the first apse of the basilica, may be seen in the courtyard of the Palazzo dei Conservatori (see entry).

Situation
Via dei Fori Imperiali

Underground station
Colosseo (line B)

Buses
11, 27, 81, 85, 87, 88, 118

Opening times
Mon.–Sat.
9am–7pm,
in winter 3pm;
Sun. 9am–2pm

Basilica di Porta Maggiore   H 6/7

This underground sanctuary (probably of the 1st c. A.D.), although well preserved, is still something of a puzzle to archaeologists. Discovered 13m/40ft below ground level in 1917, it has the form of a basilica measuring 19×12m/62×39ft, with a porch and a semicircular apse. With its mosaic pavement, stucco decoration on the ceiling and cycles of mythological scenes, it seems to have been the shrine of some mystical cult (perhaps the Neo-Pythagoreans). It has been suggested that this building, of a type which was evidently widely distributed throughout the Empire, influenced the development of the Christian basilica.

Situation
Via Prenestina 17

Buses
152, 153, 154, 155, 156, 157

Trams
13, 14, 19, 19b, 516, 517

Basilica di San Marco   D 6

This church, now partly incorporated in the Palazzo Venezia, is traditionally believed to have been founded by Pope Marcus (Mark) in honour of the Evangelist in 336. Its present form results from restoration and rebuilding about 800 and in the 15th and 18th c. Appropriately, since St Mark is the patron saint of Venice, the Palazzo Venezia was from 1564 to 1797 the residence of the Venetian ambassador to the Holy See.

Notable features of the church are the two-storey portico, the campanile adjoining the tower of the Palazzo Venezia and the mosaic in the apse of Christ transmitting the Law. Dating from the time of Pope Gregory IV

Situation
Piazza Venezia

Buses
46, 56, 60, 62, 64, 65, 70, 75, 85, 87, 88, 90, 95, 170

(827–844), this shows Christ on a dais surrounded by Apostles and saints (Gregory, being still alive, is depicted with a square nimbus), above a frieze with symbolic representations of the Lamb of the Apocalypse, amid twelve other lambs, and of two cities.

Borsa (Exchange)   D 6

Situation
Piazza di Pietra

Buses
26, 87, 94

The Exchange occupies part of the site of a large ancient temple, eleven Corinthian columns from which are preserved along one side. Long thought to have been a temple of Neptune, it is now identified as the Hadrianeum, a temple erected in honour of the deified Hadrian. The floor of the temple now lies below street level. The temple was absorbed into the new customs house, now the Exchange, built by Carlo and Francesco Fontana in 1691–1700 under Pope Innocent II.

Camera dei Deputati (Parliament)   D 5

Situation
Palazzo
Montecitorio
Piazza di
Montecitorio

Buses
52, 53, 56, 58, 58b,
60, 61, 62, 71, 81,
85, 88, 90, 90b, 95,
115

The Palazzo Montecitorio, begun by Bernini in 1650 for Pope Innocent X Pamphili and completed in 1694 by Carlo Fontana, has been occupied since 1871 by the Chamber of Deputies, the lower house of the Italian Parliament. At the beginning of this century the palace was enlarge to meet Parliamentary needs. In the Piazza di Montecitorio is an ancient Egyptian obelisk (594–589 B.C.). Here German archaeologists excavated what is claimed to be the largest sundial in the world, dating from the 2nd c. A.D., of which the obelisk was the gnomon. The great bronze base of the sundial, 60m/200ft in diameter, was brought to light behind the Chamber of Deputies at a depth of 6.5m/20ft below the present street level. Below it is the still more famous sundial of Augustus. Open to the public some weekends.

Corinthian Columns of the Exchange

Parliament

Campidoglio (Capitol)   D/E 6

The Capitol, the smallest of Rome's seven hills, was the political and religious centre of the ancient city. On its two summits stood the city's two principal temples, dedicated to Jupiter Optimus Maximus Capitolinus and Juno Moneta, on the sites now occupied by the Palazzo dei Conservatori and the church of Santa Maria in Aracoeli (see entries). The lower area between them is now occupied by the Piazza del Campidoglio. The square, flanked by palaces and approached by Michelangelo's ceremonial ramp and staircase, still conveys a feeling of the grandeur and dignity which the city has preserved down the centuries. Here victorious Roman generals came to celebrate their triumphs, making their way to the Capitol along the Sacred Way (Via Sacra); here in the Middle Ages poets were crowned and tribunes of the people were acclaimed; here in 1955 the Treaty of Rome, establishing the European Economic Community, was signed; and here, in the Palazzo dei Senatori (see entry), the Mayor of Rome has his residence and receives distinguished visitors to the city. This has been since time immemorial the political centre of Rome, the counterpart of the city's spiritual and religious centre in the Vatican.

Underground station
Colosseo (line B)

Buses
57, 85, 87, 88, 90, 90b, 92, 94, 95, 716, 718, 719

Piazza del Campidoglio (Capitol Square)

The Piazza del Campidoglio is reached from Via del Teatro di Marcellos by way of the ceremonial ramp and staircase designed by Michelangelo, passing a monument (on the left) to Cola di Rienzo, the 14th c. tribune of the people, and statues of the Dioscuri (Castor and Pollux), the Emperor Constantine and his son Constantine II.

The square, also designed by Michelangelo, is bounded by the façades of three palaces, the Palazzo dei Senatori (to the rear), the Palazzo dei Con-

Approach to the Capitol

servatori (on the right) (see entries) and the Palazzo Nuovo (see Museo Capitolino) (on the left). It is not, however, totally enclosed, since there are openings between the buildings which allow passage to streets leading down to the Forum. The palaces are not set at right angles to one another but form a trapezoid, within which Michelangelo laid out an oval (marked by steps) and a star formation (marked by lighter-coloured paving). This gives emphasis to the centre of the square, in which an equestrian statue of Marcus Aurelius (161–180 A.D.) was set up. The statue, of bronze which was originally gilded, had previously stood in front of the church of St John Lateran (see San Giovanni in Laterano). It was thought to represent the Emperor Constantine, who favoured Christianity, and was accordingly preserved from destruction in spite of its heathen origins. Its true identity was revealed by Platina, the librarian to the Vatican, in the 15th c. and in 1538 Pope Paul III had it transferred to the Piazza del Campidoglio.

The statue was taken as a model for the greatest equestrian statues of the Gothic, Renaissance and Baroque periods, including Donatello's Gattamelata in Padua and Verocchio's Colleoni monument in Venice. The statue, which had been badly damaged by air pollution, was restored in 1990 and protected against further decay, and is exhibited at the Museo Capitolino.

This work, one of the largest achievements of antique sculpture, symbolises strength and peace. The Emperor has his right hand raised in a gesture of peace, and under the raised right hoof of each horse was originally the figure of a defeated king with bound hands.

Campo Verano   H/J 5/6

Situation
Via Tiburtina

Buses
11, 63, 65, 71, 109, 111, 163, 309, 311, 411, 415, 490, 492, 495

Trams
19, 19b, 30, 30b

According to ancient Roman tradition, the Campo Verano, the main cemetery, lies outside the city walls on the Via Tiburtina (the road to Tivoli).

The cemetery mirrors the different social strata of the city. In the park-like open spaces can be seen luxurious family graves and mausoleums; poorer folk have to make do with modest "locoli-houses". These tall buildings of marble and travertine have numerous compartments into which the sarcophagi were pushed.

The Campo Verano is particularly busy on All Saints Day (November 1st), when the people of Rome visit their dead and decorate the graves.

Cappella di Sant'Ivo, in the Palazzo della Sapienza   D 6

Situation
Corso del Rinascimento

Buses
26, 46, 62, 64, 70, 81, 88, 90

One of the most distinctive landmarks of Rome is the dome, with its airy lantern and spiral finial, of the church of St Ivo in the Palazzo della Sapienza. The "Sapienza" was the home of the University of Rome from its foundation by Pope Boniface VIII in 1303 until it was able to move to more spacious accommodation in the University City in 1935. The three-storey palace, now housing the State Archives, was built by Giacomo della Porta for Pope Sixtus V in 1587.

Crossing the inner courtyard between the two massive wings of the palace, we come to the church of Sant'Ivo, a Baroque chapel with a lively façade mingling concave and convex forms. The interior with its semicircular and trapezoid elements was designed by Borromini in the form of a bee, the heraldic emblem of Pope Urban VIII, a member of the noble Barberini family.

The church as a whole is a masterly example of the work of Borromini, domestic architect of the Barberini family.

Carcere Mamertino (Mamertine Prison)   E 6

From the 4th c. B.C. onwards the state prison of Rome stood at the foot of the Capitol hill (see Campidoglio), on the side nearest the Foro Romano. It consisted of two vaulted chambers, one on top of the other. In the lower chamber, also known as the Tullianum (after a water cistern), we are told by the Roman historians that the Numidian king Jugurtha (140 B.C.), the Gallic chieftain Vercingetorix (46 B.C.) and Catiline's fellow conspirators were confined. According to Christian tradition the Apostles Peter and Paul were also imprisoned here, and during his confinement Peter is said to have baptised the other prisoners with water from the Tullianum spring. Accordingly the chapel which was later constructed in the prison was named San Pietro in Carcere (St Peter in Prison). the church above it is dedicated to St Joseph the Carpenter (San Giuseppe dei Falegnami).

Situation
Via dei Falegnami adjoining the Forum

Underground station
Colosseo (line B)

Opening times
Mon.–Sun.
9am–12.30pm
and 2–6.40pm

Castel Gandolfo

In Castel Gandolfo is the Pope's summer residence, the construction of which was begun by Urban VIII in 1624. The property enjoys extraterritorial status as part of Vatican City.

From the little town, which according to legend was founded by Aeneas' son Ascanius and which, as Alba Longa, was later destroyed by Rome, there are wide-ranging views over the Roman Campagna, extending as far as the dome of St Peters (see San Pietro), and down to the Alban Lake (see Colli Albani).

In the main square, opposite the Papal palace, is the church of San Tommaso di Villanova by Bernini.

Situation
25km/15 miles south-east of Rome

Underground station
Line A to Subaugusta (then regular bus service from Via Tito Labieno)

Rail Ferrovia Roma-Albano

Castel Gondolfo, the Pope's summer residence

★Castel Sant'Angelo

Situation
Lungotevere
Vaticano/
Lungotevere
Castello

Buses
23, 28, 28b, 34, 64

Opening times
Daily 9am–6pm
(2pm in winter).
Closed second and
fourth Tues. every
month

The Castel Sant'Angelo (now a museum) is one of the most imposing buildings to survive from antiquity. It was originally a mausoleum, begun by Hadrian (A.D. 117–138) in the closing years of his reign to provide a last resting-place for himself and his successors, and completed by Septimus Severus (A.D. 193). When Rome was endangered by Germanic raiders from the north and was surrounded by Aurelius with a new circuit of walls (see Mura Aureliane) the mausoleum, strategically situated, was incorporated in the defences and became the strongest fortress in Rome. The original name of the structure (Hadrianeum) was changed to Castel Sant'Angelo after a vision vouchsafed to Pope Gregory the Great in 590 when he saw an angel hovering over the mausoleum and sheathing his sword, heralding the end of the plague which was then raging in Rome. Hence the figure of an angel which now crowns the monument (by Piet van Verschaffelt, 1753).

In 1277 Pope Nicholas III linked the castle with the Vatican Palace (see Palazzi Vaticani) by building a wall along which ran a covered passage known as the *passetto*. Pope Alexander VI, the Borgia Pope whose adventurous policy of conquest made adequate protection against attack very necessary, fortified the passage and strengthened the castle by building four corner bastions. In times of danger the Popes were able to take refuge in the Castel Sant'Angelo, as did Gregory VII (1084) when threatened by the German king Henry IV, Clement VII during the attack on Rome by the Emperor Charles V (1527, sack of Rome) and Pius VII when in danger of capture by Napoleon's forces. Celebrated prisoners were confined in the castle, and executions took place on its walls. For a time it housed the Papal treasury and secret archives.

The Mausoleum of Hadrian consisted of a circular structure 64m/210ft in diameter and 20m/65ft high standing on a square base (84m/275ft each way, 15m/50ft high). Around the top of the walls, built of dressed travertine

Castel Sant'Angelo

and tufa, were set a series of statues, and on the highest point was a bronze quadriga (four-horse chariot). This cylindrical structure with its simple geometrical forms and massive walls, within which were the tomb chambers of the Imperial family, formed the core of the Papal stronghold. In the course of 1500 years the building was altered by successive Popes according to their particular needs (whether for defence against attack or for purposes of display, with sumptuous decoration). From 1870 until 1901 the Castel Sant'Angelo served as both barracks and prison, then it was renovated and furnished as a museum. On view in 58 rooms, some decorated with fine murals, are an interesting collection of weaponry, models of the history of the building of the fortress, several chapels and a treasury. From the upper platform there are magnificent views.

Castro Pretorio (Praetorian Barracks)   F/G 5

The barracks of the Praetorian Guard, the Emperor's personal bodyguard, were built by Tiberus' minister Sejanus in A.D. 23 on a site measuring 460×300m/500×330yd. The barracks, with their fortifications, were later incorporated by Aurelius in the city walls (see Mura Aureliane).

Situation
Via Castro Pretorio

Buses
9, 163, 310, 415, 492

Catacombe di Domitilla (Catacombs of Domitilla)   F 10

The Catacombs of Domitilla are among the most impressive of the Roman catacombs, the underground burial-places which were used by pagans as well as Christians (though the more famous and wealthier Romans might prefer to be buried beside one of the great trunk roads leading out of Rome). Domitilla was a descendant of Vespasian who, after her conversion to Christianity, allowed Christians to be buried in the family tomb.

Christians met to celebrate the commemorative day of notable members of their community; at their gravesides, but not always in the catacombs (see Practical Information, Catacombs). In the Catacombs of Domitilla is the basilica of SS Nereus and Achilleus, an underground church of highly impressive effect with its columns and marble fragments. From the basilica visitors enter the catacomb passages with their tomb chambers and wall recesses. There are well-preserved wall paintings on Christian themes.

Situation
Via Ardeatine
Via della Sette
Chiese 282

Buses
93, 671 or 118 and
change
into 94 or 218

Opening times
Mon., Wed.–Sun.
8.30am–noon,
2.30–5pm (in
summer 5.30pm)

About 300m/330yd from the catacombs lies the Fosse Ardeatine with a mausoleum to the memory of the 335 Italian hostages who were shot here in March 1944 as a reprisal for a bomb attack.

Fosse Ardeatine

Catacombe di Priscilla (Catacombs of Priscilla)   G 2

These catacombs are believed to be named after Priscilla, a member of the gens Acilia who became a Christian and was killed on the orders of Domitian. They contain a number of wall paintings of saints and early Christian symbols. Particularly notable is the "Greek Chapel", a square chamber with an arch which contains 2nd c. frescoes of Old and New Testament scenes. Above the apse is a Last Judgment. Near this are figures of the Virgin and Child and the Prophet Isaiah, also dating from the 2nd c.

Opening times: Tues.–Sun. 8.30am–noon, 2.30–5pm (in summer 6pm).

Situation
Via Salaria Nuova
430

Buses
135, 235, 319

★Catacombe di San Callisto (Catacombs of St Calixtus)   G 10

The Catacombs of St Calixtus were called by Pope John XXIII "the sublimest and most famous in Rome". These underground burial places in the

Situation
Via Appia Antica

Opening times
Mon., Tues.,
Thurs.–Sun.
8.30am–noon,
2.30–5pm
(in summer
5.30pm)

Via Appia Antica (see entry) extend over an area of 300×400m/330×440yd, with an intricate network of passages and chambers hewn from the soft Roman tufa on four levels. Some 20km/12½ miles of passages have so far been explored, and the total number of burials is estimated at around 170,000.

In six sacramental chapels, constructed between A.D. 290 and 310, are both pagan and early Christian wall paintings. In the "Papal Crypt", to which visitors descend by a flight of 35 steps, are the tombs of most of the martyred Popes of the 3rd c. identified by Greek inscriptions (Urban I, Pontius, Antherus, Fabian, Lucius, Eutychianus). To the left of the Papal Crypt is the tomb of St Cecilia, with wall paintings; the saint's remains are now in the church of Santa Cecilia in Trastevere (see entry). Also of interest are tombs of Pope Eusebius (309–311) and Pope Cornelius (251–253) and Lucina crypt with wall paintings dating from 2nd c.

Cerveteri

Situation
51km/32 miles NW,
just off the Via
Aurelia

Cerveteri (a corruption of Caere Vetus) occupies the site of the Etruscan city of Caere, which was an important commercial and political centre from the 8th to the 4th c. B.C. The necropolis of Cerveteri, to the north of the present town, introduces the visitor to the life and the funerary cult of this people, who occupied large areas of central Italy before the rise of Rome and developed a high degree of artistic achievement in architecture, painting, sculpture and metalwork.

Gold and bronze objects, vases and paintings produced by the Etruscans can be seen in the museums of Rome as well as in the British Museum and the Louvre.

There are numerous impressive tombs, among the most notable being the Tomba dei Capitelli, dei Dolii, dei Vasi Greci, dei 13 Cadaveri, dei Rilievi, della Cassetta and dei Letti e Sarcofagi, and the tumuli (burial mounds) of the Cornice and of Ophelia Maroi.

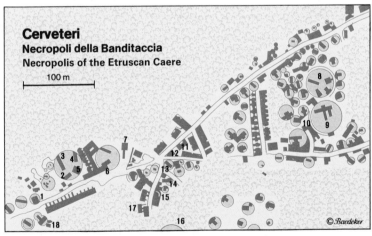

Cerveteri
Necropoli della Banditaccia
Necropolis of the Etruscan Caere

100 m

© Baedeker

1 Tomba dei Capitelli
2 Tomba dei Letti e Sarcofagi
3 Tomba della Capanna
4 Tomba dei Dolii
5 Tomba dei Vasi Greci
6 Tomba dei 13 Cadaveri

7 Tomba dei Rilievi
8 Tumulo del Colonello
9 Tumulo Mengarelli
10 Tumulo Maroi
11 Tomba di Marce Ursus
12 Tomba della Casetta

13 Tumulo della Quercia
14 Tumulo dei 2 Ingressi
15 Tumulo della Cornice
16 Grande Tumulo della Tegola Dipinta
17 Tomba dei 6 Loculi
18 Tombe della Spianata

Oratorio dei Filippini and Chiesa Nuova

★Chiesa Nuova (the "New Church": officially Santa Maria in Vallicella)   C 6

The church of Santa Maria in Vallicella was begun in 1575 on the initiative of St Philip Neri, founder of the Congregation of the Oratory. It was built on the site of an earlier (12th c.) church dedicated to St John, and is still popularly known as the "New Church". A number of different donors and architects were involved in its construction. The exterior of the church is of imposing effect with its massive façade (by Fausto Rughesi) and central dome rearing high above the close-packed houses in the older part of the city. The sumptuously decorated interior of this high cruciform three-aisled basilica is notable particularly for frescoes by Pietro da Cortona and paintings on the high altar (early works by Rubens). Left of the choir is the Chapel of San Filippo Neri, containing his tomb of marble and mother-of-pearl.

Situation
Piazza della Chiesa Nuova
(Corso Vittorio Emanuele II)

Buses
46, 62, 64

Cimitero degli Stranieri Acattolico (Protestant Cemetery)   D 8

The Protestant Cemetery lies within the Aurelian Walls (see Mura Aureliane) near the Pyramid of Cestius (see Piramide di Caio Cestio). Among the famous foreigners buried here are Keats, who died in Rome on February 24th 1821, and Shelley, drowned in the Gulf of La Spezia in 1822.
   Tues.–Sun. 9am–6pm (in winter 5pm).

Situation
Via Caio Cestio

Buses 11, 23, 57, 92, 318, 673

Opening times

Circo Massimo (Circus Maximus)   D/E 7

According to legend, the Circus Maximus, lying to the south of the Palatine, was constructed by Tarquinius Priscus on the site of the rape of the Sabine women. The Circus was, in fact, established in the 2nd century A.D. as a

Situation
Via dei Circo Massimo

Underground Station
Circo Massimo

stadium for chariot races. It consisted of two tracks, 500m/547yd in length and could accommodate 300,000 spectators. The remains of the buildings date from the time of Trajan. An obelisk erected at the Circus during the reign of Augustus, now stands on Piazza del Popolo (see entry).

Città Universitaria (University City)   G/H 5/6

Situation
Viale delle Scienze

Buses 11, 71, 109, 111, 309, 310, 311, 411, 415, 492

When the Papal University, the "Sapienza" (see Cappella di Sant'Ivo), became too small, plans were considered from 1870 onwards for replacing it with new university buildings. This large new complex was built by Mussolini in 1932–35, but it too soon became inadequate for the number of students. In the University City are a number of small museums.

Colli Albani (Alban Hills)

Situation
20–30km/12–18 miles SE

Underground station
Line A to Cinecittà (then regular bus service from Via Labieno)

Rail
Ferrovia Roma–Albano

In the past many Roman noble families and Popes built castles in these hills, and the region is therefore also known as the Castelli Romani ("Roman Castles"). Today Roman citizens have made their homes here, attracted by purer air and quieter surroundings of an area which lies considerably higher than Rome. These volcanic hills rise to a height of 949m/3114ft in Monte Cavo. The craters of the volcanoes have formed two lakes, the Lago Di Albano (Alban Lake) and the Lago di Nemi (Lake Nemi). An excellent wine known as Castelli Romani is produced from grapes grown on the slopes of the hills. Around the old castles a series of little towns have grown up, including Frascati, Grottaferrata (see entry), the picturesque Marino, Castle Gandolfo (see entry), Albano, Ariccia, Genzano, Nemi, with its small ship museum, and Rocca di Papa, surrounded by beautiful woodland on the edge of a crater known as Campo di Annibale.

Lago di Albano

This crater lake (about 3.5km/2 miles long, 2km/1¼ miles wide; alt. 293m/960ft; greatest depth 170m/560ft) is of extraordinary beauty from whatever viewpoint it is seen. The level of the lake is maintained at a constant height by an emissary or tunnel 2500m/2700yd long, 1.2m/4ft wide and 1.6m/5ft high which drains surplus water into the Tiber. The emissary was originally constructed by Roman engineers in 397 B.C., following a prophecy that Rome could not conquer the Etruscan city of Veii until the water of the lake had been drained.

Colombario di Pomponio Hylas (Columbarium of Pomponius Hylas)   F 8

Situation
Via di Porta San Sebastiano

Bus: 118

Closed for restoration

A columbarium was a communal burial chamber with niches in the walls for cinerary urns. The name comes from the resemblance of this type of structure to a dovecote (*columba* = pigeon).

A particularly well-preserved example is the columbarium built for Pomponius Hylas and his wife Vitalinis, which is situated near the Sepolcro degli Scipioni, between the Via Appia Antica and the Via Latina. Pomponius Hylas was a freed slave who seems to have risen to prosperity in the reigns of Augustus and Tiberius.

★Colonna di Marco Aurelio (Column of Marcus Aurelius)   D 6

Situation
Piazza Colonna

The Piazza Colonna, with the Palazzo Chigi (now housing the Prime Minister's office), is dominated by the column of Marcus Aurelius. After Marcus

Aurelius' defeat of the Marcomanni, Quadi and Sarmatae the column was erected by the Senate in the centre of a square flanked by temples dedicated to Hadrian and Marcus Aurelius and by other public buildings. The inscription at the foot of the column wrongly ascribes it to Antoninus Pius, and it is sometimes also known by the name of that Emperor.

The column, standing 29.6m/97ft high (42m/138ft, if the base and capital are included) and 3.7m/12ft in diameter, is constructed of 27 drums of Carrara marble. A spiral relief runs up the column, with scenes from the wars with the Germanic tribes (171–173) and the Sarmatians (174–175). The figures of soldiers and horses stand out more strongly from the background than on Trajan's Column, and like the reliefs on that column have yielded a wealth of information about the weapons and uniforms, the military techniques and the life of the period.

A staircase (190 steps) inside the column gives access to the platform on the top, once occupied by a figure of Marcus Aurelius. The monument is now crowned by a bronze statue of the Apostle Paul (by Domenico Fontana), set up in 1589.

Buses: 52, 53, 56, 58, 58b, 60, 61, 62, 71, 81, 85, 88, 90, 90b, 95, 115.

Column of Marcus Aurelius

★★Colosseo (Colosseum)   E 7

The Colosseum, or Flavian Amphitheatre, is the largest structure left to us by Roman antiquity, and has provided the model for sports areas right down to modern times; the football stadia of the present day have basically the same form as this monument created by the architects of the Flavian Emperors, Vespasian and Titus. The object of the Emperors in raising the Colosseum was to satisfy the appetite of the Roman populace for *circenses* (games), and there is no doubt that they achieved their aim.

Situation
Piazza del Colosseo

Underground station
Colosseo (line B)

Colosseum – the Flavian amphitheatre

Colosseo

View of spectators' seats and underground corridors

Buses
11, 15, 27, 81, 85,
87, 88, 118, 673

Trams
13, 30, 30b

Opening times
Daily 9am–3pm
(in summer 7pm),
Wed. and Sun.
9am–1pm

A bronze cross in the arena commemorates the Christian martyrs who were believed to have died here during the Roman Imperial period. There is some doubt, however, whether large numbers of Christians in fact met their death in the Colosseum. The structure of the Colosseum is so well preserved that it still creates a powerful impression of its original form, but it bears very evident marks of the damage and destruction it has suffered down the centuries – by fire, earthquake, neglect and dilapidation under the Christian Empire (when the games were abandoned), its conversion into a fortress of the Frangipane family, the pillaging of its marble, travertine and brick for the construction of palaces (see Palazzo Venezia, Cancelleria, Palazzo Farnese) and the constant thunder of modern traffic.

The building of the Colosseum was begun by Vespasian in A.D. 72 on the site of a colossal statue of Nero (hence the name Colosseum) which stood within the precincts of Nero's Domus Aurea (see entry). Vespasian's son Titus enlarged the structure by adding the fourth storey, and it was inaugurated in the year 80 with a series of splendid games.

The Colosseum was oval in form (though it appears to be almost circular), 186m/610ft long by 156m/510ft across, with an arena 78 × 46m/260×150ft which could be used for theatrical performances, festivals, circus shows or games. It stood 57m/190ft high and could accommodate some 50,000 spectators – the Imperial court and high officials on the lowest level, the aristocratic families of Rome on the second level, the populace on the third and fourth. Around the exterior, built of travertine, are pilasters – of the Doric order on the ground floor, Ionic on the next tier and Corinthian on the third. The interior structure was contrived with immense skill, the rows of seating and the internal passages and staircases being arranged so as to allow the 50,000 spectators to get to their places or leave the theatre within a few minutes. On the top storey there were originally 240 masts set round the walls to support an awning over the audience. Unfortunately the sumptuous decoration of the interior has been totally destroyed.

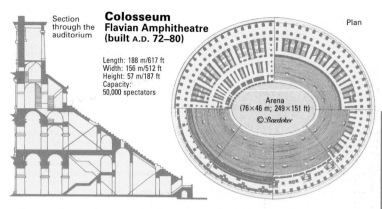

Colosseum
Flavian Amphitheatre
(built A.D. 72–80)

Section through the auditorium

Plan

Length: 188 m/617 ft
Width: 156 m/512 ft
Height: 57 m/187 ft
Capacity:
50,000 spectators

Arena
(76×46 m; 249×151 ft)

© Baedeker

Underneath the arena were changing rooms and training rooms for gladiators, cages for wild beasts and store-rooms, the walls of which are now visible since the collapse of the arena floor.

Domine Quo Vadis Church F 9

This church takes its name from the legend that the Apostle Peter, fleeing from Rome to escape martyrdom, met Christ here and, not recognising him, asked, "Sir, whither goest thou?" ("Domine, quo vadis?"); where-

Situation
Via Appia Antica,
km 0.8

Domine Quo Vadis

Bust of Henryk Sienkiewicz

upon Christ replied "I come to be crucified a second time". Then Peter realising who it was, was stricken with shame and returned to Rome.

On the basis of this legend the little church of Santa Maria in Palmis was built in the 9th c. and became known as the Domine Quo Vadis church; it was rebuilt in the 17th c. Within the church is a reproduction of the footprint of Christ and a bust of Henryk Sienkiewicz, author of the novel "Quo Vadis?".

Domus Aurea (Nero's Golden House)   E 6/7

Situation
Viale Monte Oppio

**Underground
station**
Colosseo (line B)

Buses
15, 81, 85, 87, 88

Trams
13, 30, 30b

Open:
by appointment
tel. 6 99 01 10

The burning of Rome in A.D. 64 happened very conveniently for Nero's purposes. In the huge area thus cleared of buildings he planned to erect a huge and sumptuously appointed new palace, and although the vast project, covering an area greater than that of the present-day Vatican City, was never completed, the site was used by Nero's successors for the erection of other buildings, including the Colosseum (see entry), approximately occupying the position of Nero's artificial lake.

Excavations which began at the Renaissance in the area between the Forum (see Foro Romano) and the Esquiline brought to light large numbers of works of art, frescoes and marble statues, including the famous Laocoön group, now in the Vatican Museum (see Città del Vaticano, Musei Vaticani).

★EUR (Esposizione Universale di Roma)   H–K 10–12

**Underground
station**
EUR-Fermi,
EUR-Marconi
(line B)

Buses
93, 97, 123, 197,
223, 293, 393, 493,
593, 671, 703, 707,
708, 762, 765, 775

The Italian Fascist government planned to hold a great international exhibition in Rome in 1942, but work on the project, which began in 1938, was suspended on the outbreak of war. Mussolini's plan was to create, between Rome and the sea, a satellite town the modern buildings of which should outshine the old palaces of Papal Rome, and new streets were laid out and vast buildings (Palace of Congress, Palace of Labour, museums – see Museo della Civiltà Romana) erected in the monumental style of the Fascist period.

After the war the development of the area continued, with some buildings of considerable architectural quality.

Fontana dell'Acqua Felice   E 5

Situation
Via Orlando
(corner of Piazza
San Bernardo)

Buses 16, 37, 60,
61, 63, 415

The fountain, with a figure of Moses as its central feature, was commissioned by Pope Sixtus V in 1585. The Pope, Felice Peretti (hence the name of the fountain), to whom Rome owes so many magnificent buildings, was unfortunate in his choice of a sculptor. Prospero di Brescia, who carved the figure of Moses, is said to have died of grief, or even to have committed suicide, on comparing his work with Michelangelo's Moses in San Pietro in Vincoli (see entry).

★Fontana delle Tartarughe (Tortoise Fountain)   D 6

Situation
Piazza Mattei

Buses
26, 44, 58, 60, 75,
170, 710, 718, 719

This fountain was created by the Florentine sculptor Taddeo Landini in 1581–84 to the design of Giacomo della Porta. From the marble basin rises a base decorated with four shells, and four slender youths with outstretched arms support the upper basin. The tortoises from which the fountain takes its name were added in the 17th c.

Tortoise Fountain

Triton Fountain

★**Fontana di Trevi** (Trevi Fountain) D 5/6

Rome's largest fountain, the Fontana di Trevi, stands in a small square closely hemmed in by buildings. It is supplied by an aqueduct originally constructed by Agrippa, the great art patron of the 1st c. B.C., to bring water to his baths, and later restored by the Popes. The fountain was created for Pope Clement XII between 1732 and 1751 by Nicolò Salvi, whose masterpiece it is.

The fountain, 20m/65ft wide and 26m/85ft high, is built against the rear wall of the palace of the Dukes of Poli. It depicts the "kingdom of Ocean" – the sea god Oceanus (Neptune), with horses (one wild, the other quiet), tritons and shells. The water swirls round the figures and the artificial rocks and collects in a large basin. In the basin can be seen the coins thrown into it by visitors, in virtue of the old tradition that if you throw a coin into the Trevi Fountain you will one day return to Rome.

Situation
Piazza di Trevi

Underground station
Barberini (line A)

Buses
52, 53, 56, 58, 58b, 60, 61, 62, 71, 81, 85, 88, 90, 90b, 95, 115, 415

★**Fontana del Tritone** (Triton Fountain) E 5

In Piazza Barberini stands the Triton Fountain, a masterpiece created by Bernini in 1632–37 for Pope Urban VIII, a member of the Barberini family.

Four dolphins support the Barberini coat of arms with its three bees, and on a large scallop shell sits a triton blowing a conch shell.

Opposite, at the end of Via Veneto (see entry), is the Bee Fountain (1644), also created by Bernini for Urban VIII.

Situation: Piazza Barberini

Underground station
Barberini (line A)

Buses
52, 53, 56, 58, 60, 61, 62, 71, 80, 415

53

Foro di Augusto (Forum of Augustus) E 6

Situation
Via dei Fori
Imperiali, entrance:
Piazza del Grillo 1

Little is left of the Forum of Augustus but three columns from the temple of Mars Ultor (Vengeful Mars), built by Augustus in 2 B.C. (which avenged the murder of Julius Ceasar).

Underground station
Colosseo (line B)

About 1200 the Knights of St John (later of Rhodes and Malta) used the ruins of the forum to build their palaces. In an exedra and in the Antiquarium are remains of the Priory of the Knights of Malta. (Plan: see Foro Romano.)

Foro di Cesare (Forum of Caesar) E 6

Situation
Via dei Fori
Imperiali

Underground station
Colosseo (line B)

Buses
85, 87, 88

The Forum of Caesar or Forum Julium lies at the foot of the Capitol hill (see Campidoglio), part of its area being now occupied by the gardens and car parks of the Via dei Fori Imperiali. It was built between 54 and 46 B.C. by Julius Ceasar at his personal expense, with the object both of enhancing his own fame and meeting the needs of the citizens, for which the old Forum Romanum was no longer adequate. The scanty remains give little impression of the original structure, which covered an area 170×75m/550×250ft. Around the forum were shops, the Basilica Argentaria (occupied by money-changers' offices and the exchange) and the temple of Venus Genetrix. Nothing has survived of the sculptural decoration of the forum, including an equestrian statue of Caesar which is described by ancient writers. (Plan: see Foro Romano.)

★★Foro Romano D/E 6/7

Situation
Via dei Fori
Imperiali

Underground station
Colosseo (line B)

Buses
11, 27, 81, 85, 88, 97

Opening times
Mon.–Sat.
9am–7pm,
in winter 3pm,
Sun. 9am–2pm

No other site in Europe is so pregnant with history as the Roman Forum. Although the surviving remains give only a very inadequate impression of the splendour of the Forum in ancient times, this area at the foot of the Capitol (see Campidoglio) and the Palatine (see Palatino), with its columns still standing erect or lying tumbled on the ground, its triumphal arches and its remains of walls, still have the power to impress, for it was here during many centuries that the fate of Europe was decided. For more than a thousand years the might of Rome, the magnificence of Roman art, Roman law and Roman religion found imposing and enduring expression here.

The history of the Forum was, over this long period, the history of Rome and of the western world. Originally a marshy area between the hills of Rome, it was later drained. The first buildings erected here were temples, soon followed by various public buildings, and the area became the political centre of the city, the meeting-place of the Roman courts and the assemblies which took decisions on the internal and external affairs of the republic. This in turn led to the building of market halls in which the citizens of Rome could go about their business. The Forum thus developed into a complex of buildings serving the purposes of Rome's religious, political and commercial life, increasing in splendour as the city grew in power. Consuls and senators, Caesar and later the Emperors vied with one another in developing and embellishing this focal point of the Roman world which became the meeting-place of the peoples of Europe and the Empire. By the end of the Imperial period the Forum was a densely built-up complex in which "modern" buildings rubbed shoulders with ancient ones, carefully planned structures with casually sited later buildings. Not surprisingly, it is sometimes difficult to identify individual buildings in the huddle of the surviving remains.

The last monument erected in ancient times was the undecorated column set up in A.D. 608 for the Byzantine Emperor Phocas. Thereafter the buildings fell into ruin, and the Forum began to be used for other purposes. Churches and fortresses were built amid the ancient remains, and the area served as a quarry of building stone and a pasturage for cows, becoming known as the Campo Vaccino. It was not until the 18th and 19th c. that systematic excavations brought the ancient buildings to light under a layer of earth and rubble between 10 and 15m/30 and 50ft deep. It needs a good deal of imagination (and small-scale plaster models) to summon up a picture of the Forum in Imperial times; but the site, even in its state of ruin, still retains a powerful evocative force. The entire area, however, suffers from heavy traffic surging around it, and plans are being made to impose traffic restrictions around the site and in the nearby Via dei Fori Imperiali.

The following features are especially notable:

Tempio di Antonino e Faustina (Temple of Antoninus and Faustina)

From the Via Sacra (Sacred Way) a broad flight of steps leads up to the temple of Antoninus Pius and his wife Faustina. The temple was built by resolution of the Senate in A.D. 141 in honour of the deified Empress, and was also dedicated to Antoninus after his death. This is recorded in the inscription "Divo Antonino et Divae Faustinae ex S(enatus) C(onsulto)". Of the temple there survive six columns with Corinthian capitals along the front and a number of columns along the side.

In the 12th c. the temple was converted into the church of San Lorenzo in Miranda. On the occasion of the Emperor Charles V's visit to Rome in 1536 the columns were disengaged from the medieval masonry.

Tempio di Castore e Polluce (Temple of Castor and Pollux)

The Dioscuri – Castor and Pollux – are the subject of numerous myths, partly of Greek and partly of Etruscan origin, featuring healings (in association with the god Aesculapius), beautiful women (including Helen of Troy) and horsemen with their horses. The first temple of Castor and Pollux was built in 484 B.C. by the son of the dictator Aulus Postumius in thanksgiving for the defeat of the Tarquins, which was attributed to the help of the Dioscuri. According to legend, after the victory Castor and Pollux rode to Rome and watered their horses at a spring in the Forum, the Lacus Juturnae (the position of which has been located).

The temple was rebuilt in the reign of Tiberius (1st c. A.D.), and of this temple there survive three Corinthian columns 12m/40ft high, popularly known as the "Three Sisters".

Tempio di Saturno (Temple of Saturn)

The first temple in the Forum was dedicated to Saturn, a god who was probably of Etruscan origin but was adopted by the Romans and worshipped as the supreme god. Built about 497 B.C., soon after the expulsion of the Tarquins, the temple was one of the most important and most venerated of republican Rome.

It was several times destroyed by fire (the last occasion being in the 4th c. A.D.) but was repeatedly rebuilt. It is represented by eight columns with Ionic capitals, now much weathered. Under the Republic the state treasury was kept in this temple. The celebration of the Saturnalia, observed annually on December 17th, started from the temple of Saturn.

Adjoining the temple is a fragment of the Miliarium Aureum, the "Golden Milestone" which was the starting point of the Via Sacra and all the Roman consular roads. On the stone, in golden figures, were inscribed the distance from Rome to the various provinces of the Empire.

Arco di Settimio Severo (Arch of Septimus Severus)

It was a regular practice for the Senate and people of Rome to set up triumphal arches in honour of victorious Emperors and generals, and in A.D. 203 this arch, opposite the church of Santi Martina e Luca, was erected

Foro Romano

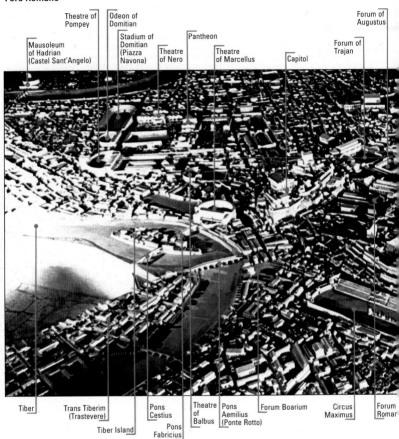

Labels (top, left to right):
Mausoleum of Hadrian (Castel Sant'Angelo) · Theatre of Pompey · Odeon of Domitian · Stadium of Domitian (Piazza Navona) · Theatre of Nero · Pantheon · Theatre of Marcellus · Capitol · Forum of Trajan · Forum of Augustus

Labels (bottom, left to right):
Tiber · Trans Tiberim (Trastevere) · Tiber Island · Pons Cestius · Pons Fabricius · Theatre of Balbus · Pons Aemilius (Ponte Rotto) · Forum Boarium · Circus Maximus · Forum Romar

in honour of Septimus Severus and his sons Caracalla and Geta after their victories over the Parthians and various desert tribes.

On the arch, 23m/75ft high and 25m/80ft wide, are four marble reliefs with vigorous representations of episodes from these wars, the figures standing out prominently from the background. Goddesses of victory with trophies and a large inscription proclaim the glory of the Emperor and his sons (though the name of Geta was later erased).

Other features of the arch are:
 The base of a column commemorating the tenth anniversary of Diocletian's accession.
 The remains of the Rostra, the ancient orators' platform, which was originally decorated with the prows (*rostra*) of captured enemy ships.
 The position of the Umbilicus Urbis, the "navel" or symbolic centre of Rome.

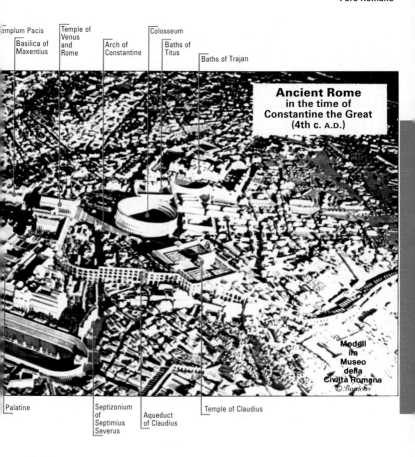

emplum Pacis | Temple of Venus and Rome | Arch of Constantine | Colosseum | Baths of Titus | Baths of Trajan

Basilica of Maxentius

Ancient Rome
in the time of
Constantine the Great
(4th c. A.D.)

Modell im Museo della Civiltà Romana
© *Baedeker*

Palatine | Septizonium of Septimius Severus | Aqueduct of Claudius | Temple of Claudius

Curia

The Curia, meeting-place of the Roman Senate, is one of the best preserved ancient buildings in the Forum. The first such building was erected in the time of the kings, and thereafter rebuilding was frequently necessary as a result of fires and other forms of destruction in the time of Sulla, Caesar, Augustus, Diocletian, Julian and Apostate, etc. Finally in the 7th c. the Curia was converted into a church and was thus preserved from further destruction. Borromini adapted its bronze doors to serve as the main doorway of St John Lateran (see San Giovanni in Laterano).

The Curia, a plain and unornamented building both externally and internally, was stripped of later accretions between 1931 and 1937. It is now sometimes used for special exhibitions.

The building measures 27×18m/90×60ft internally, and could seat some 300 senators. It preserves fragments of a coloured marble floor. Here, too, are displayed the Anaglyphs of Trajan, two travertine slabs with reliefs depicting the Emperor and the people of Rome.

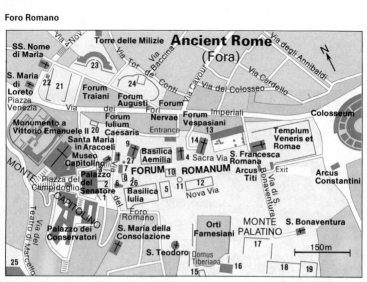

1 Portico of the Twelve Gods
2 Temple of Vespasian
3 Temple of Concordia
4 Temple of Faustina
5 Temple of Castor and Pollux
6 Temple of Saturn
7 Arch of Septimius Severus
8 Rostra
9 Curia Iulia (church of
  Sant'Adriano)

10 Temple of Caesar
11 Temple of Vesta
12 House of Vestal Virgins
13 Basilica of Maxentius
14 Church of Santi Cosma e
   Damiano
15 Temple of Cybele
16 House of Livia
17 Palace of Flavians
18 Palace of Augustus

19 Stadium
20 Temple of Venus Genetrix
21 Basilica Ulpia
22 Trajan's Column
23 Trajan's Market
24 Temple of Mars Ultor
25 Theatre of Marcellus
26 Column of Phocas
27 Lapis Niger

Tempio di Vesta (Temple of Vesta)

In ancient times the Temple of Vesta in the Forum – there is another temple
of Vesta in the Forum Boarium – contained the "Sacred Fire" which was
guarded by the Vestals (virgins selected from the best families in Rome).
The six priestesses served in the temple between the ages of 10 and 14. The
Romans attached great importance to this "eternal fire"; on the first day of
the new year (March 1st) they put out the fires in their houses and lit new
ones from the flame in the temple of Vesta. The present remains, dating
from the time of Septimus Severus (A.D. 193–211), indicate that the temple
was circular, with 20 slender columns supporting the roof. Archaeological
investigation has established that there was an opening in the centre of the
roof to let out the smoke from the sacred flame.

Atrium Vestae (House of the Vestals)

Adjoining the Temple of Vesta was the house of the Vestal virgins, also built
by Septimus Severus. It consisted of a large atrium, the lodgings of the
priestesses, and various offices. The plan of the building, with remains of
the foundations and numerous statue bases, can be readily identified. It is
known from the works of Latin writers that the sacred Palladium (an image
of Pallas Athene), which Aeneas was said to have brought from Troy to
Latium, was preserved in the House of the Vestals.

Arch of Septimus Severus

Forum Romanum

Foro Romano

Faustina Temple

Castor and Pollux Temple (on right)

Colonna di Foca (Column of Phocas)

In front of the Rostra (see above) is a Corinthian column 13.8m/45ft high, erected in A.D. 608 in honour of the Byzantine Emperor Phocas and in recognition of his presentation of the Pantheon to Pope Boniface IV for conversion into a church.

Lapis Niger (Black Stone)

Outside the Curia, protected by a low roof, is a block of black marble, under which, according to Roman legend, is the tomb of Romulus, founder of Rome. Close by is a stele, excavated in 1899, with the oldest known Latin inscription.

Arco di Tito (Arch of Titus)

At the end of the Forum farthest from the Capitol is the Arch of Titus, the oldest of the Roman triumphal arches, erected after Titus' death by his successor Domitian.

Titus, son the Emperor Vespasian, was the Roman general who captured Jerusalem in the year 70 and thus put the final seal on the defeat of the Jewish people in Palestine. The reliefs on the arch, which has a single passageway, depict this event, and also the victorious general's triumphal procession to the Capitol. Titus (who became Emperor only in the year 79) is shown in his chariot accompanied by the goddess of Victory with a laurel wreath and by the booty brought back from the Jewish War – the seven-branched candlestick, the table with the shewbread and trumpets from the treasury of the Temple.

Forum of Trajan with the Colonna di Traiano and Santa Maria di Loreto ▶

Santa Maria Antiqua Church

As its name indicates, the church of Santa Maria Antiqua (badly damaged and rarely open to the public) is the oldest and the most important Christian building in the Forum. Converted from a building of the Roman Imperial period in the 6th c. and richly furnished by various 8th c. Popes (John VII, Zacharias and Paul I), the church thereafter fell into a state of dilapidation before being restored in the 13th c.

This extensive complex at the foot of the Palatine hill is of interest for its architecture and for its wall paintings, ranging in date between the 6th and 8th c.

★ Foro di Traiano (Forum of Trajan)   E 6

Situation
Via dei Fori
Imperiali

Underground station
Colosseo (line B)

Buses
85, 87, 88

Opening times
Tues.–Sat.
9am–1pm,
(summer Thur., Sat.
until 6pm)
Sun. 9am–12.30pm

The Forum of the Emperor Trajan (A.D. 98–117), the last, largest and best preserved on the Imperial fora, comprised a considerable complex of buildings, including a temple and basilica as well as three monuments erected in honour of the Emperor himself – a triumphal arch, an equestrian statue and a victory column. The markets extended north-east up the Quirinal hill. The forum, designed by Apollodorus of Damascus, was begun in A.D. 107 and completed in 143. During the Middle Ages new buildings were erected in the area of the forum by the Colonna and Caetani families, among them the Torre delle Milizie (see entry) still to be seen in Via Quattro Novembre, and later the twin churches of Santa Maria di Loreto and the Santissimo Nome di Maria were also built here. In the first half of the present century a wide motor road and a number of smaller streets were laid out in the area (see Via dei Fori Imperiali).

Excavations carried out since 1928 have revealed the layout of the forum. A triumphal arch erected in A.D. 116 gave access to an open rectangular area, in the centre of which stood an equestrian statue of the Emperor. At the far end was the Basilica Ulpia, a hall measuring 130×125m/430×410ft. In the present state of the site it is difficult to image a building of these dimensions; and indeed it was no easy matter at the time it was built to find space for it in this crowded part of central Rome. Built on to the rear of the basilica were two libraries, one for Latin and the other for Greek literature, and between the two reared up Trajan's victory column (see below). Beyond this, at the end of the forum (between the two churches dedicated to the Virgin), was a temple of deified Trajan. Only Trajan's column is left to represent this whole complex, much admired in ancient times, dedicated to honouring the Emperor under whom the Roman Empire reached its greatest extent. (Plan: see Foro Romano.)

★ Colonna di Traiano (Trajan's Column)

This victory column which has undergone costly cleaning and renovation, is a magnificent monument to Roman Imperial power and the skill of Roman sculptors. The column 38m/125ft high and constructed of marble from the Greek island of Paros, is covered with a spiral frieze 200m/655ft long, with over 2500 figures depicting Trajan's wars with the Dacians in 101–102 and 105–106. This frieze, with its fighting soldiers, prancing horses and the whole panoply of Roman military equipment, is worth studying in detail – though this is more difficult for the modern visitor than for the ancients, who could examine the reliefs from the windows of the two libraries. A spiral staircase of 185 steps runs up inside the column, lit by 43 narrow slits in the wall of the column. In the base of the column was a golden urn containing the Emperor's ashes, and on its summit was a golden statue of Trajan. The statue was lost during the Middle Ages and in 1588 Pope Sixtus V replaced it with a figure of the Apostle Peter with his key. (Plan: see Foro Romano.)

★ Mercati di Traiano (Trajan's Markets)

To the north of Trajan's Forum was a semicircular range of market halls in three tiers, the ruins of which, with their red-brick walls and high vaulted roofs, form an impressive termination to the group of Imperial fora, rising up the slopes of the Quirinal hill to Via Quattro Novembre. The difference in level was skilfully exploited by the architect, Apollodorus of Damascus (early 2nd c.). In establishing his markets Trajan was concerned to ease the financial burdens of the population by maintaining prices at a reasonable level and to reduce social tensions by the distribution of Imperial subsidies. (Plan: see Foro Romano.)

Foro di Vespasiano   E 6

Adjoining the Forum of Nerva (see entry) at the point where Via Cavour now joins the Via dei Fori Imperiali, was the Forum of the Emperor Vespasian (A.D. 69–79), in the centre of which was the Temple of Peace (after which it was also known as the Forum of Peace). The forum, of which only a few fragments remain, was built by Vespasian and paid for from the booty won in the Jewish War. (Plan: see Foro Romano.)

Buses: 11, 27, 81, 85, 87, 88.

Situation
Corner of Via Cavour and Via dei Fori Imperiali

Underground station
Colosseo (line B)

Galleria Colonna (in Palazzo Colonna)   D 5/6

The huge palace of the Colonnas, one of Rome's leading noble families, which produced Pope Martin V (1417–31) and many other notable figures, was begun in the 15th c. and completed after successive extensions in 1730. Within the precincts of the palace are the church of Santi Apostoli (see entry) and the Galleria Colonna, built by Antonio del Grande and Girolamo Fontana in the 17th c.

The gallery contains a famous collection of pictures originally founded by Cardinal Girolamo Colonna. This consists mainly of works by 17th and 18th c. masters (including Veronese "Portrait of a Nobleman"; Tintoretto "Portrait of Onofrio Panvinios" and "Narcissus"; the "Portrait of Lucrezia Tomacelli Colonna" ascribed to Van Dyke and a ceiling painting by Sebastiano Ricci), together with pictures recording the achievements of the Colonna family: e.g. the victory won by Marcantonio Colonna as commander of the European fleet at the battle of Lepanto (1571) against the Turks.

Situation
Via della Pilotta 17, Piazza SS Apostoli

Buses
56, 57, 60, 62, 64, 65, 70, 71, 75, 81, 85, 88, 90, 95, 170

Opening times
Sat. 9am–1pm
(closed in Aug.)

Galleria Nazionale d'Arte Antica

See Palazzo Barberini

★ Galleria Nazionale d'Arte Moderna (National Gallery of Modern Art)   D 4

The National Gallery of Modern Art, founded in 1883, has the largest collection of works by Italian painters and sculptors of the 19th and 20th c. The 70 rooms (only 25 at present open to the public) of the massive building in which it is housed present a survey of Italian and foreign painting and sculpture since 1800, though some leading figures are missing and others are represented only by some minor works. Notable among the non-Italian artists are Degas, Cézanne, Mondrian and Van Gogh ("The Gardener"). Other items of particular interest are pictures by the Macchiaioli, a group of open-air painters from Tuscany comparable in style with the Impression-

Situation
Viale delle Belle Arti

Bus 26

Trams
19, 19b, 30. 30b

The Jesuit church of ''Il Jesu''

Tomb of Ignatius of Loyola (founder of the Society of Jesus)

ists, sculpture by Marino Marini and Giacomo Manzù and paintings by Giogio de Chirico.

The gallery courtyard, displaying Antoine Bourdell's "Bowman" amongst the ivy and roses, is an attractive setting.
Opening times: Tues.–Sat. 9am–7pm, Sun. 9am–1pm.

★ Gesù Church

The Gesù is the principal church of the Jesuits. The initiative for its construction came from Ignatius Loyola, founder in 1540 of the Society of Jesus, an order which spread quickly throughout the Roman Catholic countries of Europe and organised the Counter-Reformation. Adjoining the church is a house (now a Jesuit college) in which Ignatius was living at the time of the church's foundation. Cardinal Alessandro Farnese, whose heraldic lilies recur frequently in the decoration of the interior, commissioned Vignola to design and build the church, which was completed by members of the Society. The basic innovation of the design was to set a dome over the crossing of the nave and transepts of a basilican church, a type familiar in Roman, early Christian and medieval models. The Gesù was much imitated by later churches, not only in the general plan but also in details and the form of the façade.

Situation
Piazza del Gesù

Buses
46, 56, 60, 62, 64, 65, 70, 75, 81, 88, 90, 170

The façade by Giacomo della Porta, completed in 1575, shows both Renaissance and Baroque features. The two statues represent Ignatius Loyola and St Francis Xavier the venerated missionary.

Façade

The interior is notable for its unified effect. Flanking the nave are lateral chapels, which seem almost cut off from the body of the church, and beyond the spacious transepts is the choir, terminating in an apse.
The decoration of the interior is of great richness, with variegated marble, sculpture, bronze statues, stucco ornament, gilding and frescoes. In the barrel vaulting of the nave is a painting of the "Triumph of the Name of Jesus", which glorifies the great missionary achievements of the Jesuits.

Interior

Particularly notable are the altars and tombs of Jesuit saints:
In the south transept the altar of St Francis Xavier by Pietro da Cortona (1674–8).
To the right of the high altar the monument of Cardinal Ballarmine, with a bust by Bernini (1622).
In the north transept the altar and tomb of St Ignatius (1491–1556), founder of the Jesuit order, by Andrea Pozzo (1696–1700).
The present statue of the saint is a copy of the original silver statue by Pierre Legros, which Pope Pius VII was obliged to melt down to meet reparations payable to Napoleon under the treaty of Tolentino.

Grottaferrata

No tour of the Castelli Romani area (see Colli Albani) would be complete without a visit to the old abbey of the Basilians (an order of the Greek Catholic Church) at Grottaferrata, described by Pope Leo XIII at the end of the 19th c. as "a jewel from the East in the Papal tiara".

Situation
21 km/13 miles SE

Underground station
Line A to Cinecittà (then regular bus service from Via Labieno)

The abbey, situated at an altitude of 329m/1080ft, is not only a venerable old religious house with some notable works of art but an example of Renaissance defensive architecture.

Ianiculcum

See Passeggiata del Gianicolo

Isola Tiberine (Tiber Island)   D 7

Buses
15, 23, 26, 44, 56,
60, 65, 75, 170, 710,
718, 719, 774

A Roman legend has it that the Tiber Island was formed when, at some time in the distant past, a heavy laden ship sank in mid stream; and indeed the island has something of the air of a huge vessel stranded in the Tiber. The obelisk which once stood on the island must in its day have looked like a mast. Another explanation, based on historical grounds, is that the island was formed by an accumulation of silt produced by waste from cargoes of corn after the expulsion of the Tarquins. About 200 B.C. there was a sanctuary of the healing god Aesculapius and his sacred snakes on the island where, according to another legend, the god's boat had once called in.

Ponte Fabrico

The existence of the island made this a convenient place for bridging the Tiber. In 62 B.C. the consul L. Fabricius built the Ponte Fabrico, Rome's oldest surviving bridge, which links the island with the left bank of the river and the Capitol. It is popularly known as the Ponte dei Quattro Capi ("Bridge of the Four Heads") after two four-headed herms on the balustrades. On the island are the Fatebenefratelli Hospital – maintaining the

San Bartolomeo

tradition of healing associated with Aesculapius – and the church of San Bartolomeo, built at the end of the 10th c. by the Emperor Otto III on the ruins of the temple of Aesculapius and restored in the Baroque period. Notable features of the church are the beautiful Romanesque campanile and a marble well-head at the entrance to the chancel (probably over the spring belonging to the ancient sanctuary) carved with figures of Christ, St Adalbert of Bohemia, an Apostle (probably Bartholomew) and Otto III.

Ponte Rotto and Tiber Island

The island is linked with the right bank of the Tiber (Trastevere) by the Ponte Cestio, built by Lucius Cestius in 46 B.C. and renewed on a number of occasions under the Empire.

To the south of the Isola Tiberina, in the river, is the Ponte Rotto ("Broken Bridge"), all that remains of the Pons Aemilius, which was begun in timber by the censors Aemilius Lepidus and Fulvus Nobilior in 179 B.C. and completed in stone in 142 (the first arched stone bridge in Rome).

Largo di Torre Argentina   D 6

In the centre of the Largo di Torre Argentina, a few feet below the level of this busy square with its swirling traffic, is the Largo Argentina temple precinct. The name Torre Argentina is derived from the tower of a house (at Via del Sudario 44) occupied by a prelate named Burckhardt from Strasbourg (Argentoratum) who was Papal master of ceremonies at the beginning of the 16th c. An alternative explanation is that the square is named after the shops of the silversmiths (*argentarii*) who worked in this area.

The temples which were excavated here in 1926–30 are one of the few such complexes dating from the republican period.

Buses
26, 44, 46, 56, 60, 62, 64, 65, 70, 75, 87, 94, 170, 710, 718, 719

There are four temples:
The rectangular Temple A (near the bus stops), with 15 columns still standing, within which was built the medieval church of San Nicola dei Cesarini (now destroyed).
The adjoining Temple, circular in plan, with six columns, which once housed a seated effigy of the goddess Juno.
The rectangular Temple C, the smallest and oldest (4th or 3rd c. B.C.) of the temples, on a lower level than the others.
Temple D, part of which is under the roadway.
It is not known with certainty which gods were worshipped in these temples.

Lido di Ostia

The once beautiful beach of Ostia is still one of the weekend and holiday resorts most favoured by the people of Rome, and accordingly is one of the busiest and liveliest stretches of sand and promenades in the whole of Italy. In recent years, however, Lido di Ostia has grown into a town of considerable size (pop. 55,000), and since most of its sewage goes into the sea, where it is joined by the sewage carried down by the Tiber from Rome, bathing in the sea here is not to be recommended – indeed at times it is prohibited by the public health authorities.

Situation
20km/12 miles S

Railway
Rome–Ostia Lido
branch of
Underground line B

Mausoleo di Augusto   D 5

The present appearance of the Piazza Augusto Imperatore gives little hint of the importance this area once enjoyed. Here, some years before his death, the Emperor Augustus constructed a mausoleum for himself and his family (the Julio-Claudian dynasty). This took the form of a gigantic earthen mound 89m/290ft in diameter, of the kind used for the burial of kings and princes in the Mediterranean area since prehistoric times.

Outside the entrance to the mound stood two Egyptian obelisks, now to be seen behind the church of Santa Maria Maggiore (see entry) and in the Piazza Quirinale (see entry). By the entrance were the "Res Gestae", two bronze tablets on which Augustus recorded the achievements of his reign. (The original tablets are lost, but their text has been preserved in inscriptions.) During the Middle Ages the mausoleum was used by the

Situation
Piazza Augusto
Imperatore

Buses
2, 26, 81, 90, 90b, 115, 911

Opening times
Information
tel. 67 10 20 70

Mausoleum of Augustus

Colonna family as a fortress, which was pulled down by Pope Gregory IX in 1241. Thereafter the mausoleum became a vineyard, a garden, an amphitheatre and even a concert hall, before being restored to its original state in 1936.

Monte Testaccio　　　　　　　　　　　　　　　　　　　D 8

Buses
27, 92

Between the Tiber and Porta San Paolo is a small hill, 35m/115ft high and 850m/930yd in circumference, which was formed during the republican period by the deposit of rubbish, mainly broken pottery from the nearby warehouses, on the banks of the Tiber where the merchant vessels discharged their cargoes.

The site was occupied in ancient times by large trading establishments and the Portus Aemilius (2nd c. B.C.), a street of shops 487m/530yd long. The hill is now honeycombed with wine-cellars, some of which have tavernas attached.

★Monumento Nazionale a Vittorio Emanuele II　　　　　D 6
(National Monument to Victor Emmanuel II)

Situation
Piazza Venezia

Buses
46, 57, 85, 87, 88,
90, 90b, 92, 94, 95,
716, 718, 719

The National Monument to Victor Emmanuel II – a memorial to which there are varying reactions, of approval or disapproval – was built between 1885 and 1911 to celebrate the winning of Italian unity in 1870 and to commemorate the first king of united Italy, Victor Emmanuel II (d. 1878). The monument is 135m/440ft long by 130m/425ft deep and rears up to a height of 70m/230ft. Half-way up are the "Altar of the Fatherland" (Altare della Patria) and the Tomb of the Unknown Soldier, which regularly feature in city tours.

National Monument to King Victor Emmanuel II

The east part of the Monument houses the Museo Centrale del Risorgimento (museum of Italian independence; tel. 6 79 35 98) and the Museo Sacrano delle Bandiere della Marina Militare (museum of flags; closed for restoration).

Mura Aureliane (Aurelian Walls)   B 6/7–C 7

The Aurelian Walls were built by the Emperor Aurelius in A.D. 270–275 to protect Rome – which had by now far outgrown the old Servian Walls – against the fresh dangers which were threatening the city from the northern provinces of the Empire. The main threat came from the Goths, who in A.D. 268 had pushed forward from the plain of the Po into Umbria.

The Aurelian Walls had a total length of some 20km/12½ miles. They were about 4m/13ft thick and originally stood 7.2m/24ft high, but were raised by Stilicho, the great general of the Emperor Honorius (A.D. 395–423), to 10.6m/35ft and reinforced by 380 towers standing some 30m/33yd apart. There were 16 gates in the circuit. The very length of the walls, however, meant that they rarely served their military function.

The walls were kept in repair until the 19th c. Although parts of the circuit have been used as a quarry of building material in the last 100 years or so, some sections have been preserved, and in places it is possible to walk along the top.

Museo Barracco   C 6

The Museo Barracco, presented to the city by Baron Giovanni Barracco in 1902, contains a small but very interesting collection of Assyrian, Babylonian, Egyptian, Greek, Etruscan and Roman sculpture, both originals and

Situation
Corso Vittorio
Emanuele II 168

69

Buses
46, 62, 64

Opening times
Tues.–Sat.
9am–1.30pm,
Sun. 9am–1pm,
Tues. and Thurs.
also 5–8pm

copies, illustrating the development of ancient art in the pre-Christian centuries. Particularly notable items are some Assyrian reliefs of the 7th c. B.C., a sphinx with the head of Queen Hatshepsut (15th c. B.C.), Greek statues of the early classical period and Etruscan cippi. Also of interest are the head of the Diadumenos (second half of 5th c. B.C.) by Polycletus, the head of an Apollo (mid 5th c. B.C.) ascribed to Phidias, a bust of Epicurus (c. 270 B.C.), the head of the Lycian Apollo, the "Wounded Bitch" (Lysippus) and a head of Alexander Helios (late 4th c. B.C.).

★Museo Capitolino (Capitoline Museum)   D 6

Situation
Piazza del
Campidoglio

The Capitoline Museum, founded by Pope Sixtus IV in 1471, is the oldest public art collection in Europe and has a rich stock of classical sculpture.

Buses
57, 85, 87, 88, 90,
90b, 92, 94, 95, 716,
718, 719

Opening times
Tues.–Sun.
9am–1.30pm,
Tues. also 5–8pm,
Sat. also 8–11pm

In the Palazzo Nuova of the Capitoline Museum, built about 1650 on the model of the Palazzo dei Conservatori (see entry) on the opposite side of the square, the following pieces of sculpture are outstanding: the "Dying Gaul", a Roman copy of the figure of a dying warrior from the victory monument erected by King Attalus of Pergamon in the 3rd c. B.C. after he had defeated the Galatians; the "Wounded Amazon", a copy of a work by Cresilas (5th c. B.C.); the "Capitoline Venus", a Roman copy of the Cnidian Aphrodite of Praxiteles; and two Hellenistic works, "Amor and Psyche" and the "Drunken Old Woman". Also of the greatest interest are the collections of 64 portrait heads of Roman Emperors and members of their families and 79 busts of Greek and Roman philosophers and scholars.

The recently restored equestrian statue of Marcus Aurelius (see Campidoglio) stands behind glass in the courtyard of the Capitoline Museum.

Capitoline Museum: Palazzo Nuovo

★ Museo della Civiltà Romana (Museum of Roman Culture) K 11

The Museum of Roman Culture, housed in a building presented to the city of Rome by the Fiat company, seeks to illustrate the history of Rome with the help of models and reconstructions. It offers an excellent survey of the development of the Roman world empire and of the changing architecture of Rome under the Republic and the Empire.

Situation
EUR, Piazza Giovanni Agnelli

Underground station
EUR, Fermi (line B)

Opening times: Tues.–Sat. 9am–1.30pm, Tues. and Thurs. also 4–7pm, Sun. 9am–1pm.

Piazza Giovanni Agnelli

 1 Vestibule
 2 Atrium
 3 Hall of Honour
 4 Map of Roman Empire
 5 Roman legends; the earliest Roman culture
 6 Beginnings of the city
 7 Conquest of the Mediterranean area
 8 Caesar
 9 Augustus
10 Family of Augustus; the Julio-Claudian Emperors
11 The Flavians
12 Trajan and Hadrian
13 Roman Emperors Antoninus Pius to the Severans
14 Roman Emperors from Macrinus to Justinian
15 Christianity
16–19 The Roman army
20–21 The Roman navy
22 Ports

23 Central administration
24 The Imperial court
25 The Roman triumph
26 Provinces of the Roman Empire
27 Regions of Italy
28 Building, tunnelling, mining
29 Baths, aqueducts, fountains, cisterns
30 Theatres, amphitheatres, arenas, sports grounds
31 Fora, temples, basilicas
32 Arches and gates
33 Roads, bridges, milestones, vehicles
34 Gates from Aphrodisias (Asia Minor) and Leptis Magna (Libya)
35 Social relations
36 Schools
37 Model of Rome in the time of Constantine the Great
38 Plans of Roman towns

39 Tombs
40 Houses
41 Museum administration and records
42 Family life
43 Religion
44 Portraits
45 Hoards of silver
46 Roman law
47 Libraries
48 Musical instruments
49 Literature and science
50 Medicine and pharmacy
51 Casts of the reliefs on Trajan's Column
52 Industry and crafts
53 Agriculture, stock-farming, land surveying
54 Hunting, fishing, food
55 Commerce
56–58 Roman art (outstanding examples)
59 Column of Marcus Aurelius

71

Museo Nazionale d'Arte Orientale (National Museum of Oriental Art)   F 6

The National Museum of Oriental Art displays in its fourteen rooms the art of Asia from Persia to Japan, over the period from prehistoric times (5th c. B.C.) to the present day. Afghanistan and China, Korea and India, Nepal and Tibet, Iraq and Pakistan are all represented by a wide range of gold jewellery and bronzes, ceramics and clothing, sculpture and paintings, busts and vases.
Opening times: Tues.–Sat. 9am–2pm, Sun. 9am–1pm.

Situation
Via Merulana 248

Buses
11, 16, 93, 93b, 93c

★Museo Nazionale delle Arti e Tradizioni Populari   J 11

The National Museum of Folk Arts and Traditions has ten sections devoted to Italian folk art and the traditions and customs of the different parts of Italy, illustrated with displays of flags, costumes, musical instruments and models.
Gradually the museum is being rebuilt. Not all the departments are open to visitors.
Opening times are: Tues.–Sat. 9am–2pm, Sun. 9am–1pm.

Situation
EUR, Piazza
Marconi 10

Underground stations
EUR-Marconi or
EUR-Fermi (line B)

★Museo Nazionale Etrusco di Villa Giulia (National Etruscan Museum)   D 4

The Villa Giulia, built by Vignola for Pope Julius III in 1550–55, has housed the national collection of Etruscan art since 1889.

The museum provides a comprehensive survey of the high standard of art and culture attained by this mysterious people, whose achievements the Romans deliberately obscured.

Particularly notable are the finds from Etruscan cemeteries (cinerary urns, reconstruction of a tomb from Cerveteri), fine small sculpture and everyday utensils, statuary (in particular the Apollo of Veii) and the famous sarcophagus from Cerveteri (c. 530 B.C.) with the reclining figures of a husband and wife.

The museum contains much else of interest – figures and figurines, grave goods and votive offerings, pottery, glass, gold and silver jewellery.

Situation
Piazzale di Giulia 9

Bus: 26

Trams 19, 30

Opening times
Tues.–Sat.
9am–7pm,
Sun. 9am–1pm

Museo Nazionale Romano o delle Terme

See Terme di Diocleziano

Museo di Roma (Museum of Rome) Palazzo Braschi   C 6

The Palazzo Braschi, built from 1792 onwards for the Braschi family, relatives of Pope Pius VI, has housed since 1952 a collection of pictures, drawings, watercolours and prints illustrating the history of the city of Rome, together with sculpture, terracotta figures, majolica, tapestries and costumes. The exhibits also include Pope Pius IX's private train (1850) and two state carriages.

The museum's 51 rooms contain a wealth of material illustrating life in medieval and modern Rome and the history and development of the city.

On the instructions of Cardinal Carafa the remains of statues of Menelaus and Patroclus were erected, marking the site of a previous building.

Situation
Piazza San
Pantaleo 10

Buses 46, 62, 64

Closed for
restoration.
Temporary
exhibitions
sometimes on
show Tues.–Sat.
9am–11pm.
Tues. and Sat. also
5–7.30pm

◀ In the Etruscan Museum of the Villa Giulia

Museo Torlonia C 6

Situation
Via Corsini 5

The Museo Torlonia is one of the largest private collections of antiquities in Europe, with some 600 pieces of sculpture. The collection was begun by Giovanni Raimondo Torlonia (1754–1829), a wealthy Roman, who acquired a number of private collections and added to them material found in excavations on his estates.

The museum can be seen by appointment only; apply to the Amministrazione Torlonia, Via della Conciliazione 30.

Obelisco di Axum (Obelisk of Axum) E 7

Underground station
Circo Massimo
(line B)

The Obelisk of Axum, 24m/80ft high, which stands in the Piazza di Porta Capena was brought from Axum, the holy city of Ethiopia, in 1937, during the Italian war of conquest in Abyssinia.

Oratorio dei Filippini C 6

Situation
Piazza della Chiesa
Nuovo

Buses
46, 62, 64

Immediately to the left of the Chiesa Nuovo (see entry) is the Oratory, a residential house of prayer of the Congregation of Oratorians founded by St Philip Neri. The house was built for the Oratorians – an order which was very popular in Rome – by Borromini (1637–50), and was designed as a place where they could live, work and pray in common. A notable feature of the building is the finely articulated façade, which contrasts with the adjoining church in height, form and colouring.

The Sala del Borromini, in the former Oratory, is now used as a concert hall. The Oratory also contains the Biblioteca Vallicelliana, the oldest library open to the public in Rome.

Orotorio di San Giovanni in Oleo F 8

Situation
Via di Porta San
Sebastiano

Bus
118

The Oratory of St John "in the Oil" is a small octagonal chapel built by Bramante at the beginning of the 16th c. on the remains of an earlier building, and later embellished by Borromini. Here, according to legend, St John was thrown into boiling oil but emerged unharmed, thereafter being banished to Patmos.

If the Oratory is closed apply to the missionary college at No. 17.

★Ostia Antica

Situation
28km/17 miles SW

Railway
Rome–Ostia Lido
branch of
Underground
line B
Station Ostia Antica

No site in the neighbourhood of Rome gives such a vivid and comprehensive impression of an ancient city as Ostia Antica, the excavated remains of Roman Ostia.

According to Roman legend it was here, at the mouth (*ostium*) of the Tiber, that Aeneas, forefather of the Latins, landed in Italy and King Martius established a settlement in the 7th c. B.C. Archaeological investigation has shown, however, that it was only about 335 B.C. that a little fishing and trading town grew up here on the banks of the Tiber and on the sea coast. This settlement flourished and developed along with Rome, and under the Empire became one of the busiest and most important Roman commercial and naval ports, with a population of some 10,000 – a status which is clearly reflected in the extensive surviving remains.

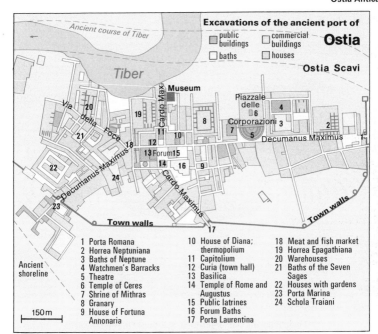

Excavations of the ancient port of Ostia

☐ public buildings ☐ commercial buildings
☐ baths ☐ houses

Ostia Scavi

1 Porta Romana	10 House of Diana; thermopolium	18 Meat and fish market
2 Horrea Neptuniana	11 Capitolium	19 Horrea Epagathiana
3 Baths of Neptune	12 Curia (town hall)	20 Warehouses
4 Watchmen's Barracks	13 Basilica	21 Baths of the Seven Sages
5 Theatre	14 Temple of Rome and Augustus	22 Houses with gardens
6 Temple of Ceres	15 Public latrines	23 Porta Marina
7 Shrine of Mithras	16 Forum Baths	24 Schola Traiani
8 Granary	17 Porta Laurentina	
9 House of Fortuna Annonaria		

In later centuries the town fell into oblivion for a variety of reasons. The importance of Rome as a political and commercial centre showed a steady decline with the division of the Empire in the reign of Constantine, the fall of the Western Empire in the 5th c. and the troubles of the medieval period; the Tiber deposited increasing quantities of silt around its mouth, so that the sea moved steadily away from Ostia; the area was plagued with malaria and finally the construction of a canal at Fiumicino in 1613 deprived the town of its maritime trade.

Excavations carried out since the 19th c. have brought to light more than half the town's area of 66 ha/165 acres, revealing streets and dwelling-houses, theatres and administrative buildings, temples and barracks, shops and workshops, tombs and warehouses, baths and city gates, inns and hostels, sports facilities and port installations, statues and mosaics. The excavations have yielded not merely a series of unrelated remains, but the layout of a complete urban organism, with its division into five wards or districts and its rectangular street plan.

It is possible to drive into the excavation site (Scavi) and leave your car in the car park. Alternatively you can start your tour on foot from the main entrance. In the latter event you follow the Via dei Sepolcri (Street of Tombs), pass through the Porta Romana and continue along the Decumanus Maximus (part of the Via Ostiense, the road from Rome) to the theatre, passing on the way the Piazzale della Vittoria (with a statue of Minerva Victoria, the goddess of victory), baths, warehouses (*horrea*) and dwelling houses.

Even a brief visit should include at least the following:

First, the theatre. Built in the reign of Augustus, altered under Septimus Severus and Caracalla and restored some years ago, it can accommodate an audience of some 2700. Performances are given here during the sum-

Ampitheatre of Ostia Antica

mer. From the auditorium there is a view of the Piazzale delle Corporazioni behind the theatre, with the offices of 70 business firms and shipping agents, their business and place of origin being indicated by mosaics on the floor. In the centre of the square is the Temple of Ceres. To the right can be seen the Caserma dei Vigili (Watchmen's Barracks), a palaestra (a sports and athletic ground) and the Baths of Neptune. On the opposite side of the Decumanus Maximus are the Warehouses of Hortensius and beyond these an area which has not yet been excavated.

Beyond the theatre are the handsome House of Apuleius (Casa di Apuleio) and a mithraeum (shrine of Mithras), and on the opposite side of the main street the Collegium Augustale and the House of Fortuna Annonaria amid a closely packed complex of dwelling-houses. From here continue south to the temple of the Magna Mater (Cybele) and return to the main street, passing on the way the Forum Baths, the Temple of Rome and Augustus and the Casa dei Triclini. In the Forum, adjoining the Temple of Rome and Augustus, is the Basilica, and at the far end of the Forum, dominating the scene, is the Curia.

The tour of the site can be extended to take in the Tempio Rotondo, the Scuola di Traiano, the Piazzale della Bone Dea, the Casa a Giardino (dwelling-houses, gardens and arcades), the Baths of Mithras, temples of the republican period, the House of Amor and Psyche, the Little Market, the Casa dei Dipinti and the Casa di Diana.

There is also an interesting museum containing finds from the site.

★★Palatino (Palatine Hill)   D/E 7

Underground station
Colosseo (line B)

The Palatine occupies a leading place among the seven hills of Rome. It is associated with the legend of the foundation of the city, and has yielded evidence of the earliest settlement in the area, strategically situated

50m/165ft above the Tiber, near the Isola Tiberina.. Under the Empire palaces (the very word "palace" comes from the Palatine) were built here by the Emperors and great aristocratic families of Rome; and although the remains of these buildings give only a very inadequate impression of their former magnificence, a walk over the Palatine nevertheless takes us into the heart of Roman history.

History

Politicians such as Agrippa, the great art patron, and writers including Cicero had houses on the Palatine. Augustus, who was born here, enlarged his father's mansion, and under Augustus and his successors a whole series of splendid palaces, temples and public buildings were erected, reaching in the reign of Domitian the form in which we see their remains today. Since each generation carried out alterations and rebuilding, it is now difficult to disentangle the different periods of construction.

During the Middle Ages the splendours of the Palatine fell into eclipse. Numbers of convents and churches – the oratory of Caesarius, Santa Anastasia, Santa Lucia, San Sebastiano – were built over the remains of the pagan buildings, and the noble Frangipane family used them to establish a fortified stronghold. In the 16th c. wealthy families, including the Ronconi, Mattei, Spada, Magnani and Barberini, laid out gardens and vineyards on the hill, and Cardinal Alessandro Farnese commissioned famous architects to give the Palatine park its final form.

The Palatine began to attract archaeological interest in the 18th c. The names of many buildings on the Palatine were known from the works of Roman writers, but some buildings of major importance could not be located on the ground, and even today have not been found. The Palatine was frequently ravaged by fire; and as a result of these and other vicissi-tudes in its history it is now reduced, like the Forum, to a great field of ruins – but highly impressive and evocative ruins. The most important and most interesting of the structures on the hill are described below.

Buses
11, 15, 27, 85, 87, 90, 90b, 118, 673

Trams
13, 30, 30b

Opening times
Mon.–Sat. Summer 9am–7pm,
winter 9am–3pm,
Sun. 9am–2pm

View from the communal rose garden to the Palatine

Access

There are four routes of access to the Palatine. The first leads from Via San Gregorio Magno through the gateway designed by Vignola as the entrance to the Farnese Gardens. The other three start from the Forum (see Foro Romano): the Clivus Capitolinus, which leads past the Arch of Titus; the flight of steps at the House of the Vestals; and the large vaulted passage at Santa Maria Antiqua. (Plan: see Foro Romano.)

Criptoportico (Cryptoporticus)

To the north of the House of Livia are the remains of the Cryptoporticus, a semi-subterranean barrel-vaulted corridor 130m/430ft long which linked the various Imperial palaces (the palace of Tiberius, Livia and Flavians) with one another. Tradition has it that the Emperor Caligula was murdered by conspirators in this corridor in A.D. 41.

Tempio de Cibele (Temple of Cybele)

The Temple of Cybele (or of Magna Mater, the Great Mother) in the Farnese Gardens was built in 204 B.C. to house the "Black Stone" of the goddess, following guidance given by the Sibylline Books. Rock-cuttings found in front of the temple represent the earliest evidence of human settlement on the Palatine (9th–8th c. B.C.), a dwelling site of the early Iron Age which has been christened the "House of Romulus".

Casa di Livia (House of Livia)

The House of Livia (Augustus' wife) was part of the palace of Augustus and is so called because the inscription "Livia Augusta" was found on a lead pipe in one of the rooms. Augustus himself may have lived in these apartments. Although the external buildings were simple, in keeping with the unpretentiousness of the first Emperor, the interior, as seen from the atrium and four rooms, reveals the comfortable lifestyle of the Romans at the time of Christ. Central heating was conducted through ceramic pipes in the walls, and the rooms were decorated with elegant paintings in the Pompeian (second period) style.

Palazzo dei Flavi (Palace of the Flavians)

The ruins of the Palace of the Flavians lie in the centre of the Palatine hill. Built by an architect named Rabirius at the end of the 1st c. A.D. for the Emperor Domitian (a member of the Flavian dynasty), the Domus Flavia was designed to provide a setting for the increased splendour and display which the Emperors now demanded. The building undoubtedly met these enhanced requirements with its large pillared courtyard (peristyle), the spacious dining-room (*triclinium*) to the south, the throne room (*aula regia*) to the north, a rectangular hall 30.5m/100ft by 38.7m/127ft with an apse at one end, the shrine of the domestic gods (*lararium*) and a basilica which probably served as a law court.

Domus Augustana (House of Augustus)

The Domus Augustana seems to have been not so much the house of Augustus himself as the residence of the Imperial house (*augusta*). Although not yet fully excavated, this building of two and three storeys is still immensely impressive, with its monumental and yet harmonious dimensions. Built, like the Palace of the Flavians, in the reign of Domitian, it was at first the residence of successive Emperors but later, right down to

Stadium near the Flavian Palace

Byzantine times, was occupied by high dignitaries of the Empire as their residence and place of work.

Orti Farnesiani (Farnese Gardens)

The Farnese Gardens were laid out in the 16th c. by Vignola for Cardinal Alessandro Farnese and were completed by Rainaldi. Like the gardens of the Villa d'Este at Tivoli (see entry), these gardens with their terraces and pavilions, their lawns and flowerbeds, their groves of trees and fountains, were designed to provide a kind of stage-setting for gatherings of like-minded people.

The Arcadia literary academy met here in the 17th c., leaving a small nymphaeum as its memorial. The stucco decoration is of interest as well as the fountains themselves.

The remains of the palace of Tiberius lie under the gardens. Excavations – still very far from complete – have brought to light remains of an atrium.

Stadio Domiziano (Stadium of Domitian)

Among the main buildings erected by Domitian (A.D. 81–96) on the Palatine was his Stadium, a running track 160m/525ft long and 47m/155ft across. It is not known whether the public were admitted to the contests and displays in this stadium or whether it was reserved for the entertainment of the Emperor and his personal guests; indeed it is not even certain whether it was actually used for sporting contests at all or whether it was merely designed as a garden in the form of a stadium.
    According to tradition St Sebastian was martyred in this stadium.

Terme di Settimio Severo (Baths of Septimius Severus)

The remains of these baths are the most imposing ruins on the Palatine. The piers and arches of the building were supported on massive substructures which have outlasted the centuries. Remains of the heating system can still be seen in some of the rooms and corridors.

From a rectangular terrace near the baths there is the finest view of Rome from the Palatine (particularly impressive at sunset), with the Colosseum (see Colosseo), the Baths of Caracalla (see Terme di Caracalla), the Caelian, the Aventine, the Janiculum and on the low ground below it the Circus Maximus (Ciro Massimo), a huge structure which could accommodate 300,000 spectators.

★Palazzo Barberini   E 5

Situation
Via delle Quattro
Fontane 13

**Underground
station**
Barberini (line A)

Buses
60, 61, 62, 71, 415

Pope Urban VIII (Maffeo Barberini), that great builder and art patron, was fortunate in having the two greatest architects of the Baroque period, Borromini and Bernini, available to work for him during his reign (1623–44).

The bees which featured in the Barberini coat of arms are found on buildings all over Rome, and so many ancient buildings were destroyed to make room for these new creations that the epigram "Quod non fecerunt barbari, fecerunt Barberini" ("What the barbarians did not destroy was destroyed by the Barberini") became current in Rome.

The palace, rearing high above the Piazza Barberini (entrance in Via delle Quattro Fontane), was begun by Carlo Maderna, with the help of Borromini in 1625 and completed by Bernini 1633. The complex layout of rectangular and oval staircase halls, suites of rooms and state apartments can be more easily appreciated on a plan than on the ground.

The central feature of the palace is the Salone, two storeys high, with a ceiling painting of the "Triumph of Divine Providence" by Pietro da Cortona (1632–39), mainly designed to glorify the Papacy and the Barberini family.

*Arms of the
Barberini*

In the Palazzo Barberini, modelled on the palaces of northern Italy, the High Baroque found its fullest expression.

Galleria Nazionale d'Arte Antica

Opening times
Tues.–Fri.
9am–2pm,
Sat. 9am–7pm,
Sun. 9am–1pm

The Palazzo Barberini now houses the Galleria Nazionale d'Arte Antica (National Gallery of Ancient Art). After the unification of Italy in 1870 the Italian state acquired many famous works of art by the expropriation of the Papal State, and also took over various private collections and acquired other works by gift and purchase, thus building up a great store of art treasures. Since the Second World War the National Gallery has acquired mainly works of the 13th–16th c. and also of the Baroque period.

Among the painters represented are Giovanni da Rimini, Simone Martini, Fra Angelico, Filippo Lippi ("Madonna and Child"), Piero della Francesca, Antoniazzo Romano, Pietro Perugino, Sodoma, Andrea del Sarto, Girolamo Sermoneta, Pietro da Cortona, Raphael ("La Fornarina", the portrait of a baker's daughter of Trastevere – though there is some controversy about this identification), El Greco ("Adoration of the Shepherds", "Nativity" and "Baptism of Christ"), Jacopo and Domenico Tintoretto, Titian ("Venus and Adonis"), Hans Holbein (portrait of Henry VIII, perhaps a copy) and Caravaggio ("Narcissus").

Palazzo Barberini

Palazzo Borghese

Palazzo Bonaparte   D 6

The Palazzo Bonaparte – still bearing the name on the façade – stands at the end of the Corso nearest Piazza Venezia.

In this 17th c. palace Napoleon's mother Letizia Ramorino lived until her death in 1836.

Situation
Via del Corso

Buses 46, 56, 60, 62, 64, 65, 70, 71, 75, 81, 85, 88, 90, 95

★Palazzo Borghese   D 5

Like other noble Roman families, the Borghese family, to which Pope Paul V (1605–21) belonged, had to have both a palace in the city and a summer or "weekend" residence in the country (see Villa Borghese). Cardinal Camillo Borghese accordingly bought a palace near the Tiber and on becoming Pope as Paul V presented it to his brothers Orazio and Francesco. The palace, begun by the architect Martino Lunghi, was completed for the Borghese family by Flaminio Ponzio to a plan which earned it the name of "Cembalo" (harpsichord), with the "keyboard" towards the Tiber.

The sumptuous appointments of the palace reflected all the magnificence of a Papal family. The courtyard with its double row of arcades, its ancient statues, its garlands, its figures of youths and putti is a haven of peace for the visitor coming in from the noise and bustle of the streets.

Opposite the Palazzo , where once the carriages stood, are the servants quarters.

Situation
Piazza Borghese

Buses
26, 28, 70

★Palazzo della Cancelleria (Papal Chancery) C 6

Situation
Piazza della
Cancelleria

Buses
46, 62, 64

In the 15th c. the leadership of Italy in the fields of art and culture was at first held by Florence under the Medici. Rome suffered during this period from the troubles in which the Papacy was involved (the Pope's exile at Avignon, the schism during which various Cardinals contested the Papal throne), and only gradually recovered its dominant position as the city of the Popes and the centre of Christendom during the second half of the century – in spite of a further setback when the Eastern churches broke away from Papal control in 1452.

The magnificent Palazzo della Cancelleria (originally the palace of Cardinal Riario, later the Papal Chancery and seat of the government of the Papal State) marked a major step in this development. It was built between 1483 and 1513, partly with blocks of travertine from the Colosseum (see Colosseo), for Cardinals Scarampo and Mezzarota and Raffaelle Riario (the latter of whom used on this project the 60,000 scudi he won in gaming from Franceschetto Cybo, nephew of Pope Innocent VIII). The architects were Andrea Bregno (Montecavallo) and Bramante. Fortune, however, turned against Cardinal Riario: having taken part in a conspiracy against Pope Leo X, he lost his property and the palace was confiscated.

The external elevations of the palace are very characteristic of Renaissance architecture with their clean geometric lines and their uniformity of pattern; the stonework is plain and uncluttered, without superfluous ornament. The most notable feature of the interior is the large Sala Dei Cento Giorni (Hall of a Hundred Days), with paintings (1546) commissioned by Cardinal Alessandro Farnese and completed by Vasari and a team of assistants in a hundred days – leading Michelangelo to make the sarcastic remark, "You can see that". The square inner courtyard, surrounded by three-storeyed ranges of rooms, is also notable for the clarity and regularity of its structure.

Palazzo Cenci D 6

Situation
Piazza Cenci

Buses
23, 26, 44, 56, 60,
65, 75, 170, 710,
718, 719, 774

The Palazzo Cenci was built in the 16th c. on the site of the ruined Circus Flaminius (221 B.C.). According to popular tradition Francesco Cenci embellished the palace chapel in 1575 to house the tombs of his children Giacomo and Beatrice, whom he had resolved to have killed, but it was the children who murdered their father and were beheaded for the murder on the Ponte Sant'Angelo in 1599. The story provided Shelley with the theme of his verse drama "The Cenci".

★Palazzo dei Conservatori D 6

Situation
Piazza del
Campidoglio

**Underground
station**
Colosseo (line B)

Buses 57, 85, 87,
88, 90, 90b, 92, 94,
95, 716, 718, 719

Opening times
Tues.–Sat.
9am–1.30pm,
Sun. 9am–1pm,
Tues. also 5–8pm,
Sat. also 8–11pm

The Palazzo dei Conservatori, built by Giacomo della Porta in 1564–75 to the design of Michelangelo, contains reception rooms used by the municipality of Rome on ceremonial occasions, and also houses part of the Capitoline Museum (see Museo Capitolino). Notable exhibits in the museum include fragments of a colossal statue of the Emperor Constantine, 12m/40ft high, and two statues of captive Barbarian princes (in the courtyard); the Capitoline She-Wolf, an Etruscan work of the 6th c. (the hindquarters were damaged by lightning in 65 B.C.; the figures of Romulus and Remus were added at the Renaissance); parts of the Fasti Consulares et Triumphales, a list of consuls and their victories; and the "Boy with a Thorn", a Hellenistic copy in bronze of a 5th c. original. One room in the palace, the Sala delle Oche, is named after the geese whose cackling was said to have saved Rome from capture by the Gauls in 385 B.C. The palace also contains the Capitoline Picture Gallery (Pinacoteca Capitolina), eight rooms with paintings by Titian ("Baptism of Christ"), Tintoretto ("The

Passion"), Caravaggio ("John the Baptist"), Rubens ("Romulus and Remus"), Veronese ("Rape of Europa"), Lorenzo Lotto ("Portrait of a Bowman") and Velázquez ("Portrait of a Man").

Palazzo Corsini

C 6

The Palazzo Corsini was built in the 15th c. for Cardinal Domenico Riario, a nephew of Pope Sixtus IV. In the 17th c. it was occupied by Queen Christina of Sweden after her conversion to the Roman Catholic faith and her abdication, and here she brought artists and men of learning together in an academy which later became the famous Arcadia. After coming into the possession of the Corsini family the palace was completely rebuilt by Ferdinando Fuga (1723–36). It now houses part of the collections of the National Gallery of Ancient Art (the former Corsini Gallery), mainly European painting of the 17th and 18th c. Much of the Corsini collection is now in the main part of the National Gallery in the Palazzo Barberini (see entry).

Situation
Via della
Lungara 10

Buses
23, 28, 28b, 65

Opening times
Tues.–Sat.
9am–1.30pm,
Sun. 9am–12.30pm

★Palazzo Doria Pamphili

D 6

The Palazzo Doria Pamphili, one of Rome's largest palaces, is bounded by the Corso, Via del Plebiscito, Via della Gatta, Piazza del Collegio Romano and Via Lata, with the Palazzo Bonaparte (see entry) forming an enclave at the south-eastern corner.

In the course of its three centuries of existence the palace, with its varied façades and courtyards has been fashioned by a number of different architects and owned by different families – first the della Rovere, then the Aldobrandini and finally the Pamphili, from whom it descended to the Doria family.

Situation
Via del Corso
(entrance to Gallery
at Piazza del
Collegio Romano
1A)

Buses
46, 56, 60, 62, 64,
65, 71, 75, 81, 85,
88, 90, 90b, 95, 170

Galleria Doria Pamphili

The Galleria Doria Pamphili contains a collection of pictures, mainly from the private collections of the Pamphili and Doria families. They include works by Tintoretto ("Portrait of a Prelate"), the fragments of an altarpiece, probably by Titian, Corregio ("Virtue"), Raphael ("Double Portrait"), Caravaggio ("Magdalena" and the masterly "Rest on the Flight into Egypt"), Velázquez (the famous portrait of Pope Innocent X), Lippi, Lotto, Bordone, landscapes by Lorrain and works by Breughel ("Sea Battle off Naples"), Jusepe Ribera ("St Jerome"), Domenichino and Solimena as well as some fine marble sculpture (including a bust of Innocent X by Bernini). Visitors are also shown the private and state apartments of the palace, with pictures and sculpture. Guided tours between 10am and noon.

Opening times
Tues., Fri., Sat. and
Sun. 10am–1pm

★Palazzo Farnese

C 6

The effect of the Palazzo Farnese is enhanced by the fact that it can be viewed across an open square. In this palace, the handsomest of all the 16th. Roman palaces, Renaissance architecture, which had begun in Rome with the Palazzo Venezia (see entry), reached its magnificent culmination.
Cardinal Alessandro Farnese, later Pope Paul III (1534–49), commissioned Antonio da Sangallo the Younger in 1514 to build the palace. After Sangallo's death it was continued by Michelangelo (from 1546) and completed by Giacomo della Porta in 1589. The palace later passed into the hands of the Bourbons of Naples, and it is now the French Embassy.
The exterior is of majestic effect with its massive structure of ashlar masonry and its restrained articulation, mainly based on simple geometric forms. The façade, 46m/150ft long, has three storeys of contrasting design

Situation
Piazza Farnese

Buses
23, 28, 28b, 46, 62,
64, 65

Palazzo Farnese (on right)

which are almost completely dominated by the fenestration. These rows of windows with their different surrounds, the main entrance doorway and the central window on the first floor create a total harmony, so that nothing could be altered, added or taken away without reducing the perfection of the whole.

The side elevations repeat the structure of the main front, but the narrowness of the streets deprives them of their full effect. The rear façade faces the Tiber.

The interior courtyard follows ancient models in having Doric columns and pillars on the ground floor, Ionic on the first and Corinthian on the second. Stones from the Colosseum (see Colosseo) were used in the construction of the palace.

A notable feature of the interior of the palaces is the gallery on the first floor, 20m/65ft long and 6m/20ft wide, with frescoes ("The Triumph of Love in the Universe") by Annibale Caracci (1597–1604).

Palazzo Laterano (Lateran Palace)   F/G 7

Situation
Piazza San
Giovanni in
Laterano

**Underground
station**
San Giovanni
(line A)

Trams 16, 85, 87,
88, 93, 218, 650

The Lateran Palace was the residence of the Pope from the time of Constantine until 1309, when Clement V was compelled to transfer the seat of the Papacy to Avignon. After the Pope's return from exile in France the Apostolic Palace in the Vatican became the Papal residence.

The original palace dating from the time of Constantine was destroyed on a number of occasions, and in 1558 it was completely rebuilt by Sixtus V.

The palace is now occupied by the Roman diocesan administration.

In 1993 it was severely damaged in a bomb attack by the "Falange Armata".

Palazzo Massimo alle Colonne

C/D 6

The Palazzo Massimo, a master work by Baldassare Peruzzi built in 1532–36, lies between the Piazza Sant'Andrea della Valle and Piazza Pantaleo. The residences of the Massimo which had previously stood here were destroyed in 1527 during the famous Sack of Rome, the plundering of the city by Charles V's troops.

Situation
Corso Vittoria
Emanuele II

Buses
46, 62, 64

The palace is a characteristic example of the Mannerist school of architecture (between the Renaissance and Baroque), which relieves the weight of the masonry by breaking up and transforming the basic geometric forms and giving them an elegant and playful effect. The portico, supported by six Doric columns, enhances the unique character of this palace.

Palazzetto Massimi

Standing behind the Palazzo, towards the Piazza Navona (see entry), is the three-storeyed Palazzetto Massimo, with traces of the graffiti decoration used in the 16th c. for some 50 Roman palaces. Here in 1467 the papal post-stage and the first printing works in Rome were established.

Palazzo Montecitorio

See Camera dei Deputati

★Palazzo Pallavicini-Rospigliosi

E 6

This palace, on the way up to the Quirinal hill, was built (1611–16) by Vasanzio and Maderna for Cardinal Scipione Borghese and later enlarged for the French statesman Cardinal Mazarin, who was of Italian origin.

Situation
Via XXIV Maggio

Buses
57, 64, 65, 70, 71, 75, 81, 170

It now belongs to the Pallavicini-Rospigliosi family and contains the Pallavicini picture collection, which includes early works by Rubens and works by Botticelli, Poussin, Lotto, Signorelli, Van Dyck and Ribera (viewing by appointment only: tel. 4 75 78 16).

Opening times
Casino: First day of month, 10am–noon and 3–5pm

In the small garden is the Casino Pallavicini, the principal room in which has a famous ceiling painting of Aurora by Guido Reni.

Palazzo di Propaganda Fide

D 5

Diagonally opposite the Palazzo di Spagna, now the Spanish Embassy to the Holy See (see Piazza di Spagna), is the Palazzo di Propaganda Fide built for Popes Gregory XV and Urban VIII by Bernini and Borromini. This is the headquarters of the Congregation for the Propagation of the Faith, an organisation established in the 16th c. to promote the missionary activities of the Church. In front of the two palaces is an ancient column bearing a figure of the Virgin, the Column of the Immaculate Conception, around the base of which are the prophets Isaiah and Ezekiel, together with Moses and David. Every year on December 8th the Pope comes to the column to commemorate the proclamation of the dogma of the Immaculate Conception in 1854.

Situation
Piazza di Spagna

Underground station
Piazza di Spagna
(line A)

Bus
115

Palazzo del Quirinale   E 6

Situation
Piazza del Quirinale

Buses
57, 64, 65, 70, 71,
75, 81, 170

In Roman times the Quirinal hill, which had legendary associations with Romulus, was occupied by a residential district of the city with numerous handsome mansions. In the 16th c. Pope Gregory VIII selected this as the site of a Papal summer residence, which was begun in 1574 and later extended stage by stage (such famous architects as Fontana, Maderna and Bernini being involved in the work), until by the time of Pope Clement XII (1730–40) it formed a gigantic complex with long ranges of buildings surrounded by gardens. From 1870 to 1946 the Quirinal was the official residence of the king; it is now occupied by the President of Italy.

Opposite stands the Palazzo della Consulta (see Piazza del Quirinale) housing the Italian supreme court.

Palazzo dei Senatori (Senatorial Palace)   C 6

Situation
Campidoglio

**Underground
station**
Colosseo (line B)

Buses
57, 85, 87, 88, 90,
90b, 92, 94, 95, 716,
718, 719

The Palazzo dei Senatori, situated at the far end of the Piazza del Campidoglio (see entry), above the Forum, was built in the 16th c. on the remains of the Tabularium, the record office of ancient Rome, and is now the seat of the Mayor and Municipal Council of the city. The double staircase leading up to the entrance was designed by Michelangelo, who also set up here two ancient statues of the river gods of the Nile and Tiber. In the centre is a fountain with an ancient statue of Minerva, which was revered as an image of Rome. The façade is the work of Giacomo della Porta and Girolamo Rainaldi; the handsome bell-tower, modelled on a medieval campanile, was added by Martino Longhi between 1578 and 1582.

Palazzo Spada   C 6

Situation
Piazza Capo di
Ferro 3

Buses
23, 28, 28b, 65

The Palazzo Spada was built by Giulio Mersi da Caravaggio in 1540–50 for Cardinal Girolamo Capo di Ferro. Later it passed into the hands of Cardinal Spada and was restored by Borromini. It is now the seat of the Italian Council of State, and also contains the Galleria Spada.

The most notable feature of the palace is the *trompe-l'œil* colonnade built by Borromini about 1635 to link two courtyards. In this passage with its twin rows of columns and coffered ceiling the apparent length is increased by a reduction in size of the structural elements from one end to the other.

The four-storeyed façade of the palace has elegant stucco decoration (by Giulio Mazzoni; 1556–60) and eight statues of famous Romans (from left to right: Trajan, Pompey, Fabius Maximus, Romulus, Numa Pompilius, Marcellus, Caesar and Augustus). The rooms have rich stucco ornament, and in one room is a statue said to be the statue of Pompey beside which Caesar was murdered.

Galleria Spada

Opening times
Tues.–Sat.
9pm–7pm,
Sun. 9am–1pm

This gallery consists mainly of the private collection of pictures assembled by Cardinal Bernardino Spada (1594–1661); they are displayed in rooms with graceful stucco decoration. Among the fine pictures to be seen here are Baciccia's sketches for the ceiling of the Gesù Church (see entry), portraits of Cardinal Spada by Guido Reni and Guercino, Andrea del Sarto's "Visitation", Titian's unfinished "Musician" and a "Landscape with Windmill" by Pieter Breughel.

Palazzo Quirinale

Palazzo della Consultà

Palazzo dei Senatori (seat of the mayor and council)

★Palazzo Venezia   D 6

Situation
Piazza Venezia

Underground station
Colosseo (line B)

Buses
46, 57, 85, 87, 88, 90, 90b, 92, 94, 95, 716, 718, 719

Opening times
Tues.–Sat.
9am–2pm,
Sun. 9am–1pm
(sometimes also pm for special exhibitions)

The Palazzo Venezia, begun in 1451 by Cardinal Pietro Barbo, later Pope Paul II, continued under a number of architects and completed in 1491, stands next to the church of San Marco in the Piazza Venezia (see entry), one of the busiest traffic intersections in the world. The palace is now occupied by the Palazzo Venezia Museum and the National Institute of Archaeology and Art History, and is also frequently used for temporary art exhibitions.

This elegant and harmoniously proportioned palace belonged between 1594 and 1797 to the Republic of Venice – hence its name – and then became the Austrian Embassy. During the Fascist period it was the official residence of Mussolini, who used to deliver his rhetorical speeches from the central balcony. Adjoining the Palazzo Venezia, with its massive façade and tower, is the smaller Palazzetto Venezia, which was moved to its present site when the National Monument to Victor Emmanuel II (see Monumento Nazionale a Vittorio Emanuele II) was built.

The Palazzo Venezia Museum (not all open to the public at present) contains a varied collection – wood and marble sculpture, weapons and textiles, tapestries and pictures, busts and terracotta models, applied arts and printed books, a map of the world in the Sala del Mappamondo, porcelain and glass – from many different periods, nations and cultures.

Palazzo (Casa) Zuccari   D/E 5

Situation
Via Gregoriana 30

Underground station
Piazza di Spagna
(line A)

Bus 115

The Palazzo or Casa Zuccari, built by the painter Federico Zuccari about 1600 as a residence and studio, stands at the east end of Piazza Trinità dei Monti, between Via Sistina and Via Gregoriana.

It was later occupied by the widowed Queen Maria Kasimira of Poland and is now the seat of the Biblioteca Hertziana, an institute of art history attached to the German Max-Planck-Gesellschaft (not open to the public). The doorway and windows of the palace are formed by the jaws of monsters.

★★Pantheon   D 6

Situation
Piazza della Rotonda

Buses
26, 87, 94

Opening times
Mon.–Sat.
9am–4.30pm,
(6pm in summer),
Sun. 9am–1pm

The architectural form of the Pantheon, the largest and best preserved monument of Roman antiquity, is so simple that the structure has survived the hazards of the centuries almost intact. The name of its builder is inscribed above the entrance: Marcus Agrippa, son-in-law of the Emperor Augustus, who dedicated it to the "most holy" (Greek *pantheon*) planetary gods – hence the dome, representing the firmament, with its opening for the sun – and not to all the gods as the name seems to imply. The Pantheon is the place of burial of the Italian kings (Victor Emmanuel II, second niche on right; Umberto I, second niche on left); the greatest Cardinal Secretary of State of modern times, Consalvi (tomb by Thorvaldsen, 1824, third niche on left) and the great Renaissance painter Raphael (between second and third niches on left) are also buried here.

The Pantheon was damaged by fire in A.D. 80 and was rebuilt in the reign of Hadrian (120–125); the brickwork of this period demonstrates the extraordinarily high standard of technical mastery achieved by the Romans. In the course of the centuries the building suffered further damage and plundering: Pope Gregory III removed the gilded bronze roof-tiles, while Urban VIII used the heavy bronze roofing of the porch in the construction of Bernini's Confessio in St Peter's (see San Pietro in Vaticano). The building was, however, regularly restored, and also received some structural additions, since removed.

Via della Palombella

Sacristy

Chapel

High altar

4

5

3

Via della Minerva

C e l l a

Via della Rotonda

6

2

7

1

8

Porch

10m

N

Piazza della Rotonda

Pantheon
St Maria ad Martyres

1 "Annunciation", a fresco by Melozzo da Forlì (15th c.)
2 Tomb of Victor Emmanuel II, first king of Italy (1820–78)
3 "St Anne and the Virgin", sculpture by Lorenzo Ottoni (?: 17th c.)
4 Monument to the Papal diplomat Cardinal Ercole Consalvi (1757–1824: tomb in San Marcello)
5 Tomb of Raphael (Raffaello Santi or Sanzio, 1483–1520)
6 Tomb of Umberto I, second king of Italy (1844–1900: assassinated at Monza); below it the tomb of Queen Margherita (d. 1926)
7 Tomb of Baldassare Peruzzi (1481–1536), architect and painter
8 On the altar "St Joseph with the Boy Jesus" by Vincenzo de' Rossi; on either side the tombs of the painters Perin del Vaga (1501–47) and Taddeo Zuccari (1529–66) and the architect and sculptor Flaminio Vacca (1538–1605); on the walls "Joseph's Dream" and "Flight into Egypt", stucco reliefs by Carlo Monaldi (c. 1720)

The first Christian Emperors forbade the use of this pagan temple for worship, and it remained disused until Pope Boniface IV dedicated it to the Virgin and all the Christian martyrs on November 1st 609 – the origin of the feast of All Saints.

From the Piazza della Rotonda (see entry) from which the Pantheon is seen hemmed in by buildings and the semicircular dome appears much flatter than it really is, steps lead down into the porch: formerly there were steps up to the entrance, but the ground level has risen considerably since then. The porch, 33m/108ft wide and 13.50m/44ft high, has 16 granite columns with Corinthian capitals (12.5m/41ft high, 4.5m/15ft apart) and two massive ancient bronze doors.

The mighty dome of the Pantheon was the supreme achievement of Roman interior architecture. The overwhelming effect of the interior results from the harmonious proportions of the whole vast structure: the height is the same as the diameter (43.2m/142ft), while the walls of the cylinder supporting the dome measure half the diameter (21.6m/71ft). In the walls of the cylinder (6.2m/20ft thick) are semicircular and rectangular niches. The interior of the dome is coffered. The only lighting for the interior comes from a circular opening 9m/30ft wide in the dome.

The restrained decoration of the interior enhances the effect of the architecture. The harmony and perfect proportions of the Pantheon – built in the image of the earth with the vault of the firmament above it – have

The Pantheon on the Piazza della Rotonda

impressed artists and visitors down the centuries. (The magnificent acoustics will be demonstrated by an organist for a small consideration.)

★Passeggiata del Gianicolo

B/C 6/7

Bus
41

The Passeggiata del Gianicolo lined with busts of Italian patriots, extends along the Janiculum from the Porta San Pancrazio to the Piazza della Rovere (near the Vatican), offering magnificent views of the whole of central Rome and the outlying districts, extending to the surrounding hills. The light-tower dates from 1911. In Piazza Garibaldi is a monumental equestrian statue of Giuseppe Garibaldi (restored in 1990), one of the great figures of the fight for Italian unity in the 19th c. Every day on the stroke of noon an Austrian cannon in this square fires a shot which resounds far over the city to announce the time. The terraces around the square offer what is perhaps the finest panoramic view of Rome.

A little way north is a statue of Garibaldi's wife Anita, her hair streaming in the wind.

★Piazza Bocca della Verità

D 7

Buses
15, 23, 57, 90, 92, 95, 716

The Piazza Bocca della Verità occupies the site of the ancient Forum Boarium or cattle market, situated conveniently close to the Tiber, which provided a ready means for the disposal of refuse. From this square there is a view, scarcely to be equalled anywhere else in Rome, which takes in both ancient and Christian buildings: the church of Santa Maria in Cosmedin (see entry), a Romanesque building with a modestly proportioned porch and a graceful campanile; the Arch of Janus (see Arco di Giano) and beyond it the handsome church of San Giorgio in Velabro (see entry) and the Arco degli Argentari, the arch of the merchants and bankers; the church of San Giovanni Decollato (see entry); the Casa dei Crescenzi, the residence of the most powerful family in Rome during the early medieval period; and two ancient temples, the Tempio della Fortuna Virile and the Tempio di Vesta, with the Baroque Fountain of the Two Tritons.

Piazza di Campo dei Fiori

C 6

It is difficult to remember that this cheerful square, in which the flower market of Rome is held every morning, was a place of execution (rarely used though it might be) during the period of Papal rule.

Buses
46, 62, 64

Here on February 7th 1600 Giordano Bruno, a monk found guilty of heresy by the Inquisition and condemned to death when he refused to recant, was burned at the stake. He is commemorated by a bronze statue, under which are medallions of other heretics condemned by the Church, including Erasmus, Wycliffe and Hus.

★Piazza Navona

C/D 6

The Piazza Navona is one of the most characteristic Baroque squares in Rome, constantly filled with crowds of visitors as well as Romans. Street musicians play popular melodies as street artists and souvenir traders offer their wares. Visitors should be prepared to pay high prices for such treats

Buses
26, 46, 62, 64, 70, 81, 88, 90

Piazza di Campo dei Fiori

Piazza Navona, with the Church of Sant'Agnese

as the legendary chocolate confection "Tartuffo" in the Tre Scaline or an ice-cream at the Café di Colombia.

The palaces and churches around the square still mark out the area of the stadium (240m/790ft long, 65m/215ft across) constructed here by Domitian. During the Middle Ages the arena was used for water festivals and horse races. It was rebuilt with its magnificent series of palaces and churches (including Sant'Agnese – see entry) by Borromini during the Baroque period.

★Fontana dei Fiumi (Fountain of the Four Rivers)

There are three fountains in the square, the most notable being the Fontana dei Fiumi (1647–51), with which Bernini won the favour of Pope Innocent X. This is a masterly and spirited composition with a large basin from which emerges a rocky crag bearing an obelisk, surrounded by plants and animals. At the four corners are figures personifying the Nile, Ganges, Danube and Rio de la Plata – the rivers then believed to be the largest in the four known continents. Each figure is accompanied by appropriate flora and fauna.

According to a traditional Roman joke the Nile has his head veiled because the source of the river was not known, or alternatively – alluding to the bitter rivalry between the two famous architects, Bernini and Borromini – the Nile is covering his eyes to avoid seeing the structural defects in Borromini's church of Sant'Agnese (see entry), facing the fountain.
The two other fountains in the square are the Fontana del Moro in front of the Palazzo Pamphili, erected by Giacomo della Porta (1575–76), and the 19th c. Fontana del Nettuno with its figure of the sea-god.

★Piazza del Popolo   D 4/5

Before the demolition of the city walls visitors arriving in Rome from the
north on the Via Cassia or Via Flaminia, two of the old Roman consular
highways, received their first impression of the magnificence of the city
when they passed through the Porta del Popolo into the Piazza del Popolo.
On the east under the Pincio hill (see entry), and on the west above the
Tiber, the square is enclosed by semicircular walls built by Giuseppe
Valadier in 1809–20. The square was enlarged in the 16th c. during the reign
of Pope Sixtus V, and the Via di Ripetta and Via del Babuino were laid out,
radiating on either side of the Via del Corso. Some decades later the twin
churches of Santa Maria dei Miracolo and Santa Maria in Monte Santo
were built flanking the end of the Corso. In the centre of the square is the
Obelisk Flaminio, an Egyptian obelisk from the Circus Maximus (see entry),
originally brought to Rome by Augustus. Beside the Porta del Popolo is the
church of Santa Maria del Popolo (see entry). On the east side of the square
the Café Rosati, traditionally the meeting place of artists, and the Canova
opposite offer many of the famous Italian sweet delicacies.

Underground station
Flaminio (line A)

Buses
2, 90, 90b, 115

★Piazza del Quirinale   E 6

The square in front of the Quirinal Palace (see Palazzo del Quirinale),
residence of the President of Italy, is one of the most beautiful in Rome,
offering a panoramic view of the city extending west to St Peter's (see San
Pietro in Vaticano). In the centre of the square is the famous Dioscuri
Fountain, with the 14m/46ft high obelisk which formerly stood at the
entrance to the Mausoleum of Augustus and the 5.6m/18ft high figures of
the Dioscuri (Castor and Pollux as horse-tamers) from the nearby Baths of
Constantine.

Opposite the Quirinal Palace is the sumptuously decorated Palazzo della
Consulata, built by Ferdinando Fuga in 1734 for Pope Clement XII to house
the Papal court, the Tribunale della Sacra Consulta. The palace is now
occupied by the Corte Costituzionale, the Italian supreme court.

Buses
57, 64, 65, 70, 71,
75, 170

Piazza della Rotonda   D 6

The Piazza della Rotonda in front of the Pantheon (see entry), the heart of
the Centro Storico, is a popular meeting place for all ages, particularly in
the summer months. The pleasant cafés, bars and tea rooms which encircle
the square and its fountain, create a lively atmosphere late into the night.
After visiting the Pantheon visitors may wish to take some refreshment
here and sample the delicious "bignes" pastries at Di Rienzo.

Buses
26, 87, 94

Piazza San Giovanni in Laterano   F 7

The Piazza San Giovanni in Laterano, at the end of Via Merulana, is
bounded by the Lateran Palace, the side entrance to the church of St John
Lateran (see San Giovanni in Laterano) and the baptistery of San Giovanni
in Fonte (see entry). It is dominated by an Egyptian obelisk, the tallest
(31m/102ft high, or 47m/154ft including the base) and also the oldest in
Rome. It was brought from Thebes to Rome in a specially constructed ship
in A.D. 357 and set up in the Circus Maximus. In 1587, during the reign of
Sixtus V, it was transferred to its present site, and the equestrian statue of
Marcus Aurelius which stood here was moved to the Capitol (see
Campidoglio).

Underground station
San Giovanni
(line A)

Buses
16, 85, 87, 88, 93,
93b, 93c, 218, 650

Piazza della Rotonda

★Piazza di Spagna and Scalinata della Trinità dei Monti   D 5
(Spanish Steps)

Underground station
Piazza di Spagna (line A)

Bus 115

The Piazza di Spagna, a large irregularly shaped square named after the Spanish Embassy to the Holy See, which was established here in the 17th c., is one of Rome's most typical squares and a special attraction for every visitor.

Spanish Steps

The feature which first catches the tourist's eye is the elegant Scalinata della Trinità dei Monti or Spanish Steps, constructed by Francesco de Sanctis in 1723–25 in a bewildering pattern of steps and landings, now wider and now narrower, now turning this way and now that, with a terrace on which to rest and enjoy the view half-way up. The steps were paid for by the French ambassador, Gueffier – hence the fleurs-de-lis which can be seen here and there.

Trinità dei Monti

At the top of the steps is the French church of Trinità dei Monti, begun by Louis XII in 1502 and consecrated by Pope Sixtus V in 1585. It was restored after the Napoleonic occupation of Rome. The interior still preserves some of the original Gothic arches and contains an "Entombment" by Daniele da Volterra, a pupil of Michelangelo.

Via Dei Babuino

The Via Dei Babuino, from the Piazza di Spagna to the Piazza del Popolo, is a busy street with many art galleries and antique shops. Parallel to it, below the slopes of the Pincio, is the Via Margutta, the haunt of artists and intellectuals.

Via Condotti

From the Piazza di Spagna the Via Condotti leads south-west to the Corso. This is Rome's most fashionable shopping street, with the famous Caffè Greco, long frequented by artists, writers and musicians. Among its

Spanish Steps, with La Barcaccia Fountain ▶

patrons have been Goethe, Gogol, Schopenhauer, Mendelssohn, Berlioz, Wagner and Liszt.

Barcaccia Fountain   The fountain at the foot of the Spanish Steps, in the shape of a boat, is known at the "Barcaccia". It is said that Pietro Bernini, Gian Lorenzo's father, who created the fountain in 1627–29, got the idea when the Tiber overflowed its banks and a boat was stranded in the square.

Piazza Venezia   D 6

Buses
46, 56, 57, 60, 62, 64, 65, 70, 71, 75, 81, 85, 87, 88, 90, 90b, 92, 94, 95, 170, 716, 718, 719

The Piazza Venezia is one of the busiest traffic intersections in Europe, at the meeting of five roads – the Via del Corso, the main street of the city, running north-west to the Piazza del Popolo; Via del Plebiscito, running south-west to St Pietro's (see San Pietro in Vaticano); the Piazza Aracoeli, leading to the Capitol (see Campidoglio); the Via dei Fori Imperiali, running south-east to the Imperial fora (see Foro di Traiano, Foro di Cesare, Foro di Augusto, Foro di Nerva, Foro di Vespasiano), The Forum Romanum (see Foro Romano) and Colosseum (see Colosseo); and Via Battista, climbing to the Quirinal. The square is dominated by the Palazzo Venezia (see entry) and the church of San Marco, an early 20th c. office building, similar in proportions to the Palazzo Venezia, and the National Monument to Victor Emmanuel II (see Monumento Nazionale a Vittorio Emanuele II).

★Pincio Gardens   D 4/5

Underground station
Flaminio (line A)

Buses
1, 2b, 90b, 115, 202, 203, 205, 490, 492, 495

The Pincio Gardens, lying above the Piazza del Popolo below the grounds of the Villa Medici (see entries), were laid out at the beginning of the 19th c. by the architect Giuseppe Valadier, in an area occupied by gardens belonging to old Roman families, including the Pinci after whom they are named.
  The paths in the gardens are lined with busts of Italian patriots. The views from the terraces, looking down on the Piazza del Popolo and across the whole of central Rome to St Peter's (see San Pietro in Vaticano), are among the finest in the city, particularly at sunset.

Piramide di Caio Cestio (Pyramid of Cestius)   D 8

Situation
Piazza di Porta San Paolo/
Piazza Ostiense

Underground station
Piramide (line B)

Buses
11, 23, 27, 57, 94, 95, 318, 673, 716

The Pyramid of Cestius, more steeply pitched than the Egyptian pyramids on which it was modelled, was built in 12–11 B.C. as the tomb of Caius Cestius, who had been praetor, tribune of the people and one of the Septemviri Epulones (the committee of seven which organised religious festival banquets). It was later incorporated, together with the Porta San Paolo (the ancient Porta Ostiense), in the Aurelian Walls.
  The pyramid, 22m/72ft square and 27m/89ft high, is faced with Carrara marble and was built, as the inscription records, within the space of 330 days. The tip of the pyramid is said to have originally been gilded. It contains a tomb chamber measuring 6×4m/20×13ft. A similar tomb stood near the Castel Sant'Angelo (see entry) until the early 16th c.

★Ponte Milvio (Ponte Molle, Milvian Bridge)   C 2

Buses
1, 31, 201, 202, 203, 204, 205, 220, 301, 391, 446

The bridge, to the north of the city in a direct line from the Forum (see Foro Romano) and the Piazza del Popolo (see entry) by way of the Via Flaminia, was originally constructed over the Tiber during the republican period. Four of the piers are ancient. The first reconstruction of the bridge was undertaken in 109 B.C. and a tower was added in the 3rd c. A.D. as part of the city defences. Pope Pius VII ordered further reconstruction in the early 19th c., but the bridge was subsequently blown up by Garibaldi's troops to halt the advancing French army. A year later, under Pope Pius IX, the present bridge was constructed.

The Ponte Milvio was the scene of the fateful battle on 28 October A.D. 312 in which Constantine defeated his fellow Caesar Maxentius. Attributing his victory to the God of the Christians, Constantine showed his gratitude by granting them freedom of worship.

There is a colourful local market on weekdays on the Piazzale di Ponte Milvio, the north side of the bridge.

★Ponte Sant'Angelo

C 5

The Ponte Sant'Angelo, the finest of Rome's bridges, was built by Hadrian in A.D. 136 to give access to his Mausoleum (see Castel Sant'Angelo) and was known as the Pons Aelius (after one of the Emperor's forenames). The three central piers are original. The entrance to the bridge, which is closed to traffic, is guarded by statues of Peter, by Lorenzetto (1530) and Paul, by Paolo Romano (1463), erected in the mid 16th c. under Clement VII. Clement IX commissioned Bernini, who was 70, to carve the ten figures of angels which line the bridge. The figures, carrying the instruments of Christ's passion, were executed by Bernini's pupils (Antonio Raggi, Antonio Giorgetti and Ercole Ferrata) between 1660 and 1668 to Bernini's design.

Buses
23, 28, 28b, 34, 41, 42, 46, 46b, 62, 64

Ponte Milvio over the Tiber

Statue of an angel on the Ponte San Angelo   *St Paul, by Lorenzetto, guards the bridge*

Porta Maggiore   G 6/7

Situation
Piazza di Porta
Maggiore

Buses
152, 153, 154, 155,
156, 157

Trams
13, 14, 19, 19b, 30,
30b, 516

The Porta Maggiore, now surrounded by the swirl of modern traffic, was one of the most imposing structures in ancient Rome. It was built by the Emperor Claudius in A.D. 52 at the point where two important roads, the Via Praenestina (the road to Praeneste, present-day Palestrina) and the Via Casaline (the road to Labici), left the city, passing under two aqueducts, the Aqua Claudia and the Anio Novus (the River Aniene). They were later incorporated in the Aurelian Walls.

Adjoining the gate is the tomb of a Roman master baker, Virgilius Eurysaces and his wife.

Porta Pia   F 5

Situation
Piazza di Porta Pia

Buses
36, 37, 60, 61, 62,
63, 65, 136, 137,
490, 495

The Porta Pia, a town gate in the Aurelian Walls (see Mura Aureliane) near the ancient Porta Nomentana, was built by Michelangelo for the Medici Pope Pius IV in 1561–64.

Near here on September 20th 1870 Italian troops entered the Papal city, an event which heralded the end of the Pope's temporal authority in the Papal State.

Porta San Sebastiano (formerly Porta Appia)   F 8

Situation
Via Appia Antica

This gate in the Aurelian Walls was refortified at the end of the 4th c. A.D. in view of the increasing threat to Rome from the Germanic tribes, and was again renovated in the 6th c. by Belisarius and Narses. The Porta Appia, later renamed after the church of San Sebastiano outside the city on the Via Appia (see entry), was the principal entrance to the ancient city.

The so-called Arch of Drusus (Arco di Druso) inside the Porta San Sebastiano probably dates from the time of Trajan; in the reign of Caracalla it was used to support an aqueduct.

Bus
118

Porta Tiburtina   G 6

The Porta Tiburtina, the city gate on the road to Tivoli (see entry), the Via Tiburtina, was originally built in the reign of Augustus as an arch supporting the Marcia, Tepula and Julia aqueducts. A gate flanked by towers was built in front of the arch in the reign of Honorius (beginning of the 5th c.).

Situation
Via Tiburtina

Buses
11, 71

Portico di Ottavia (Portico of Octavia)   D 6

The Portico of Octavia was originally built by Quintus Merellus Macedonius in 149 B.C., and dedicated to his sister Octavia, whose name it now bears; it was later rebuilt by Septimus Severus and Caracalla. It is now represented by a number of columns and remains of the entablature, which are incorporated in the porch of the church of Sant'Angelo in Peschiera. The portico, adjoining the Theatre of Marcellus (see Teatro di Marcello), originally covered an area 115m/375ft×135m/445ft in extent and contained numerous pieces of Greek and Roman sculpture.

Situation
Via del Progresso

Buses
15, 23, 57, 90, 90b, 92, 94, 95, 716, 774

San Bernardo alle Terme (church)

See Terme di Diocleziano

San Carlo ai Catinari (church)   D 6

St Charles Borromeo, to whom this church is dedicated, was born at Arena in 1538. In 1560 he was made Cardinal Archbishop of Milan by his uncle Pope Pius IV. He died in 1584 and was canonised in 1610. Soon after his canonisation this church, built by Rosato Rosati, was dedicated to him by the Barnabite order.

San Carlo ai Catinari (named after the manufacturers of washtubs, *catinari*, whose workshops were near here) has an imposing travertine façade and a very fine interior.

Situation
Piazza Benedetto Cairoli

Buses
26, 44, 46, 56, 60, 65, 75, 87, 94, 170, 710, 718, 719

San Carlo al Corso (church)   D 5

Although officially dedicated to St Ambrose and St Charles Borromeo, both bishops of Milan, this church is always known simply as San Carlo al Corso.

This "national church" of the Lombards was given its present form by Onorio and Martino Lunghi, together with Pietro da Cortona and Carlo Fontana, in the 17th c. Its most impressive feature is the dome (by Pietro da Cortona), whether this is seen from within the church (which has a 72m/236ft long nave) or from outside in a general prospect of central Rome, above which it rears up in imposing bulk. Carlo Maratta's altarpiece ("The Glory of St Ambrose and St Charles Borromeo") and the paintings in the dome pendentives by Giancinto Brandi are of interest.

Situation
Via del Corso

Buses
2, 26, 81, 90, 90b, 115, 911, 913

San Carlo alle Quattro Fontane (church)   E 5

Situation
Via del Quirinale

Buses
57, 64, 65, 70, 71, 75, 170

This masterpiece by Borromini, situated at the intersection of Via del Quirinale and Via delle Quattro Fontane, is only a short distance away from a masterpiece by Bernini (see Sant'Andrea al Quirinale). It is named after the four Baroque fountains at the intersection, with reclining figures representing respectively the Tiber, the River Aniene, Fidelity and Valour.

Borromini began building this church, his first church in Rome, in 1638. Its total area is no greater than one of the piers at the crossing in St Peter's (see San Pietro in Vaticano). The building shows a lively interplay of convex and concave lines with no attempt at regular form. "Harmony and divergence, symmetry and asymmetry, passion and serenity blend here into an inexhaustible play of forms" (Anton Henze).

The façade of the church is strongly articulated. In the interior, an elongated oval, the richness of the decoration largely conceals the basic architectural structure.

Borromini died in 1667, shortly before the church was completed.

★San Clemente (church)   F 7

Situation
Via San Giovanni in Laterano

Buses
85, 88

San Clemente is one of the most venerable and beautiful of Rome's churches.

On a site previously occupied by a house containing a shrine of Mithras – now far below street level – an early Christian church was built at some time before A.D. 385 and dedicated to St Clement, third bishop of Rome after Peter. After the destruction of this church by the Normans in 1084 a new basilican church was built over its ruins at the beginning of the 12th c.

Fountain of San Carlo alle Quatro Fontane   *San Giorgio in Velabro*

Upper Church of San Clemente

The upper church reflects the old basilican structure with its sequence of   Upper church
entrance porch, atrium with a fountain, the nave where the congregation
worshipped and the area reserved for the clergy (the *schola cantorum*),
with the high altar and the apse. Notable features of the interior are the
ancient columns and the intarsia work by the Cosmati family in the marble
pavement, the screens, the Easter candlestick, the tabernacle and the
bishop's throne. The triumphal arch and apse are decorated with mosaics
of Old and New Testament scenes, the most richly decorated in Rome, with
the Tree of Life and the Cross, saints and symbolic devices, animals and
plants combined in intricate patterns.

In the little St Catherine's Chapel at the west end of the north aisle are
early Renaissance frescoes by Masolino (before 1431) depicting scenes
from the life of St Catherine of Alexandria, of particular importance as
showing the earliest use of perspective painting in Rome.

The lower church, a three-aisled pillared basilica of the 4th c., has frescoes   Lower church
dating from different centuries in the Romanesque period. Notable among
them are a Ascension in the central aisle, in which the donor, Pope Leo IV, is
shown with a square nimbus, indicating that he was still alive, episodes
from the Passion, and scenes from the life of St Clement.

A passage leads underground to the excavated foundations of a 2nd c.
Roman dwelling with the shrine of Mithras in a barrel-vaulted chamber.
The altar, in the middle of the shrine, has a relief depicting Mithras (the
Persian sun-god) killing a bull.

San Crisogono (church)   C/D 7

The church of San Crisogono, situated at the end of the Viale di Trastevere   **Situation**
nearest the Tiber, was originally built at some time before 499 in honour of   Viale di Trastevere/
St Chrysogonus, martyred in the reign of Diocletian, and rebuilt in 1129.   Piazza Sonnino

San Francesco a Ripa

Buses 26, 44, 56, 60, 65, 75, 170, 710, 718, 719

Situated in the busy Piazza Sonnino, the church attracts large numbers of worshippers. The two porphyry columns of the triumphal arch are the largest in Rome.

San Francesco a Ripa (church)   C/D 7

Situation
Piazza San
Francesco d'Assisi

Buses 23, 26, 28, 97, 170, 718, 719

Trams: 13, 30

The present church of San Francesco a Ripa was built in 1231, replacing an earlier chapel belonging to the pilgrim hospice of San Biagio, in which St Francis was said to have stayed when visiting Rome. The church was rebuilt by Mattia de'Rossi in 1682–89. In the fourth chapel in the north aisle is a famous statue of the Blessed Ludovica Albertoni, a major late work by Bernini (1674).

San Giorgio in Velabro (church)   D 7

Situation
Via del Velabro

Buses
15, 23, 57, 90, 90b, 94, 95, 716, 774

The name Velabro refers to the marshy area on the banks of the Tiber where according to Roman legend Faustulus found the twins Romulus and Remus. The first church on the site was built by Leo II (682–683), the second by Gregory IV (827–844); the campanile and porch were added in the 12th c. The present church, a handsome Romanesque building incorporating ancient elements (columns and capitals), stands near the Arch of Janus (see Arco di Giano). It is a popular wedding church. In 1993 the church was partly destroyed in a bomb attack by the "Falange Armata".

Arco degli
Argentari

Adjoining the church is the Arco degli Argentari (Arch of the Moneychangers), erected in honour of Septimus Severus, his wife Julia Domna and their sons Caracalla and Geta, by merchants and bankers of the Forum Boarium and later incorporated in the church of San Giorgio. It has reliefs, some of them remarkably well preserved, depicting the Imperial family attending a sacrifice and barbarian prisoners. Some of the names in the original dedication were later erased.

San Giovanni Decollato (Church of the Beheading of St John)   D 7

Situation
Via di San Giovanni
Decollato

Buses
15, 57, 90, 90b, 94, 95, 716

There was in Papal Rome a "Fraternity of Mercy" (Confraternità della Misericordia), established in 1488 (of which Michelangelo was a member), which had undertaken responsibility for accompanying condemned prisoners to execution and had the right, once a year, to secure the pardon of a prisoner. This body erected the church of San Giovanni in honour of the beheading (decollation) of St John the Baptist; begun in 1535, the church was completed in 1555. The paintings in the church and in the oratory adjoining the cloisters depict scenes from the life of the saint as it is described in the Bible, with particular emphasis on his beheading.

San Giovanni dei Fiorentini (church)   C 6

Situation
Via Giulia

Buses
23, 28, 28b, 41, 42, 46b, 62, 64, 65, 98, 98c, 881

Pope Leo X, a member of the Florentine ruling dynasty of the Medici, being desirous of providing a church for his fellow countrymen in Rome, held an architectural competition in which both Michelangelo and Raphael took part. The competition was won, however, by Sansovino, who enlisted other architects in the building of the church – Sangallo, Michelangelo (in an advisory capacity), della Porta, Maderno, and Alessandro Galilei who was responsible for the façade. The church is impressive for its size, the exactly contrived spatial effect of the interior and the rich Baroque decoration and furnishings, including many fine paintings. The famous architects Francesco Barromini and Carlo Maderno are buried in the church.

★San Giovanni in Fonte (Baptistery)

F 7

The baptistery of St John was built by Constantine on the site of a Roman nymphaeum in the Lateran Palace. This octagonal building, the oldest baptistery in Christendom, provided a model for later baptisteries.

The doors of the chapel of St John the Baptist emit a ringing sound when they are opened or closed.

Buses: 16, 85, 87, 88, 93, 218, 650.

Situation: Piazza San Giovanni in Laterano

Underground station San Giovanni (line A)

★San Giovanni in Laterano (Basilica of St John Lateran)

F/G 7

The inscription on the façade of St John Lateran claims the status of "Mater et caput omnium ecclesiarum urbis et orbis" ("Mother and head of all the churches of the City and the world").

A beginning was made in A.D. 313 with the building of a large church dedicated to the Saviour on the ruins of the palace of the Laterani and of a barracks. This was accordingly the first of the four "patriarchal" basilicas – the others being St Peter's (see San Pietro in Vaticano), San Paolo fuori le Mura and Santa Maria Maggiore (see entries) – and the most venerable of the seven pilgrimage churches of Rome (the four patriarchal churches, together with Santa Croce in Gerusalemme, San Sebastiano and San Lorenzo fuori le Mura: see entries). This status was confirmed by the holding of general councils of the Church in St John Lateran in 1123, 1139, 1179, 1215 and 1512.

Before the Popes established their residence in the Apostolic Palace in the Vatican after their return from exile in Avignon they lived mainly in the Lateran; and St John Lateran has remained the episcopal church of the Pope. Various additions and alterations were carried out in the 5th, 8th, 10th, 13th and 15th c., and in the 16th and 17th c. the church was almost completely rebuilt. The west porch, the interior and the main façade were entirely refashioned at this period. During medieval times the church was put under the patronage of St John the Baptist and St John the Evangelist.

The basilican plan of the church, with its porch, narthex, five-aisled apse, presbytery and apse, was established in the original Constantinian church and respected in the Baroque rebuilding. The wide façade with its huge

Situation Via Vittorio Emanuele Filiberto (main entrance); Piazza San Giovanni in Laterano (side entrance)

Underground station San Giovanni (line A)

Buses 16, 85, 87, 88, 93, 218, 650, 673

San Giovanni in Laterano

San Giovanni in Fonte

Coro

Chiostro

100 m

N

1 Bronze doors (Roman)
2 Holy Door
3 Statue of Constantine the Great
4 Frescoes by Giotto (Boniface VIII)
5 Orsini Chapel
6 Torlonia Chapel
7 Massimo Chapel
8 St John's Chapel
9 Papal altar
10 Tomb of Pope Martin V (crypt)
11 Baroque organ
12 Side door
13 Monument of Pope Leo XIII Entrance to Portico of Leo XIII
14 Choir chapel
15 Sacristies
16 Chapterhouse
17 St Hilary's Chapel. Entrance to cloister
18 Chapel of St Francis of Assisi (monument of 1927)
19 Santorio Chapel
20 Chapel of Assumption
21 Corsini Chapel
22 Baptistery

San Giovanni a Porta Latina

Papal arms of Pius VI . . .　　　　. . . *Basilica of San Giovanni in Laterano*

Note
The baptistery was badly damaged in a bomb attack in 1993 and is still being restored

statues by Alessandro Galilei (*c.* 1735) is a masterpiece of late Baroque architecture. Note also the bronze doors of the main doorway which came from the ancient Curia in the Forum, and the Holy Door (far right). The interior, 130m/427ft long, was refashioned by Borromini on the occasion of Holy Year 1650, with massive piers along the nave and tall figures of Apostles (4.25m/14ft high), by various sculptors, in the niches. The magnificent timber ceiling dates from the 16th c.

Above the Papal altar (Altare papale) is a tabernacle-like baldachin in which the heads of the Apostles Peter and Paul are preserved (shown by custodian: tip). Here, too, is a wooden altar at which the earliest Popes, Peter's immediate successors, are said to have officiated. In the Confessio at the foot of the altar is the bronze tomb of Pope Martin V (on which it is a Roman custom to throw a coin) – one of the numerous tombs of great persons, both ecclesiastical and lay, which the church contains.

In the apse (beyond the presbytery), which was widened by Pope Leo XIII (1878–84), are some very fine mosaics – faithful copies of early Christian originals, renewed by Torriti in the 13th c. – depicting Christ surrounded by angels and (below, on either side of a jewelled cross) various saints, including St Francis of Assisi and St Antony of Padua.

The valuable decoration and furnishings of the church have given it an air of rather cold magnificence.

The Cloister (Chiostro: entrance in left-hand aisle), a masterpiece of 13th c. architecture by a family of Roman artists, the Vassalletti, should not be missed.

San Giovanni a Porta Latina (church)　　　　　　　F 8

Situation
Via di Porta Latina

The early Romanesque church lies hidden behind the ancient city walls in Via di Porta Latina.

The basilica of "St John at the Latin Gate", was founded in the 5th c., rebuilt about 720 and restored in 1191 during the reign of Pope Celestine III. It is in the familiar form of the Roman basilica, with a portico supported by columns and a tall campanile of classical type.

The church contains an important cycle of early 13th c. frescoes depicting 46 Old and New Testament scenes which are among the finest medieval frescoes in Rome.

Bus
118

San Girolamo (degli Illirici or degli Schiavoni)   D 5

After the Turkish victory in the battle of Kosovo in 1387 many refugees from Dalmatia and Albania fled to Rome, and this church (built during the reigns of Sixtus IV and V and completed in 1588) was thereafter known as the church "degli Illirici" or "degli Schiavoni".

It is now the Croatian national church and has a priests' college attached to it.

Situation
Via Ripetta/
Via Tomacelli

Buses
2, 26, 28, 70, 81, 88,
90, 115

San Gregorio Magno (church)   E 7

The church of San Gregorio, which is approached by a large flight of steps, was founded in 575 – before he became Pope – by Gregory the Great, a member of the Antitii family, who converted his family house on this site into a convent. It was rebuilt in the medieval period and completely re-fashioned in the Baroque period, by Giovanni Battista Sorià (1629–33), on the model of the church of Sant'Ignazio, though on a smaller scale. The interior was remodelled by Francesco Ferrari in the mid 18th c.; the ceiling painting (1727) is by Placido Constanzi.

The atrium, the church itself, the oratory and the three chapels of St Andrew (frescoes by Guido Reni and Domenichino, 17th c.), St Silvia ("Angel fresco" by Reni, 1608) and St Barbara (wall painting by Antonio Viviani, 1602) combine to form a unity of impressive effect.

Situation
Via de San
Gregorio

Buses
11, 15, 27, 118, 673

Trams
13, 30, 30b

San Lorenzo in Lucina (church)   D 5

The church of San Lorenzo in Lucina, dedicated to the martyr St Lawrence, who is much venerated in Rome, has had an eventful history. Originally built in the 4th and 5th c. over the house of a Roman woman named Lucina, it was rebuilt in the 12th c. and received its present form in 1650.

On the high altar is a "Crucifixion" by Guido Reni, one of his finest works. The fourth chapel in the south aisle, the Fonseca Chapel, was designed by Bernini.

Situation
Piazza di San
Lorenzo in
Lucina

Buses
52, 53, 56, 58, 60,
61, 62, 71, 81, 88,
90, 95, 115

★San Lorenzo fuori le Mura (St Lawrence outside the Walls)   H 5

This early Christian basilica, one of the seven pilgrimage churches of Rome, is dedicated to St Lawrence, who was martyred in A.D. 238 by being roasted on a gridiron. (The other pilgrimage churches are San Giovanni in Laterano, San Pietro in Vaticano, San Paolo fuori le Mura, Santa Maria Maggiore, San Sebastiano and Santa Croce in Gerusalemme: see entries.) The church was founded by Constantine the Great and thereafter frequently rebuilt and restored – most recently after suffering damage in an Allied air raid on Rome in July 1943.

San Lorenzo, situated beside the Campo Verano, Rome's largest cemetery, has preserved through all rebuildings (particularly in the 13th c.) the

Situation
Piazza San Lorenzo

Buses
11, 71, 109, 111,
309, 311, 411, 415,
492

Trams
19, 19b, 30, 30b

structure of an early Christian basilica, with its porch (containing ancient sarcophagi), its wide, high nave with narrow lateral aisles, its chancel on a higher level and its handsome columns. Lower down, on the level of the first basilica, is the tomb of Pope Pius IX (1846–78). Particularly fine is the Cosmatesque work (coloured stones inlaid in marble) on the two marble ambos (pulpits for the reading of the Gospels and Epistles: the one on the epistle side, to the right, is the finest in Rome), the Easter candlestick, the floor, the tabernacle, the bishop's throne and the tomb of Cardinal Fieschi.

The mosaics on the triumphal arch depict Christ surrounded by saints, with elaborate representations, to left and right, of Jerusalem and Bethlehem.
There is a plain cloister dating from the late 12th c.

★San Luigi dei Francesi (church)   D 6

Situation
Piazza di San Luigi
dei Francesi

Buses
26, 70, 81, 87, 88,
90, 94

San Luigi dei Francesi, dedicated to St Louis (Louis IX of France), is the French national church in Rome. It was begun by Cardinal Giulio de'Medici, later Pope Clement VIII, but work was then suspended and not resumed until 1580 (under the direction of Domenico Fontana). The church was dedicated in 1589.

The Renaissance façade was probably the work of Giacomo della Porta (c. 1540–1602). The church itself, a three-aisled pillared basilica, contains three major pictures (scenes from the life of St Matthew) by Caravaggio (c. 1597). Masterpieces of realistic painting, with Caravaggio's new composition of light and shade and striking chiaroscuro effects, they were not universally admired at the time. A self-portrait of the artist can be seen to the left of the executioner in the martyrdom scene.

"St Matthew", by Caravaggio . . .

. . . in the Church of San Luigi dei Francesi

San Paolo fuori le Mura

★San Paolo fuori le Mura (St Paul outside the Walls)   D 10

The remains have so far been found of the early Christian chapel built in the time of Constantine (4th c.) over the grave of St Paul, well outside the city on the road to Ostia; but it seems certain that Paul – who according to tradition was beheaded in A.D. 67 and buried by the Via Ostiensis – was venerated in early times at the site of the present church. In order to do honour to the Apostle the Emperors of the 4th and 5th c. built a basilica which until the rebuilding of St Peter's (see San Pietro in Vaticano) was the largest in the world. This church was damaged on various occasions by earthquake and fire, and finally was completely destroyed by fire as a result of the carelessness of a plumber on July 15th 1823. Thereafter it was rebuilt, with financial assistance from many countries, and reopened in 1854. San Paolo is one of the four patriarchal churches of Rome (the others being St John Lateran, St Peter's and Santa Maria Maggiore) and one of the seven pilgrimage churches (the patriarchal churches together with Santa Croce in Gerusalemme, San Lorenzo fuori le Mura and San Sebastiano).

Following its 19th c. rebuilding San Paolo is notable particularly for its basilican plan, following the early Christian model, and for a number of fine works of art. The church is entered by way of a colonnaded forecourt which leads into the porch (19th c. mosaics high up on the façade), with the Holy Door, on the inner side of which can be seen the old bronze door, cast in Constantinople in the 11th c. The interior of the church is dark, since the alabaster windows admit little light. The nave (120m/395ft long, 60m/195ft wide and 23m/75ft high) is divided into five aisles by a forest of 80 columns leading up to the triumphal arch (5th c. mosaic), the altar with its ciborium and the apse (mosaics). High up on the walls of the church are 265 portrait medallions of all the Popes from Peter onwards. Apart from the 13th c. mosaics by Venetian artists, commissioned in 1220 by Honorius III, which

Situation
Piazzale San Paolo

Underground station
San Paolo (line B)

Buses
23, 123, 170, 223, 673, 707, 766

were extensively restored, the decorations in the apse, including the Bishop's throne, are copies dating from the 19th c.

Particular features which should not be missed are the ciborium (by Arnolfo di Cambio, 1285) over the Papal altar which, like the altar in St Peter's, probably marks the spot where the Apostle was buried; a magnificent medieval Easter candlestick, 5m/16ft high, to the right of the altar; and the Chapel of the Crucifix and the baptistery.

In the sacristy is the entrance to the cloister of the Benedictine abbey, decorated with mosaics by the Vassalletti family (1204–41). The variety of form of the columns and the colour of the mosaics make this one of the most attractive cloisters in the West.

San Pietro in Montorio (church)   C 7

Situation
Via Garibaldi

Buses
41, 44, 75, 710

The church of "St Peter on the Golden Mountain" (from the name of Mons Aureus or Monte d'Oro which was given in early times to the Janiculum), an early Renaissance building of the late 15th c., owes its foundation to the medieval legend – without historical foundation – that the Apostle Peter was crucified on this spot.

The church was built for King Ferdinand IV of Spain by Baccio Pontelli (after 1481). The chapels on the left-hand side contain notable pictures ("Scourging of Christ" by Sebastiano del Piombo, 1519–25, a Madonna by Pomarancio and the "Conversion of St Paul" by Giorgio Vasari) and monuments.

In a court to the right of the church is the famous Tempietto di Bramante (a small round pillared temple), a chapel built in 1502 to commemorate the crucifixion of St Peter, which is recognised as a classic example of High Renaissance architecture, demonstrating the characteristic return to antiquity and the revival of Greco-Roman architectural forms. The harmony of its proportions and symmetry of its forms make this little temple an architectural delight.

★ Tempietto
di Bramante

★San Pietro in Vincoli (St Peter in Chains)   E 6

Situation
Piazza San Pietro in Vincoli

Underground station
Cavour (line B)

Buses
11, 27, 81

San Pietro in Vincoli is one of the oldest churches in Rome, having been begun in 431. It was originally dedicated to SS. Peter and Paul, but when Pope Leo the Great was presented with the chains which Peter was traditionally believed to have worn in the Mamertine Prison, St Peter became sole patron of the church; the chains are now preserved as a precious relic in the high altar. The gold decoration on the tabernacle is attributed to Christoforo Caradossa. The church has been considerably altered by later additions (restoration 1990/91). The impressive portico is the work of Meo da Caprino and the marble porch bears the coat-of-arms of the architect Giuliano della Rovere. The most notable features are the 20 columns with Doric capitals in the nave; the tomb of Cardinal Nicholas of Cusa (Kues on the Mosel, Germany; d. 1465) in the north aisle; and above all the monument of Pope Julius II in the south transept. This monument to the great Pope of the della Rovere family (1503–13) was originally conceived by Michelangelo on a larger scale for erection in St Peter's. Of the sculpture originally planned Michelangelo himself executed only three figures – the central figure of Moses, together with Rachel and Leah, the two wives of Jacob. The statues of Rachel and Leah, symbols of the active and contemplative life, are late works of outstanding quality; but the figure of Moses (1513–16), designed also to celebrate the great Pope and Prince of the Renaissance, ranks among the finest achievements in the sculpture of the world. Moses is depicted at the moment when he has received from God the tables of the Law, which he holds under his right arm, and is

San Pietro in Vincoli: St Peter in Chains . . .   . . . and the Tomb of Julius II

watching his people dancing round the golden calf, his face reflecting both divine illumination and wrath over the faithlessness of his people. (The horns on his forehead reflect a mistranslation of the Biblical text.)

San Sebastiano (church)

The church of St Sebastian on the Via Appia is one of the seven pilgrimage churches of Rome (the others being San Giovanni in Laterano, San Pietro in Vaticano, San Paolo fuori le Mura, Santa Maria Maggiore, Santa Croce in Gerusalemme, and San Lorenzo fuori le Mura: see entries), built in the 4th c. on the site of old cemeteries and catacombs. St Sebastian, a Christian officer in the Praetorian Guard who was martyred in the reign of Diocletian, was buried here.

In the 13th and early 17th c. three Roman tombs and a series of Christian catacombs were brought to light. Also found here were the foundations of the Constantinian basilica and remains of Roman houses. (A conducted tour of the whole underground complex of catacombs is to be strongly recommended.) Beneath the centre of the church is a meeting-hall (*triclia*) in which commemorative services were held, with large numbers of scratched inscriptions dating from the turn of the 3–4th c. Here can be seen numerous examples of the symbolic language of the early Christians – the fish (Greek *ichthys*, made up of the initials of the words "Jesus Christ, Son of God, Saviour"); the lamb, referring to Christ's sacrificial death; the anchor, a sign of trust; the dove as a symbol of peace. It is believed that the remains of Peter and Paul, who are particularly venerated here, were brought from the Vatican and the Via Ostiense for safe keeping in St Sebastian's during the persecutions in the reigns of Decius and Valerian.

Here too, are tomb chambers on several levels (1st c. A.D.) with fine paintings, stucco decoration and inscriptions.

Situation
Via Appia Antica

Bus
118

Opening times
Mon.–Wed.,
Fri.–Sun.
8.30a.m.–noon,
2.30–7pm

From the apse steps lead down to the Platonia, the tomb of the martyr Quirinius. To the left of this is a cell known as the Domus Petri (4th c. wall paintings).

★Sant'Agnese (church)   C 6

Situation
Piazza Navona

Buses
46, 62, 64, 70, 81, 88, 90

The church of Sant'Agnese, on the west side of the Piazza Navona (see entry), is dedicated to the Roman martyr St Agnes. It is built on the foundations of one side of the Stadium of Domitian, on the spot where, according to legend, the saint was about to be exposed naked to the populace when her hair suddenly and miraculously grew long to cover her nakedness. St Agnes is supposed to have been executed at the place where the church of Sant'Agnese fuori le Mura (see entry) stands.

Sant'Agnese, which adjoins the Palazzo Pamphili (see entry), was founded by Pope Innocent X, a member of the Pamphili family, and built by a succession of architects – first Girolamo Rainaldi (1652), then Borromini (1653–57) and finally Carlo Rainaldi (1672). The façade, campanile and dome (heightened by Borromini) present a lively interplay of convex and concave forms, gables, canopies, windows, columns and piers. The interior shows the same sense of movement and yet of unity. The crypt contains Alessandro Algardi's portrayal of "The Miracle of St Agnes" (1653) and the remains of a Roman mosaic pavement.

Sant'Agnese provided a model which was followed in many churches of the Baroque and Rococo periods, both in Italy and in other countries.

★Sant'Agnese fuori le Mura (St Agnes outside the Walls)   H 3

Situation
Via Nomentana 349

Buses
36, 37, 60, 136, 137, 310

According to legend, Agnes was a young and beautiful Roman girl who steadfastly refused to marry the son of the pagan governor of the city and was martyred for her faith. Constantine's daughter Constantia built a church in her honour in the 4th c. outside the city on the Via Nomentana. The present church was built by Pope Honorius I (625–638), but has undergone much alteration and restoration since then.

Notable features of this church, a basilica with a high narrow nave, are the sixteen antique columns, the richly decorated wooden ceiling (17th c.), the marble candelabra and the bishop's throne in the chancel. Finest of all, however, is the apse mosaic (7th c.) which depicts St Agnes with Popes Honorius and Symmachus, Relics of St Agnes and her sister, St Emerentiana, are contained in the high altar.

Beneath the church are the Catacombe di Sant'Agnese (A.D. 300), part of the complex being preserved in its original state. They extend over three stories and have a total length of 7km/4 miles. Open daily, 9am–12.30pm and 3.30–6pm; visits on application to the verger.

★Sant'Agostino (church)   D 6

Situation
Piazza
Sant'Agostino

Buses
26, 70

Sant'Agostino, situated near the Piazza Navona (see entry), is noted for its image of the Madonna del Parto (Madonna of Childbirth) who is invoked by pregnant women seeking a safe delivery and by married couples wanting a child. The church, built between 1479 and 1483 (probably by Giacomo da Pietrasanta) and rebuilt in 1750, has a severe travertine façade, one of the earliest Renaissance façades in Rome.

The interior, with a high nave barely wider than the aisles, is dominated by the dome which is flanked by the transepts. In addition to the Madonna del Parto (by Jacopo Sansevino, 1421) the church has a painting of the prophet Isaiah by Raphael (1512; third pillar on left) and Caravaggio's "Madonna of the Pilgrims" (1605; third chapel in north aisle).

Sant'Andrea al Quirinale

To the right of the church is the Biblioteca Angelica (state-owned since 1873), a library specialising in philology.

★Sant'Andrea al Quirinale (church)

E 6

Sant'Andrea al Quirinale, built by Bernini (1658–71) for Cardinal Camillo Pamphili as the church of a Jesuit seminary, is a jewel among the smaller churches of Rome, and forms a counterpoint with the nearby church of St Carlo alle Quatro Fontane (see entry), built by Bernini's great rival Borromini.

Situation
Via del Quirinale

Buses
57, 64, 65, 70, 71, 75, 170

Sant'Andrea, which was the court chapel of the Italian royal house from 1870 to 1946, is notable both for the consummate perfection of its design and the richness of its decoration. The circular ground plan of the Renaissance is here extended into the oval which was favoured by Baroque architects, and this, opened out still further by eight lateral chapels, creates the sense of space and movement which appealed to the Baroque taste.

The lively architectural pattern is matched by the lavish interior decoration with its pilasters and friezes, arches and recesses, coffered domes, cornices and windows, marble and stucco of many colours (old rose, white, gold). There are also fine frescoes and pictures, mainly of the Baroque period.

Sant'Andrea della Valle (church)

D 6

The beauty of the façade and dome of the church of Sant'Andrea della Valle is best seen from the Corso del Rinascimento; a distinctive feature is the angel with outspread wings on the left-hand side, taking the place of

Situation
Corso Vittorio Emanuele

111

a volute (there is no corresponding feature on the right-hand side). Sant'Andrea, served by the Theatines (a preaching order), is very popular with the people of Rome – as is evidenced by the fact that Puccini sets the first act of "Tosca" in the Cappella Allavanti, the first chapel in the south aisle of the church.

The architects responsible for Sant'Andrea (Francesco Grimaldi, Giacomo della Porta, Carlo Maderna and Carlo Rainaldi) followed the model of the Gesù church, some 500 yards away; many features are clearly reminiscent of that church – the two-storey travertine façade with its plastic structure, the nave (high and wide, but yet creating an effect of harmony and unity) with its side chapels, transept, choir and apse, and the mighty dome (the second largest in Rome, after the dome of St Peter's) – and indeed the ground plan of Sant'Andrea is almost indistinguishable from that of the Gesù (see entry).

The side chapels contain some fine pictures and statues, but the most notable features of the interior are the tombs of two Popes belonging to the Piccolomini family of Siena which were brought here from St Peter's in 1614 and now stand in the nave near the north transept: the humanist Pope Pius II (Aeneas Silvius Piccolomini, d. 1464) on the left and Pope Pius III (Francesco Todeschini Piccolomini, d. 1503) on the right. Both tombs were the work of Paolo Taccone and Andrea Bregno.

The magnificent frescoes in the dome and the semi-dome of the apse were painted by Domenichino (1624–28).

Sant'Ignazio (church)   D 6

Situation
Piazza di
Sant'Ignazio

Buses
28, 56, 60, 62, 71,
81, 85, 87, 88, 90,
90b, 94, 95

The Society of Jesus, founded by Ignatius Loyola in 1540, soon attracted an increasing following and a large membership in Rome and throughout Europe, and to honour the memory of their founder, who died in 1556 and was canonised in 1622, the Jesuits built the church of Sant'Ignazio – the second Jesuit church in Rome, following the Gesù (see entry) – between 1626 and 1650, with financial assistance from Cardinal Ludovico Ludovisi, a nephew of Pope Gregory XV. Both the architect, Orazio Grassi, and the painter, Andrea Pozzo, were Jesuits.

The square in which the church stands, with something of the air of a stage set, and its imposing façade are very much in the Baroque spirit, the interior even more so. The spacious wide nave (equally suitable for preaching purposes and for conducting the service from one central spot), the linked side chapels and the sumptuous decoration and furnishings, with their use of precious materials and elaborate ornamental patterns, were all calculated to draw the faithful back to the Church (this was the period of the Counter-Reformation). The harmony of the interior does not suffer from the fact that the central dome originally planned was not built; in its place and on the ceiling Andrea Pozzo created a *trompe l'œil* painting celebrating the triumph of Sant'Ignatius, his entry into paradise and the four missionary regions of the world, in which the painted representation of Heaven appears to break up the illusionist architecture and the sham dome. (A marble disc in the floor marks the spot from which the illusion is most effective.) In Sant'Ignazio architecture, sculpture and painting merge into one another; the eye of the believer was to be caught and held by art, his heart to be opened to the teaching of the Church.

In the south transept is the tomb of St Aloysius (Luigi Gonzaga, 1568–91), in the north transept that of St John Berchmans, both Jesuit saints.

Santa Cecilia in Trastevere (church)   D 7

St Cecilia, described in her Life as "Coeli Lilia" (the Lily of Heaven), was one of the early Christian martyrs who were always much venerated in Rome and became the subject of numerous legends.

Traditionally the church occupies the site of the house belonging to Cecilia's husband Valerian. Originally founded in the 5th c., it was much altered and rebuilt in later centuries. It is of basilican type, with forecourt, porch (façade by Ferdinando Fuga, 1725), a Romanesque campanile, a wide nave with rows of columns, chancel and apse.

In the chancel are a marble ciborium by Arnolfo di Cambio (1283) and a figure of St Cecilia carved by Stefano Maderna in 1600 (a year after the discovery of a tomb containing the body of a young girl in this position). The apse has a mosaic dating from the reign of Pope Paschal I (9th c.). In the crypt can be seen the excavated foundations of a Roman house.

Special permission is required to visit the adjoining convent, which contains a magnificent "Last Judgment" by Pietro Cavallini (1293).

Buses
23, 26, 28, 44, 75, 97, 170, 710, 718, 719, 774

★Santa Costanza (church)   H 3

Close to the church of Sant'Agnese fuori le Mura (see entry), on the Via Nomentana, is a church with one of the most beautiful interiors of all the Roman churches – Santa Costanza, a round church erected at the beginning of the 4th c. as a mausoleum for Constantine's daughter Constantia (or rather Constantina) and Helen, wife of Julian the Apostate. This little architectural masterpiece, measuring 22.5m/74ft in diameter, is simple in conception, with an unpretentious brick-built exterior, but constructed internally with costly and valuable materials (12 double columns with capitals). The mosaics depict both sacred and pagan figures, with animals playing amid vines. In the church Roman architecture, the mosaic art of late antiquity and early Christian symbols are blended into a harmonious whole.

Situation
Via Nomentana

Buses
36, 37, 60, 136, 137, 310

Santa Croce in Gerusalemme (church)   G 7

Santa Croce in Gerusalemme is one of the seven pilgrimage churches of Rome, the others being San Giovanni in Laterano, San Pietro in Vaticano, San Paolo fuori le Mura, Santa Maria Maggiore, San Sebastiano and San Lorenzo fuori le Mura (see entries). Pilgrims like to attend services at these churches on the eve of important Catholic festivals.

The church was built in the reign of Constantine for the purpose – so the legend goes – of housing the relics of Christ's Passion which Constantine's mother Helen had brought from the Holy Land. It received its present Baroque form in the 18th c. (architect, Domenico Gregorini).

Situation
Piazza Santa Croce in Gerusalemme

Underground station
San Giovanni (line A)

Buses
3, 9, 15, 81

Santa Francesca Romana (church)   E 7

To replace the church of Santa Maria Antique a new church dedicated to the Virgin, Santa Maria Nuova, was built in the second half of the 10th c. on the other side of the Forum, on what is now the Via dei Fori Imperiali. The church occupied part of the site of the old temple of Venus and Rome. The tower, a characteristic example of a medieval Roman campanile, was added in the 13th c. The church received its present name when it was dedicated to the foundress of the Oblates, St Frances of Rome.

Notable features of the interior, which is richly adorned with marble stucco and pictures, are the Confessio, the apse mosaic and the 6th c. Madonna on the high altar (ascribed to St Luke).

Underground station
Colosseo (line B)

Buses
11, 27, 81, 85, 87, 88

Santa Francesca Romana

Santa Maria in Aracoeli

Santa Maria degli Angeli (church)

See Terme di Diocleziano

Santa Maria dell'Anima (church)   C 6

Situation
Via di Santa Maria
dell'Anima
(entrance in Piazza
della Pace)

Buses
28, 70, 81, 88, 90

Pilgrims to Rome expected to find a hospice where they could stay and a church belonging to their particular nation. Santa Maria dell'Anima, situated near the Piazza Navona (see entry), was built in 1501–14 for German pilgrims – that is, all pilgrims from the Holy Roman Empire – and it is still a church of the German Catholic community in Rome.

Soon after the church was built Pope Adrian VI (1522–23) – a native of Utrecht and the last non-Italian Pope before John Paul II – was buried here. His tomb, on the south side of the choir, is flanked by allegorical figures representing the four cardinal virtues, Prudence, Justice, Fortitude and Temperance. The experience of this sorely tried Pope, who reigned during the early days of the Reformation, is summarised in a Latin inscription referring to the effect on a man's life of the age into which he is born. The interior of this tall hall-church is richly decorated.

Santa Maria in Aracoeli (church)   D 6

Situation
Via del Teatro di
Marcello

The church of Santa Maria in Aracoeli occupies a venerable sacred site on the Capitol (see Campidoglio), having been built by Franciscans in the 13th c. on the foundations of the ancient temple of Juno Moneta, which dated from the 6th c. B.C. The steep flight of 124 steps leading up to the church (which young couples like to climb after their wedding) was constructed in 1348. In the Middle Ages the church was at the centre of Roman political life, being the meeting place of the municipal parliament. The interior was redecorated after the defeat of the Turkish fleet at Lepanto in 1571.

Buses
57, 90, 90b, 92, 94, 95, 716, 718, 719

The majestic flight of steps leads up from the Via del Teatro di Marcello to a bare brick façade which makes the interior appear all the more sumptuous, in spite of its simple basilican plan (with side chapels added later). Notable features of the church are the 16th c. wooden ceiling, the Cappella Bufalini at the near end of the south aisle, which has frescoes by Pinturicchio (1485), and the numerous grave-slabs and monuments in the floor and on the walls.

In the north transept is an elegant aedicula (miniature temple) marking the spot where the Sibyl prophesied to Augustus that a virgin would bear a divine child who would overthrow the altars of the gods; whereupon the Emperor set up an altar on the spot with the inscription – now on the triumphal arch – "Ecce ara promogeneti Dei" ("Behold the altar of the firstborn of God"). Beneath the aedicula are the remains of St Helen, Constantine's mother, who searched for the True Cross and the relics of Christ's Passion in the Holy Land and brought them back to Rome.

In the sacristy can be seen the "Santo Bambino", a figure of the Child Jesus which legend says was carved from the wood of an olive-tree in the garden of Gethsemane and which is popularly credited with miraculous qualities. At Christmas the image is set up in the nave, and children preach "sermons" in front of it.

Santa Maria della Concezione (church of the Capuchins)   E 5

Consisting of a single central aisle, the church of the Capuchins was commissioned by Cardinal Antonio Barberini, a Capuchin friar, and built at the beginning of the 17th c. by Antonio Casoni. The Cardinal's memorial in front of the high altar bears the Latin inscription "Hic iacet pulvis, cinis et nihil!" ("here lie dust, ashes and nothing"). The altarpieces contained in the church, Guido Reni's "Archangel Michael battles with Satan" (to the right in the first chapel) and Domenichino's "Francis and the Angel" (third chapel) are particularly impressive.

Situation
Via Veneto 37

Buses
52, 53, 56, 58, 90b, 95, 490, 492, 495

The most unusual feature of the church is the marble cemetery in five chapels, where the skulls and bones of some 4000 Capuchin friars have been arranged to form an intricate decoration.

Cimitero dei Cappuccini

★Santa Maria in Cosmedin (church)   D 7

On the south side of the Piazza Bocca della Verità, overlooking the Tempio di Fortuna Virile, the Arco di Giano and the church of San Giorgio in Velabro (see entries), is the church of Santa Maria in Cosmedin (probably given this name by Byzantines after a square in their city).

This is one of the finest examples of medieval church architecture in Rome. Begun in 772, during the reign of Pope Adrian I, and completed in its present form in about 1124 under Calixtus II, it is an architectural gem (suggesting an alternative derivation of the name Cosmedin from the Greek *cosmos*, which means "perfect order" or "ornament").

The noble harmony of the church's proportions begins with the seven-storey campanile and is continued in the wide two-storey porch with its projecting canopy; it reaches even sublimer heights in the interior, with its tall nave and carefully structured layout to meet liturgical needs, and is infinitely repeated in the intarsia (inlaid marble) work by the Cosmati.

The alternation of columns and piers, the irregular dimensions, the three apses, the aisles with their famous frescoes, the Cosmatesque work in the

Situation
Piazza Bocca della Verità

Buses
15, 23, 57, 90, 90b, 94, 716

Santa Maria in Cosmedin

Bocca della Verità (mouth of truth)

floor and the marble screens of the *scola cantorum* (the area reserved for the clergy), the marble ambos (reading pulpits), the bishop's throne with its two lions' heads and the ornamental disc behind it, the twisted Easter candlestick, the ciborium over the altar; all these details combine to make Santa Maria in Cosmedin one of the most beautiful of the smaller churches of Rome.

In the crypt are early Christian tombs and the foundations of a pagan temple.

Bocca della Verità

At the left-hand end of the porch is the large stone mask known as the Bocca della Verità, the "Mouth of Truth". According to popular belief, the Romans when taking an oath would put their right hand into the mouth of the mask, which would then close and hold them fast if they perjured themselves. (Nowadays the "Mouth of Truth" serves only as a threat to troublesome children.)

★Santa Maria Maggiore (church) F 6

Situation
Piazza di Santa
Maria Maggiore

Underground
station
Termini
(lines A and B)

Buses
3, 4, 16, 27, 70, 71,
93, 93b, 93c

Santa Maria Maggiore is the largest of the 80 Roman churches dedicated to the Virgin. It is also one of the four patriarchal basilicas (coming after San Giovanni in Laterano, San Pietro in Vaticano and San Paolo fuori le Mura – see entries) and one of the seven pilgrimage churches (the patriarchal churches together with Santa Croce in Gerusalemme, San Lorenzo fuori le Mura and San Sebastiano – see entries). It is the only church in Rome in which mass has been celebrated every day without interruption since the 5th c.

According to legend, on the night of the 4th/5th August in the year 358 the Virgin appeared to Pope Liberius and a Roman patrician named Johannes and told them to build a church on the spot where snow fell on the

Santa Maria Maggiore

Crypt of Santa Maria Maggiore, with relics of the crib of Bethlehem

Trams
14, 516, 517

Opening times
7am–7pm
(in summer 8pm)

following day (in the month of August!). Snow did fall on the following morning on the Esquiline hill, outlining the plan of a basilica; since then the feast of Our Lady of the Snow has been celebrated on August 5th. Archaeological research has been unable to establish, however, whether the church was erected in the 4th or the 5th c. The original church was added to in later centuries; a new apse was built in the 13th c; the campanile (75m/245ft high; the tallest in Rome) in 1377. Alexander VI built the golden coffered roof with the first gold from America; two side chapels, the Cappella Sistina and the Cappella Paoline were added, and between the 16th and 18th centuries the church was surrounded by a whole series of extensions prelates's house). From the square with the obelisk (14.80m/49ft high) from the Mausoleum of Augustus (see Mausoleo di Augusto) an imposing flight of steps leads up to the entrance at the chancel end of the church. The main entrance (façade by Ferdinando Fuga, 1743) is reached by way of the column from the Basilica of Maxentius, now crowned by a figure of the Virgin (see Basilica di Massenzio).

The interior is perhaps the finest and most majestic church interior in Rome; 86m/282ft long, three-aisled, with 36 marble and four granite columns, mosaics (4th or 5th c., the oldest in Rome) on the upper part of the walls, Cosmatesque work in the floor (mid 12th c.) and a coffered ceiling by Giuliano da Sangallos (15th c.).

The Cappella Sistina on the right and the Cappella Paoline on the left are in effect transepts. The Cappella Sistina, built by Domenico Fontana (1584–90) for Pope Sixtus V, contains a bronze tabernacle and the tombs of Sixtus V and his predecessor Pius V. The Cappella Paolina was built for Pope Paul V by Flaminio Ponzo; the richly decorated altarpiece was designed by Girolamo Rainaldi. On the canopied high altar, by Ferdinando Fuga, is a much venerated image of the Virgin (the "Salus Populi Romani"), traditionally attributed to St Luke but in fact a 13th c. work. The Confessio contains a glass case displaying relics of the manger in Bethlehem, in front of which is the kneeling statue of Pius IX by Ignazio Iacometti (1880).

A further contribution is made to the magnificence of the decoration by the mosaics on the triumphal arch and in the apse, depicting Old and New Testament themes, scenes from the life of the Virgin and a "Coronation of the Virgin" Jacopo Torriti (end of 13th c.), the supreme achievement of the art of the Roman mosaic-workers (best light early in the morning).

The canopy over the Papal altar is supported on four porphyry columns from Hadrian's villa at Tivoli (see entry).

⋆ Santa Maria sopra Minerva (church)   D 6

Situation
Piazza della
Minerva

Buses
26, 87, 94

Elephant obelisk

The Piazza della Minerva, behind the Pantheon (see entry), is graced by a charming monument – the marble elephant by Bernini which Ercole Ferrata (1667) used as the base supporting a small Egyptian obelisk (6th c. B.C.). The inscription on the plinth of the monument is to the effect that great strength is required to bear wisdom.

The church, served by the Dominican order (the headquarters of which are to the left of the church), is built on the site of a temple of Minerva; hence its name. It was begun, in Gothic style, about 1280 but was completed only in 1453 with the vaulting of the nave. It is thus the only Gothic complex of any size in Rome.

Situated in the centre of the city and served by St Dominic's preaching order, the church was popular with the people of Rome, and the number of grave-slabs in the floor and on the walls of this three-aisled basilica and in the side chapels with their numerous pictures bears witness to the part it played in the religious life of the city. The best known of the funerary chapels is the Caraffa Chapel at the end of the south transept, also known as the Chapel of the Annunciation of St Thomas, which contains the tomb of Cardinal Oliviero Caraffa (1347–80) and is famous for its frescoes by Filippo Lippi (1489). These glorify both the Virgin (Annunciation and Assumption) and St Thomas Aquinas, a member of the Dominican order (the triumph of the saint and scenes from his life).

The high altar contains the relics of St Catherine of Siena (1347–80), author of numerous letters to the exiled Popes at Avignon urging them to return to Rome. In front of the altar, on the left, is a statue of the Risen Christ by Michelangelo (1521) which has been unjustly deprecated in comparison with his other works. It was criticised during Michelangelo's lifetime for looking more like a youthful pagan god than the founder of Christianity, and later a loincloth was added to cover its nakedness. Quiet contemplation is needed to appreciate the full expressiveness of the statue, but the masterly skill with which the marble is fashioned is evident at the first glance. Michelangelo's genius so impressed other artists that the painter Sebastiano del Piombo, for example, maintained that Christ's knees were worth more than all the buildings in Rome. In a passage to the left of the presbytery is the tomb of the painter Fra Angelico, a member of the Dominican order.

Santa Maria di Monserrato (church)　　　　　　　　　　　C 6

About the same time as the church of Santa Maria dell'Anima was built for the Germans this church was built by Antonio da Sangallo the Elder (1495 onwards) for the Aragonese and Catalans. The initiative came from the famous (or notorious) Pope Alexander VI, a member of the Spanish family of Borja (which became in Italian Borgia), who is buried in the church. Santa Maria di Monserrato (named after the famous Marian pilgrimage centre of Monserrat near Barcelona) has been since 1875 the Spanish national church in Rome.

Notable features of the church are the tombs of the two Borgia Popes, Calixtus III and Alexander VI, and a number of marble statues, including a bust of Cardinal Pietro Molto by Bernini (1621).

Situation
Via di Monserrato/
Via Giulia 151

Buses
23, 28, 28b, 65

★Santa Maria della Pace (church)　　　　　　　　　　　　C 6

Santa Maria della Pace, one of Rome's most beautiful churches, reached its present form in a number of stages. In 1482 Pope Sixtus IV rebuilt an earlier church of the Virgin on this site in thanksgiving for the peace with Milan. The architect is thought to have been Bacio Pontelli, who created a rectangular church to which another architect, perhaps Bramante, added an octagonal structure and a cloister. In 1656 Pietro da Cortona restored the church, adding the Baroque façade and a semicircular porch (pronate). This spirited entrance gives access to the nave and octagon, which contains famous frescoes by Raphael (1415) depicting the ancient Sibyls, to which figures of prophets and saints were later added by other painters.

The admirably proportioned cloister, built for Cardinal Oliviero Caraffa in 1504, was Bramante's first work in Rome.

Situation
Via della Pace

Buses
26, 70, 81, 90

★Santa Maria del Popolo (church)　　　　　　　　　　　　D 4

Beyond the pines of the Pincio Gardens (see entry) stands the church of Santa Maria del Popolo, with its fine Renaissance façade, dome and campanile. Legend has it that there was once a chapel here, built to drive away the evil spirit of Nero, which Pope Sixtus IV (1471–84) enlarged into a church. This was extended by Bramante in 1505, occupied by Augustinian canons and later restored by Bernini. Martin Luther, an Augustinian, lived in the Augustinian house during his visit to Rome in 1510–11; after the Reformation the altar at which he had celebrated mass was shunned by other members of the order.

Situation
Piazza del Popolo

Underground station
Flaminio (line A)

119

Santa Maria della Pace

Santa Maria del Popolo in the Piazza del Popolo below the Pincio

As a parish church Santa Maria del Popolo, built on a Latin cross plan with three aisles and many side chapels, contains numerous tombs including those of Cardinal Ascanio Sforza (d. 1505) and Cardinal Girolamo Basso della Rovere (d. 1507), both by Andrea Sansovino, in the choir. On the vaulting of the choir are frescoes by Pinturecchio depicting the Coronation of the Virgin, with Evangelists, Sibyls and Fathers of the Church. The side chapels are particularly fine. The first on the right was built for the family of della Rovere, the second (by Carlo Fontana, 1682–87) for Cardinal Cybo, the second on the left (designed by Raffael, 1513–15) for the Chigi family. The Cesari Chapel, in the north transept, contains two famous pictures by Caravaggio, the "Conversion of St Paul" and the "Crucifixion of St Peter".

Buses
1, 2, 2b, 90, 95, 115, 202, 203, 205, 490, 492, 495

Santa Maria in Trastevere (church)

C 7

Santa Maria in Trastevere (the densely populated part of Rome on the right bank of the Tiber; see Trastevere) is the oldest church of the Virgin in Rome. According to legend it stands on the spot where a spring of oil flowed 38 years before Christ's birth as an intimation of the future Saviour. This may also be the place where Christians were able for the first time to hold services in public.

The building of the church began between 221 and 227, in the reign of Pope Calixtus I, and was completed in 340, in the reign of Julius I. It was rebuilt by Innocent II (1130–43), who came from the Trastevere district, and redecorated in the Baroque period. It is now one of the finest and most imposing churches in Rome.

The church has a Romanesque campanile, a façade decorated with mosaics (the Virgin with ten female saints) and a portico containing early Christian sarcophagi and various medieval fragments.

Notable features of the interior are the Cosmatesque (marble intarsia) work in the floor, the coffered wooded ceiling, partly gilded by Domenichino (1617), the 22 massive Ionic columns in the nave, and a 15th c. tabernacle by Mino del Reame (at the west end of the nave on the right).

The mosaics in the apse are masterpieces of medieval art. In the conch (c. 1140) are Christ, the Virgin and saints above a frieze of lambs, and below this are scenes from the life of the Virgin – Nativity, Annunciation, Nativity of Christ, Three Kings, Presentation in the Temple, Assumption (by Pietro Cavallini, c. 1291). The mosaics at the exit of the church were supposed to remind worshippers of the glory of Heaven, portraying the saints against a celestial background of gold.

Situation
Piazza Santa Maria in Trastevere

Buses
22, 28, 28b, 56, 60, 65

★Santa Maria della Vittoria (church)

E 5

Santa Maria della Vittoria commemorates the Emperor Ferdinand II's victory in the battle of the White Mountain near Prague in 1620 during the Thirty Years' War, which was attributed to the intervention of the Virgin. The church, previously dedicated to St Paul, then received an image of the Virgin, found at Pilsen and reputed to be miraculous, and was re-dedicated under its present name.

This attractive Baroque church, built by Carlo Maderna in 1608–20 (restoration 1990–91) for Cardinal Scipione Borghese, is of imposing effect with its finely contrived decoration of coloured marble, rich stucco ornament and paintings. The most impressive thing in the church, however, is the altar of St Teresa of Avila (fourth chapel on the left), created by Bernini for Cardinal Cornaro. St Teresa (1515–82), the mystic and writer who refounded the order of Carmelite nuns, is depicted in a state of ecstatic rapture, pierced by the love of God which is symbolised by the arrow of the angel who hovers over her.

Situation
Via XX Settembre

Underground station
Reppublica or Barberini (line A)

Buses
60, 61, 62, 415

In the sacristy are pictures and flags commemorating the battle of the White Mountain.

★Santa Prassede (church)   F 6

Situation
Via San Martino ai Monti

Buses
16, 93, 93b, 93c

A legend relates that two daughters of a Roman senator named Pudens, Pudentiana (see Santa Pudenziana) and Praxedes, were converted to the Christian faith by St Peter. The church, dedicated to St Praxades, has gone through a number of different building stages but has preserved the spatial character of an early Christian basilica, its high pillared nave rising into the presbytery with its triumphal arch and apse mosaics (9th c., in the reign of Pope Paschal I). The mosaics are among the finest in Rome. On the triumphal arch is a representation of the heavenly Jerusalem; in the apse is the apocalyptic Lamb of the Revelation, and in the conch of the apse, above a frieze of lambs, SS. Peter and Paul leading Praxedes and Pudentiana, accompanied by Pope Paschal as the donor and by St Zeno. In addition to glorifying the saints the representations had a didactic purpose: the object, as in other religious painting, was to instruct the worshippers, who in the Middle Ages were mostly illiterate, in the doctrines of the faith. The Chapel of St Zeno (in the south aisle), built by Pope Paschal I to house the tomb of his mother Theodora, is like a medieval picturebook, every part of the walls and vaulting being covered with mosaics depicting saints and Biblical symbols.

★Santa Pudenziana (church)   F 6

Situation
Via Urbana

Buses
27, 70, 71, 81

Santa Pudenziana is said to occupy the house of the Roman senator Pudens, whose daughters Pudentiana and Praxedes (see Santa Prassede) were converted by St Peter while staying in the house. The church was originally built in the reign of Pope Siricius (384–399); it has undergone much subsequent alteration, but the original apse with its mosaic decoration has been preserved.

The church, now lying below the present street level, is entered from Via Urbana. Externally its most notable features are the campanile and the remains of a Romanesque doorway. The finest thing in the interior is the mosaic in the apse (end of 4th c.), now rather cramped by later building. It shows Christ surrounded by Apostles and women against a lively background based on ancient models, with a skilful use of perspective. Above the central group are the buildings of a city, a cross and the (partly obliterated) symbols of the four Evangelists, the man, the lion, the bull and the eagle.

★Santa Sabina (church)   D 7

Situation
Piazza Pietro d'Illiria

Buses
23, 57, 92, 94, 95, 716

Both externally and internally the church of Santa Sabina preserved the character of an early Christian basilica. Built by Peter of Illyria in 425–432 over the house of a Christian woman named Sabina, it was embellished with marble by Pope Eugenius II in 824. In 1222 Pope Honorius II presented the church to the Dominicans.

The central doorway in the porch has the oldest carved wooden doors in Christian art (432), of African cedar-wood with delicate and expressive reliefs by unknown artists depicting Old and New Testament scenes. Of the original 28 panels 18 have survived, though not in their original positions. The scenes can be readily identified (from top to bottom and left to right):

1st row: Crucifixion. Healing of the Blind Man. Multiplication of the Loaves, Marriage in Cana, Doubting Thomas, Moses and the Burning Bush, Christ before Pilate.

Central doorway of Santa Sabina: relief in wood on the door

2nd row: Resurrection, Miracles of Moses, Christ's Appearance to the Women.

3rd row: Three Kings, Ascension, Peter's denial, Crossing of the Red Sea, Miracle of the Serpent.

4th row: Christ between Peter and Paul, Triumph of Christ, Assumption of Elijah, Moses before Pharaoh.

The nave is flanked by 20 Corinthian columns (20m/65ft high) of Parian marble. On the wall above the entrance is one of the oldest mosaics in Rome – two female figures symbolising the Church of the Gentiles (pagans) and the Church of the Circumcision (Jews), with an inscription commemorating the erection of the church. The choir has fine marble screens with intarsia ornament.

Adjoining the church is a Dominican monastery in which St Thomas Aquinus was a monk, with a beautiful Romanesque cloister.

From the terrace next to the church there is a magnificent view across the Tiber towards Trastevere, Piazza Venezia and the Vatican City (see entries).

★Santi Apostoli (church)

D/E 6

The Church of the Apostles in the Palazzo Colonna, originally dedicated to SS. Philip and James, was probably founded by Pope Pelagius I (556–561) after the expulsion of the Goths from Rome. It was altered and renovated by later Popes and finally rebuilt by Francesco and Carlo Fontana (1702 onwards) as the last basilican church erected in Rome. Extensive restoration work was carried out in 1990. In the porch, which lies at an angle to the church, are examples of ancient and medieval art. Notable features of the interior (63m/207ft long) are the ceiling frescoes (Triumph of the Franciscan order), the tomb of Pope Clement XIV, a masterpiece by Canova (1787), and the tomb of Cardinal Pietro Riario (d. 1474).

Situation
Piazza SS. Apostoli

Buses
56, 57, 60, 62, 64, 65, 70, 71, 75, 81, 85, 88, 90, 95, 170

★Santi Cosma e Damiano (church)   E 6

Situation
Via dei Fori
Imperiali

**Underground
station**
Colosseo (line B)

This church, dedicated to the two Oriental doctor saints Cosmas and Damian, was converted in the 6th c. from a Roman building in Vespasian's Forum of Peace (see Foro di Vespasiano), hence its aisleless ground plan. In the 17th c. the interior was decorated in Baroque style.

The church has a fine wooden ceiling of 1632 and a medieval Easter candle with Cosmatesque decoration. It is, however, notable for the mosaics on the triumphal arch and in the apse, which date from the reign of Pope Felix IV (526–530). On the triumphal arch are scenes from the Book of Revelation. In the apse the "transmission of the Divine Law", in which Christ is depicted handing the scroll of the Law to Peter and Paul, flanked by SS. Cosmas and Damian, St Theodore and Pope Felix IV.

The Christmas crib (Nativity scene) in the vestibule is one of the largest in Rome and of considerable artistic quality.

Santi Giovanni e Paolo (church)   E 7

Situation
Piazza dei Santi
Giovanni e Paolo

Buses
11, 15, 27, 118, 673

Trams
13, 30, 30b

According to legend a church was built on this site in the 5th c. by a Roman senator names Byzantius and his son Pammachius in honour of the martyrs John and Paul, officers in the Roman army who were executed in the time of Julian the Apostate. The church is said to have been built over the remains of the house on the Caelian hill in which they were killed. Around 1150 it was rebuilt by Cardinal Giovanni di Sutri, with the addition of the porch, the campanile and the dwarf gallery in the apse. During the Baroque period the interior was redecorated.

Excavations in the present century have revealed the Roman house under the church, so it is now possible to follow the history of the site in an unbroken line from the original Roman house with its fine brick masonry and lively frescoes (the best preserved wall paintings in Rome, depicting Venus and a male divinity), the antique columns and the two lions in the porch, by way of the medieval building, with its marble columns and the campanile built over the walls of the large temple of Claudius on the Caelian, to the basilica we see today.

Santi Quattro Coronati (church)   F 7

Situation
Via dei Santi
Quattro Coronati

Buses
15, 81, 85, 87, 88,
118, 673

Trams
13, 30, 30b

The first church on this site was built in the 4th c. in honour of four martyrs. According to one legend they were Roman soldiers who refused to do honour to a statue of Aesculapius; another version states that they were sculptors of Pannonia who refused to carve a pagan idol. By virtue of the second of these legends the church is popular with stonemasons. The martyrs are said to have been killed by having an iron crown driven on to their heads; hence they are "crowned" martyrs.

The present church was erected in the reign of Pope Paschal II (*c.* 1100) after the destruction of an earlier church by the Normans in 1084.

The principal features of the church are the nave and apse, with the tall campanile; the Cappella di San Silvestro, with scenes from the life of Constantine, selected for their relevance to the conflict between the Pope and the Emperor in the Middle Ages; frescoes depicting the discovery of the Cross by Empress Helen; the crypt and the famous early 13th c, cloister.

Santo Stefano Rotondo (church)   F 7

Situation
Via di Santo
Stefano Rotondo

Santo Stefano Rotondo was, architecturally, one of the great churches of Rome, but its state of dilapidation destroys the full effect of this imposing structure, with its ground plan of a Greek cross set within a circle. The church dates from the 5th and 7th c. (Popes Simplicius and Adrian I). Of the two original ambulatories, only the inner one is preserved. The 34 pillars, which used to divide them, can be seen today in the outer wall. On the ambulatory wall is a cycle of badly preserved frescoes depicting the cruel martyrdom of the Saints.

In addition to St Stephen the Protomartyr (feast December 26th) St Stephen of Hungary is honoured here.

The church of Santo Stefano Rotondo merits thorough renovation, and although a beginning has been made with this work progress is lamentably slow.

Buses
85, 88, 673

Scala Santa (Holy Staircase)   G 7

Diagonally across the main front of San Giovanni in Laterano (see entry) is the church of the Scala Santa, on the position of the dining-room (triclinium) of the Lateran Palace (see Palazzo Lateran). It contains the Papal chapel of the palace (Cappella Sanctum Sanctorum, with 13th c. mosaics) and the Holy Staircase, a flight of 28 marble steps (now clad with wood) which is believed to be a staircase from Pilate's palace in Jerusalem, brought to Rome in the 4th c. by St Helen. It is the practice for the faithful to climb the staircase on their knees in memory of Christ's Passion.

Situation
Piazza San
Giovanni in
Laterano

**Underground
station**
San Giovanni
(line A)

Buses: 16, 85, 87, 88, 93, 218, 650, 673.

Spanish Steps

See Piazza di Spagna

★Teatro di Marcello (Theatre of Marcellus)   D 6

The Romans had seen in Greece how theatres with a semicircular auditorium could be built against the slope of a hill, thus avoiding the necessity of a costly building operation to provide support for the tiers of seating, and the same technique could well have been applied in Rome, which had plenty of hills. The desire to display Roman power, artistic achievement and technological skill, however, led Pompey to erect a free-standing theatre in 55 B.C. and Augustus followed his example in the theatre built for his nephew and son-in-law Marcellus, predestined to be the Emperor's successor had he not died before his time.

The theatre, originally planned by Caesar, was begun in 13 B.C. and completed two years later. The auditorium was now supported by a massive system of arcades, and the disposition of the stage and the tiers of seating was matched to the external elevation. The remains are still impressive, in spite of the fact that the theatre was converted into a fortress and residence by the Fabi, Savelli and Orsini families during the Middle Ages.

In the 16th c, a new palace was built by Baldassare Peruzzi for the Savelli family on the ruins of the theatre, but this still preserved the form of the original structure. The restoration of the theatre, begun in 1989, is expected to continue into the mid-1990s.

Situation
Via del Teatro di
Marcello

Buses
15, 23, 57, 90, 90b,
92, 94, 95, 716, 774

On a high platform in front of the Theatre of Marcellus (on the right) are three corner columns from the Temple of Apollo Sosianus, originally built in 435–433 B.C., restored in 179 B.C. and rebuilt in 32 B.C. by the consul Sosianus.

In ancient Rome the Theatre of Marcellus was adjoined on the south-east by the Foro Oblitorio (fruit and vegetable market), leading to the Forum

Temple of Apollo
Sosianus

Teatro di Marcello (left) and Temple of Apollo Socianus

Boarium (cattle market) on the site of the present Piazza Bocca della Verità (see entry).

Tempietto di Bramante

See San Pietro in Montorio

★Terme di Caracalla (Baths of Caracalla)   E 8

Situation
Via delle Terme di Caracalla

Underground station
Circo Massimo (line B)

Buses
11, 27, 90, 90b, 94, 118, 673

Trams
13, 30, 30b

The Baths of Caracalla to the south of the city, begun by Septimus Severus in A.D. 206 and completed by Caracalla in 216, were much more than public baths. Nowadays they would be called a "leisure centre", containing as they did a whole system of baths (hot and cold baths, a swimming pool, sweat baths with both dry and damp heat), facilities for gymnastics and sport, pleasant rooms for social intercourse, gardens to walk in, lecture rooms and libraries, hairdressers and shops.

These various needs were met in a massively imposing structure covering an area 300m/1100ft square, a complex of gigantic halls with huge columns and piers, domes and semi-domes, barrel vaulting and cross vaulting, which could accommodate some 1500 people at a time. The floors and walls were covered with marbles, mosaics and frescoes. The leisure needs of the population have never been catered for with such magnificence as in the Roman baths; even in ruin their splendour is still apparent.

Opening times: Tues.–Sun. 9am–6pm (in winter 2pm); Mon. 9am–1pm.

Terme di Diocleziano (Baths of Diocletian) F 5

Diocletian built these baths to serve the northern districts of the city, the southern districts having been catered for by the Baths of Caracalla. (For the functions of Roman baths, see Terme di Caracalla.) The Baths of Diocletian, measuring 356×316m/1170×1035ft, were even larger than those of Caracalla. Their huge scale can be appreciated when it is seen how widely separated from one another are the surviving parts of the structure, many of them now incorporated into later buildings – the Museo Nazionale Romano or Museo delle Terme (National Museum, Baths Museum), with a collection of Greek and Roman art; the church of Santa Maria degli Angeli, built by Michelangelo, the round church of San Bernardo; the Planetarium; the Piazza dell'Esedra, in an exedra of the Baths; and the cloister and other structures belonging to a Carthusian monastery.

Situation
Piazza dei Cinquecento/
Piazza dell'Esedra

Underground stations
Repubblica or Termini
(line A)

Buses
3, 4, 16, 36, 38, 57, 60, 61, 62, 64, 65, 170, 319, 910

The baths could no longer be used after the Acqua Marcia was cut in A.D. 536, and thereafter the buildings fell into decay.

★★Museo Nazionale Romano or Museo delle Terme
(National Museum, Baths Museum)

This museum, housed in part of the Baths of Diocletian, has the largest collection of ancient art in Rome after that of the Vatican museums (see Vatican, Musei Vaticani).

Among the most notable exhibits are pre-Christian and Christian sarcophagi and a great range of Greek, Hellenistic and Roman sculpture, including a fine Apollo, a Nereid, the "Young Dancing Girl", the "Discus Thrower" from Porziano Castle, the "Wounded Niobe" from the Gardens of Sallust (5th c. B.C.), the Venus of Cyrene (4th c. B.C.), a "Defeated Boxer" (3rd c. B.C.), the "Maiden of Anzio", the Lancellotti "Discus Thrower" (an excellent copy of the statue by Myron), the Ostia Altar, etc.

Situation
Viale delle Terme

Underground station
Repubblica or Termini (line A)

Buses
3, 4, 16, 36, 38, 57, 60, 61, 63, 64, 65, 170, 319, 910

Opening times
Tues.–Sat
9am–2pm;
Sun. 9am–1pm.
Only part of the collection can be seen here and in its new home at Palazzo Massimo on Piazza del Cinquecento which is gradually being restored.

The Museum also contains the Ludovisi Collection, with the "Ludovisi Throne" (5th c. B.C.) and statues of the "Dying Galacian", Ares, Athena Parthenos (a copy of Phidias' statue in the Parthenon), Juno and Orestes and Electra.

The Great Cloister (Grande Chiostro) of 1565, with a fountain, contains marble sculpture, architectural fragments, sarcophagi, mosaic and inscriptions.

On the first floor of the Museum are a collection of mosaics, stucco work and frescoes and wall paintings from the Villa of Livia at Prima Porta.

San Bernardo alle Terme (church)

In a rotunda at the north-west corner of the Baths is the church of San Bernardo alle Terme, built at the end of the 16th c. The dome is similar to that of the Pantheon but only half its size (22m/72ft in diameter, as compared with 43.2m/142ft).

Situation
Piazza di San Bernardo

Underground station
Repubblica (line A)

Santa Maria degli Angeli (church)

The central complex of the Baths was preserved by being incorporated into this church dedicated to the Virgin and her attendant archangels. It was designed by Michelangelo, taking in parts of the ancient structure, in particular the tepidarium (warm bath), a hall 90m/295ft long, 27m/90ft wide and 30m/100ft high. The church is in the form of a Greek cross (with arms of

Situation
Piazza della Repubblica
(Piazza dell'Esedra)

127

Museo delle Terme (National Baths Museum)

Underground station
Repubblica (line A)

Buses
57, 60, 61, 62, 65, 75, 415, 910

equal length), with chapels at the angles. In order to keep the church dry its floor was raised 2m/6½ft above ground level, so that the bases of the ancient columns were buried. The building of the church was continued after Michelangelo's death, and thereafter it was restored and redecorated on a number of occasions.

Many well-known personalities are buried in the church, which is also used by the State for solemn services on special occasions.

Fontana delle Naiadi (Fountain of the Naiads)

Situation
Piazza della Repubblica

The Fountain of the Naiads in the Piazza della Repubblica – also known as the Piazza dell'Esedre since it is laid out on the site of the exedra of the Baths – was erected between 1885 and 1914. It consists of four groups of female figures playing with marine animals, with a figure of "Man Victorious over the Hostile Forces of Nature" in the middle.

★Tivoli

Situation
31km/19 miles E

Buses
Buses to Tivoli from Via Gaeta (Statione Termini)

Tivoli, the ancient Tibur, situated on the Via Tiburtina is now a town of 52,000 inhabitants. In Imperial times it was a favourite summer residence of Roman aristocrats.

Tivoli has two main tourist attractions – the Villa d'Este and the Villa Adriana, the latter situated a short distance from the town. Also worth seeing are the Villa Gregoriana with its impressive park and the Tempio di Vesta, a round temple with Corinthian columns, dating from the 2nd c. B.C.

Villa d'Este

The Villa d'Este, situated in its beautiful gardens, ranks as the "Queen of Villas". Originally laid out by Pirro Ligorio for Cardinal Ippolito d'Este, of the great Ferrara family of Este, in the 16th c., the whole complex blended the natural landscape (a gently sloping hillside), the play of water in fountains and cascades and the architectural forms of the buildings into a harmonious and refreshing whole. The villa was completed in the early 17th c. by Luigi and Alessandro d'Este. It later passed into the hands of the Habsburg family and in 1918 was taken over by the State.

From the villa itself a series of terraces and flights of steps leads down into the spacious gardens, in which hundreds of fountains, cascades and basins toss water into the air, collect it or allow it to pass on its way downhill. The gardens are filled with the sound of plashing and running water. The whole system, with its playful sculptural forms, is designed with a single purpose in mind – to please the eye and delight the senses.

Opening times
Daily
9am–1 hour
before sunset
"Son et Lumière"
in summer

Villa Adriana (Villa of Hadrian)

The mighty ruins of Hadrian's Villa give an overwhelming impression of Imperial grandeur and the splendour of the Roman Empire in its heyday. In the extensive grounds of the villa (5km/3 miles south-west of Tivoli) Hadrian built small-scale copies of all the places and buildings which had particularly impressed him on his wide travels about the Empire, including the vale of Tempe in Thessaly, a canal from the Egyptian Canopus valley near Alexandria and the Academy of Athens. Here, too, everything was provided to meet the needs of the Imperial court. Visitors can now walk about the site and see the remains both of the reproductions of famous buildings and the residences of the Emperor and his court. Of particular interest are the Greek Theatre (at the entrance); the "garden room" of a

Opening times
Daily
9am–1 hour
before sunset

Fountains at the Villa d'Este

small palace, showing the restless architectural style of the period with its interplay of convex and concave lines; the Piazza d'Oro (Golden Square), which was surrounded by 60 columns; the Teatro Marittimo ("Maritime Theatre"); a small villa with a marble colonnade and the "Island of Solitude"; two sets of baths, one large and one small, the Canopus, a long basin or canal, with the Temple of Serapis and the Academy; the Stadium; the Caserma dei Vigili ("Watchmen's Barracks"); the Library; and the Imperial palace proper.

A general impression of the whole complex is provided by a model housed in a building near the entrance.

★Tomba di Cecilia Metella (Tomb of Caecilia Metalla)

Situation
Via Appia Antica

Bus
118

Opening times
Tues.–Sat.
9am–1 hour before sunset; Sun. and Mon. 9am–1pm

The tomb of Caecilia Metella and her husband, one of the best known of ancient Roman monuments, stands in a conspicuous position in the picturesque setting of the Via Appia Antica. This tall 11m/35ft cylindrical structure, 20m/65ft in diameter, was erected by the famous family of the Metelli in the 1st c. B.C. Caecilia Metella was the daughter of a general, Quintus Metellus Cretius, conqueror of Crete, and her husband was a son of Crassus who was a member of the Triumvirate together with Caesar and Pompey. The sarcophagus of Caecilia Mettela may be seen in the courtyard of the Palazzo Farnese (see entry).

In 1302 the Caetani family incorporated the tomb in their castle which they equipped with battlements. The fortifications, stretching along both sides of the Via Appia, defended the strategic approach to the city.

Sculptured reliefs on the outer walls . . .   *. . . of the tomb of Cecilia Metella*

Torre delle Milizie

The Torre delle Milizie is one of the oldest and strongest fortified towers in Italy and the largest in Rome. It is popularly believed that Augustus is buried under the tower and the Nero watched the burning of Rome from the top.

The tower was built by Pope Gregory IX in the 13th c. and probably takes its name from a nearby barracks of Byzantine militia. It belonged to a succession of different noble families and played a part in their endless feuds. In 1312 the German king Henry VII used it as his base during his successful attempt to secure his coronation as Emperor in spite of the hostility of the Roman nobility. The tower began sinking on one side soon after its erection, so that Rome, like Pisa, has its leaning tower. From the top of the tower there are magnificent views of central Rome and the ancient remains.

Situation
Via Quatro Novembre

Buses
46, 56, 57, 60, 62, 64, 65, 70, 75, 80, 81, 88, 90, 95, 170

Trastevere

Trastevere (from *trans Tiberim*), the district of Rome beyond the Tiber, has preserved much of the character of old Rome, with its narrow and irregular streets, its little squares and its venerable churches, such as Santa Maria in Trastevere (see entry).

The people of Trastevere claim that their district is older than Rome. There is a constant bustle of life and activity in the Viale Trastevere and the little lanes and squares opening off it. This liveliness is at its height in the evening, but visitors who go across to Trastevere for their evening meal should take care to give thieves no opportunity to ply their trade.

Buses
26, 28, 44, 56, 60, 65, 97, 170, 710, 718, 719

Città del Vaticano (Vatican City)

The extensive territories of the Papal States in central Italy, originally presented to the Pope by the Frankish king Pippin the Short, father of Charlemagne, were incorporated in the new kingdom of Italy in 1870. The Pope thereafter regarded himself as a prisoner in the Vatican, and this rift between Church and State was not finally healed until 1929, when Mussolini concluded the Lateran Treaty with the Holy See under which the Pope gained full sovereignty over the more restricted territory of the Vatican State.

Underground station
Ottaviano (line A)

Buses
23, 34, 41, 42, 46, 49, 62, 64, 65, 98, 492, 881, 907, 991

Trams: 19, 30

The Vatican State is the smallest independent state in the world with an area of 0.44sq.km/110 acres and a population of some 400. It consists essentially of the Vatican palace and gardens, St Peter's and St Peter's Square, most of the area being enclosed by the Vatican walls, with a white strip across St Peter's Square marking the boundary on that side. (During the period of German occupation in the Second World War this line was of some significance.)

Vatican State

The Pope, since 1978 Jean Paul II, formerly the Polish Cardinal Karol Wojtyla, supreme head of the Roman Catholic Church (membership over 825 million), is invested with legislative, executive and judicial powers. In external affairs he is represented by the Cardinal Secretary of State, while the administration is headed by a Governor responsible only to the Pope.

Since the dissolution of the Guardia Nobile and Guardia Palatina in 1970 the Pope's bodyguard consists only of the Gendarmerie and the Swiss Guard. Membership of the Swiss Guard is restricted to Roman Catholic citizens of Switzerland aged between 18 and 25 who must be unmarried and of a minimum height of 1.8m/5ft 8½in. The period of service is from 2 to 20 years. According to the Papal decree of 1979 the Swiss Guard consists of exactly 100 men (4 officers, 1 chaplain, 23 sergeants, 70 halbadiers and

State flag of the Vatican

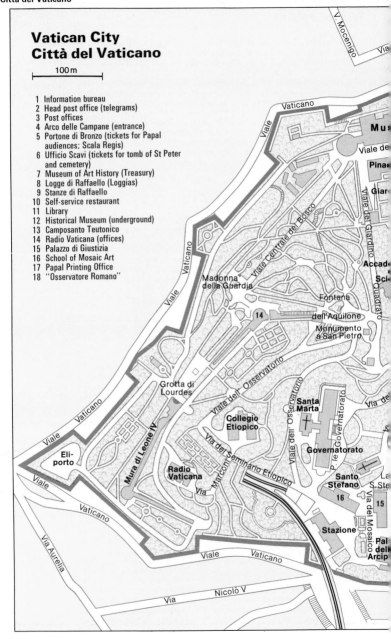

Vatican City
Città del Vaticano

├─ 100 m ─┤

1 Information bureau
2 Head post office (telegrams)
3 Post offices
4 Arco delle Campane (entrance)
5 Portone di Bronzo (tickets for Papal audiences; Scala Regis)
6 Ufficio Scavi (tickets for tomb of St Peter and cemetery)
7 Museum of Art History (Treasury)
8 Logge di Raffaello (Loggias)
9 Stanze di Raffaello
10 Self-service restaurant
11 Library
12 Historical Museum (underground)
13 Camposanto Teutonico
14 Radio Vaticana (offices)
15 Palazzo di Giustizia
16 School of Mosaic Art
17 Papal Printing Office
18 "Osservatore Romano"

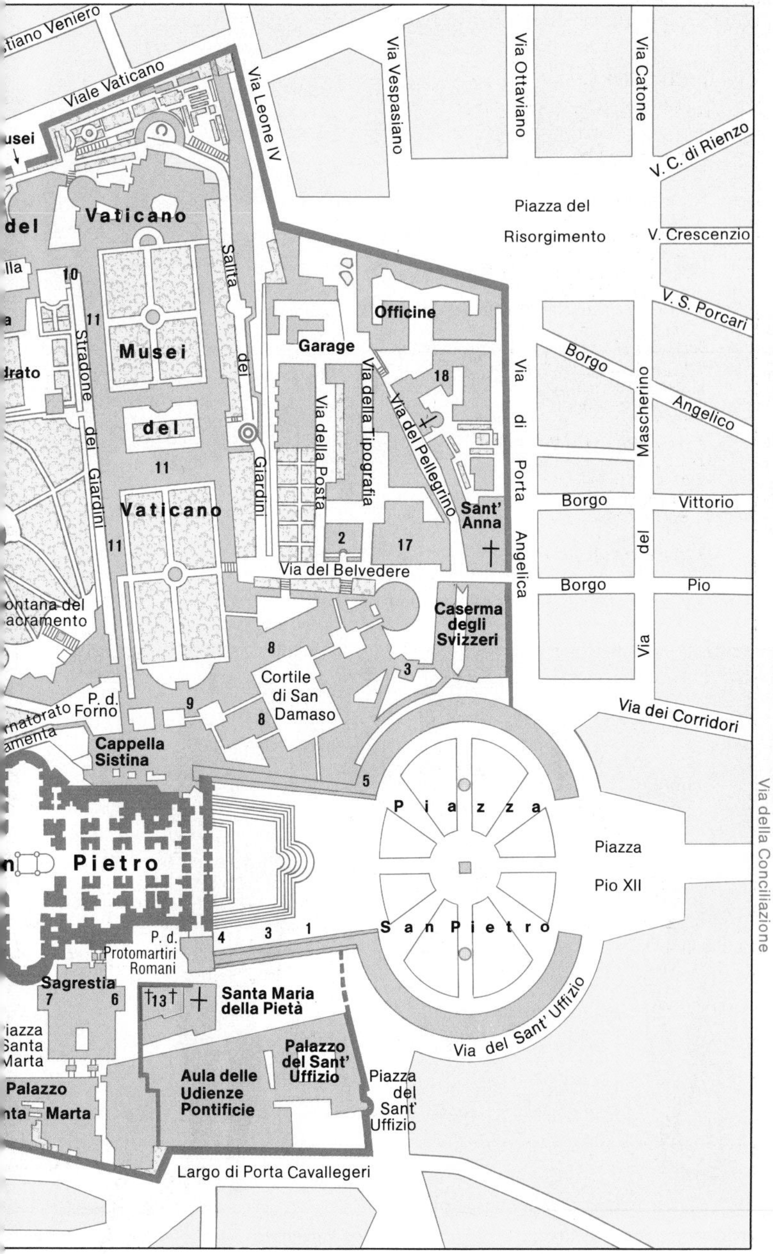

Via Sebastiano Veniero

Viale Vaticano

Via Leone IV

Via Vespasiano

Via Ottaviano

Via Catone

V. C. di Rienzo

Musei

del

Vaticano

V. Crescenzio

V. S. Porcari

Piazza del

Risorgimento

lla

10

a

11

M u s e i

Officine

Garage

Borgo

Angelico

Mascherino

Via della Tipografia

Via del Pellegrino

18

Via di Porta Angelica

drato

d e l

Via della Posta

Stradone dei Giardini

Santa dei Giardini

Borgo

Vittorio

Vaticano

11

2

17

Sant'
Anna

del

11

Via del Belvedere

Borgo

Pio

ontana del
acramento

**Caserma
degli
Svizzeri**

Via

8

3

rnatorato P. d.
amenta Forno

9

8

Cortile
di San
Damaso

Via dei Corridori

**Cappella
Sistina**

5

P i a z z a

Via della Conciliazione

n

Pietro

Piazza

Pio XII

S a n   P i e t r o

P. d.
Protomartiri
Romani

4

3

1

Sagrestia

7

6

†13† +

**Santa Maria
della Pietà**

Via del Sant' Uffizio

iazza
Santa
Marta

Palazzo
nta **Marta**

**Aula delle
Udienze
Pontificie**

**Palazzo
del Sant'
Uffizio**

Piazza
del
Sant'
Uffizio

Largo di Porta Cavallegeri

Vatican City: View of the Governor's Palace from the dome of St Peter's

Papal Guard: a Swiss sentry . . .　　　　*. . . and Vigilanza*

2 drummers). Members of the Guard wear medieval uniforms in the colours of the Medici Popes (yellow, red and blue).

The Vatican City has its own currency (1 Vatican lira = 1 Italian lira), postal service (issuing stamps which are valid throughout Rome), telephone and telegraph services, newspapers and periodicals (in particular the "Osservatore Romano", with a circulation of 60,000–70,000), radio station (Radio Vaticana: transmissions on medium and short waves in some 35 languages), a fleet of about 100 vehicles (registration letters SCV) and its own railway station and helicopter pad.

The Vatican flag has vertical stripes of yellow and white, with two crossed keys below the Papal tiara (triple crown) on a white ground.

Papal possessions outside Vatican City – the basilicas of San Paolo fuori le Mura, San Giovanni in Laterano and Santa Maria Maggiore (see entries), the Papal administrative offices and the Pope's summer residence at Castel Gandolfo (see entry) – enjoy extra-territorial status and are not subject to Italian law.

The territory of Vatican City, with the exception of certain permitted areas (St Peter's, the museums, the Camposanto Teutonico, etc.) can be entered only with special permission. Visitors who desire a Papal audience or who wish to take part in one of the religious ceremonies should write to the Prefetto della Casa Pontifica (Città del Vaticano; tel. 4876).

Musei Vaticani (Vatican Museums)

B 5

The Vatican Museums, which occupy much of the Vatican Palace, (see Palazzi Vaticani) in Viale Vaticano, contain some of the world's greatest art collections.

The history of the museums goes back to 1506, when Pope Julius II, pursuing the ideals of the Renaissance, began to collect ancient works of art. The collections were increased over the centuries from the territories of the Papal States, works of art presented to the Popes and items related to the work of the Roman Catholic Church.

In addition there are works of art created specifically for the Vatican Palace, including the paintings in the Sistine Chapel and the Stanze di Raffaello.

There are four tours of the museums marked with signs in different colours (one-way is indicated). Visitors should be correctly attired (i.e. bare shoulders covered; shorts are not permitted).

Underground station
Ottaviano (line A)

Buses
23, 32, 49, 51, 64, 81, 492, 907, 990, 991, 994; shuttle service from Piazza San Pietro (south side)

Trams 19, 30

Opening times
Mon.–Sat. 8.45am–1.45pm, last Sun. in month 8.45am–1.45pm (in summer and Easter until 4.45pm) (Admission free last Sun. in month)

★★Pinocoteca (Picture Gallery)

The Pinocoteca, founded by Pius VI and later robbed of many of its treasures by Napoleon, contains in its sixteen rooms a collection of pictures ranging in date from the Middle Ages to the present day, giving an excellent survey of the development of Western painting. The pictures are arranged in chronological order.

Pictures of particular note include the following:

Room I: medieval art (Byzantine, Sienese, Umbrian and Tuscan), including a liturgical vestment (*pluviale*) which belonged to Pope Boniface VIII (13th c.).

Room II: triptych of Cardinal Stefaneschi (Giotto).

Room III: "Madonna" and "St Nicholas of Bari" by Fra Angelico; triptych by Filippo Lippo.

Room V: "Pietà" by Lucas Cranach the Elder.

Room VII: "Coronation of the Virgin" by Pinturicchio; "Madonna" by Perugino

Vatican Museums
Musei Vaticani

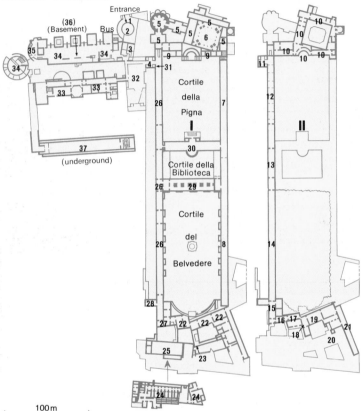

1 Lift
2 Stairs
3 Vestibule (tickets, information)
4 Atrio dei Quattro Cancelli
5 Museo Pio-Clementino
6 Cortile Ottagono
7 Museo Chiaramonti
8 Galleria Lapidaria
9 Museo Gregoriano Egizio (Egyptian Museum)
10 Museo Gregoriano Etrusco (Etruscan Museum)
11 Sala della Biga
12 Galleria dei Candelabri
13 Galleria degli Arazzi (Tapestry Gallery)
14 Galleria delle Carte Geografiche (Map Gallery)
15 Pius V's Chapel
16 Sala Sobieski
17 Sala dell'Immacolata
18 Urban VIII's Chapel
19 Stanze di Raffaello
20 Nicholas V's Chapel (Beato Angelico)
21 Logge di Raffaello (Loggias of Raphael)
22 Appartamento Borgia
23 Salette Borgia
24 Collezione d'Arte Religiosa Moderna (Museum of Modern Religious Art)
25 Sistine Chapel
26 Vatican Library
27 Museo Sacro della Biblioteca
28 Sala delle Nozze Aldobrandine
29 Salone Sistino
30 Braccio Nuovo
31 Museo Profano della Biblioteca
32 Cortile della Pinacoteca
33 Pinacoteca (Picture Gallery)
34 Museo Gregoriano Profano (Museum of Secular Art)
35 Museo Pio Cristiano
36 Museo Missionario Etnologico
37 Museo Storico (Historical Museum)

Vatican gardens and museums (on right)

Room VIII: tapestries from cartoons by Raphael, and Raphael's famous "Transfiguration" (1517; his last picture) and "Madonna of Foligno" (1512–13).

Room IX: "St Jerome", an unfinished work by Leonardo da Vinci.

Room X: "Madonna" by Titian.

Room XII: "Entombment" by Caravaggio.

Room XIV: Dutch and Flemish masters (school of Rubens).

Room XV: portraits of Popes.

Museo Gregoriana Egizio Egyptian Museum

The Egyptian Museum in the Cortile della Pigna, re-founded by Pope Gregory XVI (the first collection having been assembled by Pius VIII), contains a small but valuable collection of Egyptian art from the 3rd millennium to the 6th c. B.C., including basalt and wooden sarcophagi, heads of gods and pharaohs, mummified heads, stelae, statues of gods and animals, and papyri.

★Museo Pio Clementino

The Vatican Museums have the largest collection of ancient sculpture in the world, mainly found in Rome and the surrounding areas. The collection was arranged on a systematic basis by Popes Clement XIV (1769–74) and Pius VI (1775–99). Among outstanding items are the following:

Sala a Croce Greca: the porphyry sarcophagi of Constantia (Constantine's daughter) and St Helen (his mother), richly decorated with figures and symbols.

Sala Rotonda: Zeus of Otricoli, a copy of a work by Bryaxis (4th c. B.C.).

Sala delle Muse: Belvedere Torso, a work by Apollonius of Athens (1st c. B.C.) which was admired by Michelangelo; statues of Apollo and the Muses.

Sala degli Animali: numerous realistic marble and alabaster statues of animals; statue of Meleager with a dog and a wild boar's head (Roman copy), and Minotaur bust.

Galleria delle Statue: Apollo Sauroctonus (Apollo the Lizard Killer; Roman copy of a bronze original by Praxiteles); the reclining figure of Ariadne; the Candelabri Barberini (the finest ancient candelabras known), from the Villa Adriana at Tivoli.

Gabinetto delle Maschere (Cabinet of Masks): mosaic paving of theatrical masks from the Villa Adriana (see Tivoli); Cnidian Venus, a Roman copy of the Aphrodite of Praxiteles (4th c. B.C.).

Galleria dei Busti: lunette frescoes by Pinturicchio; statue of Jupiter Verospi.

Cortile del Belvedere: the most famous statues in the Vatican – the Apollo Belvedere (Roman copy of an original by Leochares c. 330 B.C.). Canova's Perseus, a Hermes of the Hadrianic period (copy of an original by Praxiteles) and above all the celebrated Laocoön group, a masterpiece of Hellenistic sculpture (at the finding of which in 1506 Michelangelo was present), depicting the Trojan priest Laocoön and his sons in a mortal struggle with two huge snakes.

Gabinetto del Apoxyomenos: the Athlete Apoxyomenos, a copy of a bronze statue by Lysippus, found in Trastevere in 1849.

★Museo Chiaramonti

The Museo Chiaramonti, founded by Pope Pius VII (1800–23), a member of the Chiaramonti family, is housed in a long gallery leading to the Papal palace and contains numerous works of Greek and Roman art, of varying quality.

There are also works of Greek and Roman sculpture in the Galleria Lapidaria (not open to the public) and the Braccio Nuovo, which links the

Belvedere torso　　　　　*Laocoön group*

two long wings extending from the entrance to the museums to the Palazzi Vaticani.

Notable items in the Braccio Nuovo are the Augustus of Prima Porta, a statue of the Emperor found in 1863 in the country villa of his wife Livia; a statue of the god of the Nile; and the Doryphorus ("Spear Carrier"), a copy of the work by Polycletus. In the Sala della Biga, near the entrance, are two Discus-Throwers, copies of works by Myron and Polycletus (5th c. B.C.) and a carriage and pair ("Biga" 1788) by Antonio Franzoni.

Sala della Biga

★Museo Gregoriano Etrusco (Etruscan Museum)

The Etruscan Museum, founded by Pope Gregory XVI (1831–46), contains in its eighteen rooms works of art and everyday objects which throw light on the life of the Etruscans and their idea of the afterlife. The collection also includes Greek and Roman works.

Particularly notable items are the rich grave goods from the Regolini-Galassi tomb at Cerveteri, the Mars of Todi, the Stele del Palestrita (from Attica; 5th c. B.C.), a head of Athena and numerous fine vases.

★Museo Gregoriano Profano (Museum of Secular Art)

The museum of secular art was also founded by Gregory XVI. Until 1963 it was housed, together with the Museo Pio Cristano and the museo Epigrafico Cristano in the Lateran Palace (see Palazzo Laterano). It now occupies a modern museum building adjoining the Pinacoteca which was built during the reigns of Popes John XXIII (1958–63) and Paul VI (1963–78). The works of ancient sculpture in this excellently arranged museum were mostly found in the territories of the Papal States. The collection includes Roman copies of Greek sculpture and originals of Roman Imperial sculpture – statues, reliefs, funerary monuments and sarcophagi, together with works of political and religious content.

First section: Roman copies and re-workings of Greek originals (including Sophocles, 4th c. B.C.); Niobe Chiaramonti; head of Athena; Marsia torso.

2nd section: Roman sculpture (1st and early 2nd c. A.D., including a portrait of Livia, wife of Augustus).

3rd section: sarcophagi (including the sarcophagus from the Porta Viminalis).

4th section: Roman sculpture (2nd and 3rd c. A.D., including a Mithras sculpture).

★Biblioteca Apostolica Vaticana (Vatican library)

Judged by the value of its contents, the Vatican Library is the richest in the world. Since its foundation by Nicholas V in 1450 the library has been systematically built up, and now contains, in addition to books printed since the end of the 15th c., some 7000 incunabula, 25,000 medieval handwritten books and 80,000 manuscripts. In the library hall, 70m/230ft long, built by Domenico Fontana, are cases displaying some of its greatest treasures – Biblical codices, illuminated Gospel books, finely printed books, valuable parchments and ancient papyri and scrolls.

Museo Sacro

At the end of the long range housing the Vatican Library is the Museum of Sacred Art, containing material found during the excavation of catacombs and early Christian churches in Rome and the surrounding area. Pope Pius XI (1922–39) showed a particular interest in the smaller works of Christian

"Parnassus", by Raffael, in the stanza della Signatura

art. In a side room is the "Aldobrandini Wedding" (Nozze Aldobrandine), a sensitively painted and well-preserved ancient fresco which was found about 1600 and until 1818 was kept in the Aldobrandini Gardens.

★Appartamento Borgia

The Borgia Pope Alexander VI (1492–1503) had a private residence built for himself and his family within the Vatican Palace, and commissioned Pinturicchio to decorate it with wall and ceiling paintings. between 1492 and 1495 the painter and his assistants and pupils painted a series of scenes, combining Renaissance, humanist and ancient themes with Christian subjects.

1st room: prophets and Sibyls.
2nd room: the Creed, with prophets and Apostles.
3rd room: allegories of the seven liberal arts.
4th room: legends of saints.
5th room: scenes from the life of Christ and the Virgin.
The Papal portraits formerly in the 6th room have not survived.

★★Stanze di Raffaello (Raphael Rooms)

These rooms above the Appartamento Borgia, built by Pope Nicholas V, contain a magnificent series of frescoes by Raphael, who was commissioned by the art-loving Pope Julius II in 1508 to repaint the rooms. Raphael, in re-discovering the traditions of historical painting, established a trend in art which was to be followed in subsequent centuries. As a classicist he adhered to strict compositional symmetry in the frescoes. The characters are positioned, according to their roles in the story, around a perspectival and pictorial focal point, usually in the centre of the picture.

The Stanza della Segnatura and the Stanza di Eliodoro are both by Raphael's own hand: the Stanza dell'Incendio di Borgo was executed by his pupils under his supervision; the Stanza di Constantino was painted after Raphael's death by Guilio Romano and Gian Francesco Penni.

Room 1 (Sala dell'Incendio di Borgo, Room of the Burning of the Borgo):
Ceiling painting by Perugino and four paintings of historical scenes by pupils of Raphael (1517 onwards) and the burning of the Borgo (the district around St Peter's) in 847; coronation of Charlemagne by Leo III in 800; Leo IV's naval victory over the Saracens off Ostia in 849; and Leo III's oath (denying false accusations) in 800. These paintings commemorating his predecessors of the same name were commissioned by Pope Leo X (1513–21).

Room 2: (Sala della Segnatura, the meeting place of an ecclesiastical tribunal):
The frescoes in this room, painted by Raphael in 1508–11, represent the supreme achievement of Renaissance painting. They depict the culture of the period in all its richness and splendour.
The Disputa del Sacramento, a theological disputation on the doctrine of transubstantiation, depicts the world of religious faith. In the lower zone, around the altar, are Popes, bishops, teachers and theologians, including Pope Innocent III, St Bonaventure and Dante. Above them, under God the Father are Christ with the Virgin and John the Baptist, attended by saints.
The Scuola d'Atene (School of Athens), set in the newly built St Peter's, represents the field of the natural sciences – attainable without divine revelation – and depicts representatives of philosophy (the two central figures, Plato and Aristotle, together with Socrates), architecture (Bramante), history (Xenophon) and mathematics (Archimedes, Pythagoras, Euclid), together with Raphael himself (in the corner, second from right).
Above one window is an associated scene depicting Parnassus, with Apollo playing a violin, the blind Homer, the Muses and other ancient poets (Virgil, Sappho, Ovid, Catullus and Horace). Above the other are a scene depicting the glorification of canon and civil law and allegorical representations of the virtues of Prudence and Temperance. On the ceiling, corresponding to the scenes on the walls below, are allegories of theology, philosophy, poetry and justice.

Room 3 (Sala d'Eliodoro, Room of Heliodorus):
The paintings by Raphael in this room (1512–14) show still greater expressive power and a livelier sense of movement than those in the Sala della Segnatura. They depict four scenes: Leo the Great repulsing Attila, the Mass of Bolsena (in which an unbelieving priest was convinced of the truth of the doctrine of transubstantiation), the expulsion of Heliodorus from the Temple and the liberation of St Peter from prison, Raphael's first depiction of a night scene, with effective use of light. As in the "Mass of Bolsena" the dungeon scene consists of three events which flow into each other without disrupting the unity of the picture.

Room 4 (Sala di Constantino, Room of Constantine)
The painting dates almost entirely from the reign of Clement VII, after Raphael's death. On the long wall is a fine picture by pupils of Raphael of Constantine's victory over Maxentius at the Milvian Bridge, with the scene depicting Constantine's vision of the Cross. Other scenes include Constantine's baptism and the "Presentation by Constantine".

★Cappella di Niccolo V (Nicholas V's Chapel)

Nicholas V's Chapel, near the Stanze di Raffaello, has frescoes by Fra Beato Angelico on the life and martyrdom of SS. Stephen and Lawrence (1447–49).

Galleria delle Carte Geografiche (Map Gallery)

The Map Gallery, 120m/395ft long, has maps of all the different parts of Italy, often with views of cities and prospects of scenery (1580–83). The maps, originating from the studio of Antonio Dantes, contain valuable cartographical detail and were designed to be used as decoration for a palace.

Galleria dei Candelabri e degli Arazzi (Gallery of Cadelabras and Tapestries)

Beyond the Map Gallery (when coming from the Vatican palace) is the gallery of Cadelabras and Tapestries, with valuable tapestries of the 15th–17th c. and Roman marble candelabras.

★★Cappella Sistina (Sistine Chapel)

The Sistine Chapel, built by Pope Sixtus IV in 1473–84, is a plain rectangular hall 40.4m/133ft long, 20.7m/68ft wide and 13.2m/43ft high with large wall and ceiling surfaces. The division of the chapel into presbytery and nave is achieved by the varying geometric design of the coloured marble floor and by a marble balustrade (by Mino da Fiesole and Andrea Bregno). The chapel is the Pope's domestic chapel, and is also used for services and special occasions. After the death of a Pope the conclave to elect his successor is held here. There are frescoes of the side walls, the ceiling and the altar wall. From 1980 to 1994 the Sistine Chapel, the pinnacle of Renaissance painting, was extensively restored. Layers of candle-soot, dust, varnish, oil and grease, as well as overpainting and damage were removed from the Michelangelo frescoes and once again the remarkable luminous colours can be admired.

Paintings on side walls

The side walls are covered with large frescoes painted for Sixtus IV (1481–83) by the most celebrated painters of the day – Perugino, Botticelli, Rosselli, Pinturicchio, Signorelli and Ghirlandaio – depicting Biblical scenes against the background of the Umbrian and Tuscan scenery familiar to the artists. These late 15th c. paintings already reflect the discovery of man as an individual and his importance in the historical process, and with consummate artistic skill depict him acting within an architectural and landscape setting, thus preparing the way for the further development of this trend by Michelangelo.

The left-hand wall has scenes from the life of Moses, liberator of the Jewish people from their captivity in Egypt; the circumcision of Moses; Moses with the shepherds and the burning bush; the crossing of the Red Sea; Moses receiving the tablets of the law on Mount Sinai; the destruction of the company of Korah; and the death of Moses.

The right-hand wall depicts events in the life of Christ, the liberator of mankind from sin – his baptism in the Jordan; the cleansing of lepers (a magnificent work by Botticelli); the calling of Peter and Andrew; the Sermon on the Mount; Christ giving the keys to Peter; and the Last Supper.

Paintings on ceilings

The frescoes on the ceiling were painted by Michelangelo in the reign of the great Pope and Renaissance prince Julius II, most of them being his own unaided work. They were painted between the autumn of 1508 and August 1510 and, after a pause, completed in 1511–12. Michelangelo's idea was an ambitious one, never attempted on such a scale before; no less than to depict the Creation as it is described in Genesis.

The central part of the ceiling (beginning at the near end) depicts God separating light from darkness, creating the sun and the moon, separating land and sea, creating Adam and then Eve; the Fall; Noah's thank-offering; the Flood; Noah's drunkenness. In the lower ranges of the vaulting are colossal figures of the prophets and sibyls who conveyed God's message

"Creation of Adam" and . . .   *. . . "Delphic Sibyl", by Michelangelo*

to the Jews and the Gentiles. The restoration of the chapel has revealed an unexpected luminosity of colour in Michelangelo's frescoes, which caused controversy about the restoration process, even though the intensive use of colour is consistent with the traditions of the Florentine school. The restorers only removed dirt and later repainting to reach the protective top layer of paint applied in Michelangelo's fresco technique. The colours which they revealed are bright and intensive tones of blue, green, ochre, red and white. The figures are all depicted in vigorous and passionate movement.

Michelangelo began work on the large fresco on the altar wall 22 years later (1534), in the reign of Pope Paul III, when he was 59. As a counterpart to his depiction of the Creation on the ceiling he painted on this wall the final scene in the story of the world, the Last Judgment, depicting Christ returning as the Judge to summon the righteous to paradise and consign the damned to hell. The theme in all its details is based on the scriptural account. With its dramatic presentation of his subject, which Michelangelo sees as a judgement on the life of the individual human being, this ranks as one of the greatest achievements of European painting.

Painting on altar wall

In the Last Judgment Christ is depicted as a powerful youthful god standing on a cloud, surrounded by the Virgin, the Apostles and other saints. The righteous (to the left) rising up into heaven, and the damned (on the right) tumbling into hell form a powerful upward and downward movement which determines the eternal fate of mankind, while below the dead are seen rising from their graves. In the middle are angels blowing their trumpets to summon all men to judgement, and up above other angels carry in triumph the instruments of the Passion.

The 381 figures are represented with athletic forms, and many of them have readily recognisable attributes (Peter with his key, Sebastian with his arrows, Lawrence with his gridiron, Bartholomew with his flayed skin, which bears a portrait of Michelangelo himself, Catherine with her wheel).

Museo Profano

This collection of secular art includes a variety of Etruscan, Roman and medieval material.

Museo Pio Cristino

This museum, founded by Pope Pius IX in 1854, contains material which until 1963 was housed in the Lateran Palace (see Palazzo Laterano). There are two sections, one devoted to architecture, sculpture and mosaics, the other to inscriptions.

Museo Missionario Etnologico

Objects brought back from the various mission fields of the Church were originally (from 1927 onwards) displayed in the Palazzo Laterno (see entry). Pope Pius XI directed that they should be brought together in a systematic arrangement, and in 1970 all material of interest (to scholars as well as to the general public) was transferred to the Museo Missionario Etnologico.

Museo delle Carroze

The coach museum, opened in 1973, is housed in a building under the Giardino Quadrato (Square Garden), near the Pinacoteca. The museum contains the Papal carriages (including the coach of Pope Leo XII), vintage cars and a model of the jet in which Pope Paul VI flew to the UN.

Collezione d'Arte Religiosa Moderna

Pope Paul VI (1963–78) was interested in modern religious art and made available 55 rooms in the Vatican for the display of works of art presented to the Popes or acquired by them. The collection contains more than 800 works by artists of many different countries, including Rodin, Barlach, Matisse, Modigliani, Kokoschka, Dali, Munch, Vlaminck, Feininger, Ernst Beckmann, Nolde, Le Corbusier, Kadinsky, de Chirico, Greco, Marini, Rouault, Hartung, Hansing and Sutherland.

★Palazzi Vaticani (Vatican Palace)   A/B 5/6

Underground station
Ottaviano (line A)

Buses
23, 32, 41, 47, 62, 64, 492, 990

Trams
19, 30

Some impression of the size of the Vatican Palace, which lies immediately to the right of St Peter's Square (see Piazza San Pietro) and St Peter's itself (see San Pietro in Vaticano), can be gained by starting from the fountain on the left-hand side of St Peter's Square, from which the huge bulk of the main range of buildings can be seen rearing up above the square, and then continuing along outside the walls to the entrance to the Vatican Museums (see Musei Vaticani).

There would no doubt be some form of lodging for the Bishop of Rome near Old St Peter's (then well outside the city) as early as the 6th c., but the Papal residence was for long in the Palazzo Laterano (see entry).The first Pope to consider the Vatican as a residence was Nicholas III (1277–80), and this alternative seemed all the more attractive when the Pope returned from exile in Avignon in 1377 and found the Lateran Palace in a state of dilapidation. From 1450 onwards successive Popes embellished and enlarged the Vatican, enlisting in this task the best architects in Rome. The

Piazza San Pietro and Via della Conciliazione ▶

most notable contributions were made by Nicholas V, Sixtus IV (Sistine Chapel), Alexander VI (Appartamento Borgia), Julius II (Cortile del Belvedere, Loggias in the Cortile di San Domaso), Paul III (Cappella Paolina, with frescoes by Michelangelo), Pius V and Sixtus V (the present private apartments, reception rooms and library).

The total area covered by buildings, excluding the gardens, is 55,000sq.m/13½ acres, of which 25,000sq.m/8 acres are accounted for by courtyards. The total number of rooms and chapels is 1400. Surely no other palace in the world can compare with the Vatican in historical and artistic importance. In addition to the Pope's own residential apartments and offices the palace house a number of ecclesiastical bodies as well as the Vatican Museums (see Musei Vaticani). The main entrance is the bronze door at the end of the right-hand colonnade which leads into the Corridorio del Bernini and, at the far end of this, Bernini's Scala Regia.

Giardini Vaticani (Vatican Gardens)

Guided tours
Mar.–Oct. Mon.,
Tues., Fri., Sat.
10am
(Booking at Uffizio
Informazioni,
Piazza San Pietro)

The Vatican Gardens, behind St Peter's and the Vatican Palace, occupy a large part of the area of Vatican City. In the gardens are a variety of buildings serving particular purposes, churches and offices, towers and fountains, the Casina di Pio IV (seat of the Pontifical Academy of Sciences) and a coffee-house. The north end of the gardens is bounded by the Leonine Walls, the railway station, the radio transmitter and the Vatican Museums.

★★Piazza San Pietro (St Peter's Square)   B 5

**Underground
station**
Ottaviano (line A)

Buses
23, 32, 34, 46, 49,
51, 62, 64, 65, 81,
98, 280, 490, 492,
881, 907, 982, 991,
994, 999

Trams
19, 30

The Piazza San Pietro in front of St Peter's was laid out by Bernini between 1656 and 1667 to provide a setting in which the faithful from all over the world could gather; the square he created – perhaps the most famous square in the world – has maintained its fasciation right down to our own day. It is in two parts – a large ellipse measuring 340×240m/372×263yd and a smaller trapezoid area, the Piazza Retta, from which a broad flight of steps, flanked by statues of the Apostles Peter and Paul, leads up to the church. The oval is enclosed at each end by semicircular colonnades formed by 284 columns and 88 pillars of travertine in four rows. Around the balustrade on the roof of the colonnades are set 140 statues of saints. On either side of the oval are fountains 8m/26ft high with large granite basins, the one on the right erected in 1613 is by Maderna, the one on the left (1675) probably by Bernini. Two discs set into the paving mark the focal points of the ellipse (Centri del Colonnato).

In the centre of the oval, towards which the square slopes gently down, is an Egyptian obelisk 25.5m/87ft high. This was brought from Heliopolis to Rome by Caligula in A.D. 39 and set up in his circus (later known as the Circus of Nero). Throughout the Middle Ages this obelisk remained in its original position – the only one in Rome to do so – until Pope Sixtus V directed in 1586 that it should be moved to St Peter's Square. Domenico Fontana was charged with the very difficult task of transporting this huge mass of stone weighing 350 tons to its new site. The operation took four months (from April 30th until September 10th) and involved the employment of 900 workmen, 140 horses and 44 winches. It is said that at one point the ropes were on the point of breaking under the strain when one of the workmen, disregarding the Pope's strict order that there should be absolute silence, shouted "Pour water on them" and saved the situation. The story goes that the Pope then granted him and his family the privilege of supplying the palm branches used in the Palm Sunday services, a practice which his descendants have maintained until the present day. On May 13th 1981 Pope John Paul II was seriously wounded in an attempt on his life in St Peter's Square.

View from Centro del Colonnato of the pillars of the left-hand colonnade

★★San Pietro in Vaticano (St Peter's Church)   B 5

The most famous church in Christendom is St Peter's, dedicated to the Apostle who is believed to have been the first Bishop of Rome, and whose successor each Pope, as supreme head of the Roman Catholic Church, feels himself to be. The history of St Peter's reflects the history of the Papacy.

The original church of St Peter was dedicated by Pope Sylvester I in A.D. 326, thanks to the patronage of the Emperor Constantine. It must have been evident at that time that the site, on the slopes of the Vatican hill, was a difficult one to build on, involving considerable differences of level which had to be allowed for in the foundations; and in addition it was well outside the city. That this inconvenient site was nevertheless selected for the building of St Peter's suggests – with some archaeological evidence in support – that it was honoured in the long memory of Rome as the position of the Apostle's tomb; for Peter was traditionally believed to have been martyred in 64 or 67 in the Imperial gardens on the Vatican hill. Old St Peter's, a five-aisled basilica of the classical type which we know from medieval descriptions, was frequently restored and richly embellished, but after the Pope's return from exile in Avignon and the western schism (when there were a number of Popes at the same time) it was in an advanced stage of dilapidation.

Pope Nicholas V accordingly resolved in 1452 to build an entirely new church and to seek the help of all Christendom in building it. (One source of income for this purpose was the sale of indulgences, which provoked Martin Luther to his protest.) Construction began in 1506 and was pushed ahead with all speed, but the completion and embellishment of the church involved every Pope from Julius II (1503–13) to Pius VI (1775–99). A number of architects took part in the work. The first plan was prepared by Bramante, who was accused of embezzlement of funds and the use of poor materials;

Situation
Piazza San Pietro

Underground station
Ottaviano (line A)

Buses
23, 32, 34, 46, 49, 51, 62, 64, 65, 81, 98, 280, 490, 492, 881, 907, 982

Trams
19, 30

Opening times
Daily 7am–6pm (7pm in summer). Dome: daily 8am–4.15pm (6.15pm in summer)

147

Piazza San Pietro: St Peter's Church and Apostolic Palace

then followed Raphael, Fra Giocondo, Giuliano da Sangallo, Baldassare Peruzzi, Antonio da Sangallo and finally Michelangelo, who took over in 1547 at the age of 72. He was responsible in particular for the design of the dome, the drum of which was completed by the time he died in 1564. Other architects were Vignola Ligorio, della Porta, Fontana and Maderna (who at Paul V's request, extended the original centralised building towards the square by the addition of a nave).

Façade

In addition to calling for the lengthening of the church towards the square Paul V desired that St Peter's should be linked with the Palazzo Apostolico (Vatican Palace), and for the sake of symmetry this involved a corresponding extension on the other side, giving the façade a total length of 114.7m/376ft. The height (45.5m/149ft) could not be increased, however, since this would have hidden still more of Michelangelo's dome. Maderna sought to palliate these unfortunate proportions by an elaborately articulated pattern of columns and pillars, doorways, balconies and windows.

From the central balcony on the façade the senior member of the college of cardinals proclaims the name of a new Pope elected by the conclave, and from this balcony, too, the Pope pronounces his blessing "urbi et orbi" on certain festivals, and beatifications and canonisations are announced. On top of the façade are statues of Christ flanked by Apostles, 5.7m/19ft high. The two clocks at the ends of the façade were added by Giuseppe Valadier in the 19th c.

Portico

The portico (71m/233ft long, 13.5m/44ft deep and 20m/66ft high) is entered through five doorways with bronze grilles. On the outer side are two equestrian statues – Charlemagne to the left, Constantine (by Bernini) to the right. Above the main doorway are fragments of a mosaic by Giotto from Old St Peter's, the "Navicella" (the Apostles' ship in the storm). The double bronze doors, also from Old St Peter's, were the work of the Florentine sculptor Filarete (1433–45); they depict Christ and the Virgin, the

N

Sacre
Grotte
Vaticane

Papal altar

S. Transept   Confessio   N. Transept

©*Baedeker*

St. Peter's Church
San Pietro in Vaticano

|— 50 m —|

Nave

Portico

St Peter's Square

1 Main entrance
2 Porta Santa
3 Michelangelo's "Pietà"
4 Monument to Christina of
  Sweden
5 St Sebastian's Chapel
6 Monument to Margravine
  Mathilda of Tuscany
7 Chapel of the Sacrament
8 Gregorian Chapel
9 Altar of St Jerome
10 Statue of St Peter
11 Entrance to Vatican Sacred
   Grotto
12 Entrance to Dome
13 Altar of Archangel Michael
14 Altar of St Peter (restoring
   Tabitha to life)
15 Tomb of Pope Urban VIII
16 Cathedra Petri (by Bernini)

17 Tomb of Pope Paul III
18 Chapel of the Column
19 Altar of St Peter (healing the
   lame man)
20 Tomb of Pope Alexander VII
21 Altar of the Crucifixion of St
   Peter
22 Statue of St Andrew
23 Tomb of Pope Pius VIII
24 Clementine Chapel
25 Altar of St Gregory

26 Monument to Pope Pius VII
27 Choir Chapel
28 Tomb of Pope Innocent VIII
29 Monument to Pope Pius VII
30 Chapel of the Presentation
31 Monument to Maria Sobieska
32 Baptistery
33 Sacristy
34 Museo Storico Artistico
   (Treasury)
35 Canons' Sacristy

Apostles Peter and Paul and their martyrdom, and historical scenes. To the
left is the "Door of Death", a modern work by Giacomo Manzù. To the right
is the Porta Santa which is kept closed except in Holy Years.

The huge dimensions of the interior are of overwhelming effect. The
church is 185m/610ft long, rises to a height of 46m/150ft in the nave and
119m/390ft in the dome, covers an area of 15,000 sqm/18,000 sqyd and can
accommodate a congregation of over 60,000. In the pavement of the nave,
for purposes of comparison, are marked the lengths (measured from the
apse) of other great churches. In spite of its enormous size, however, the
simple architectural plan (in the form of a Latin cross, with the nave longer

Interior
(Visitors must
obey the
rules of dress)

149

than the transepts) and the great dome which crowns it allow the church to be seen and appreciated as a whole.

The following features are worth particular note in going round the church.

A few yards from the main doorway is a red porphyry disc in the floor marking the spot on which Charlemagne was crowned in Old St Peter's by Pope Leo III on Christmas Day in the year 800.

Right-hand aisle

In the Capella della Pietà (on the right of the north aisle) is Michelangelo's famous "Pietà" (1498–1500), since 1972 protected by a reinforced glass panel. It depicts a youthful Virgin holding in her arms the body of Christ just taken down from the cross. A ribbon on her breast is inscribed with the sculptor's name. The facial expressions and the consummate skill of the carving reveal Michelangelo as a great artist even at the early age (24) at which he created this work. On the adjoining pier is a monument commemorating Queen Christina of Sweden, who abdicated as queen and became a Roman Catholic.

Just beyond this is St Sebastian's Chapel, with a fine mosaic above the altar (after a painting by Domenichino) depicting the saint's martyrdom. Most of the paintings in the church have been replaced by mosaics; the originals are in the Musei Vaticani – see entry.

By the near pier is the mausoleum (designed by Bernini) of Countess Matilda of Tuscany, who played a prominent part in the conflict between the Emperor and the Pope in the 11th c. Next comes the richly decorated Chapel of the Sacrament, to which both Bernini (the tabernacle) and Borromini (the bronze grille) contributed. The chapel was built for Pope Urban VIII of the Barberini family: hence the bees from the Barberini coat-of-arms which feature in the decoration. Just beyond this chapel is the tomb of Pope Gregory XIII, reformer of the calendar (1572–85), with the heraldic dragon of the Buoncompagni family to which he belonged.

The right transept was the meeting-place of the First Vatican Council (1869–70), in which 650 bishops took part. The Second Vatican Council (1962–65), when the number of bishops had risen to over 3000, was held in the nave. In the passage beyond the transept is the monument of Clement XIII, a youthful work by Canova (1788–92).

Crossing and dome

Four massive pentagonal piers with a diameter of 24m/79ft and a circumference of 71m/233ft bear the dome, designed by Michelangelo as the culminating point of the church, over the tomb of St Peter. The dome, set over a drum with 16 windows, has a diameter of 42.34m/139ft (slightly less than the dome of the Pantheon, 43m/142ft). It consists of an inner dome and an outer protective shell, with enough space between the two for a man to stand upright. Above the dome is the lantern, giving a total interior height of 119m/390ft. In niches in the piers are figures of St Veronica with her napkin, St Helen with the True Cross, St Longinus with his lance and St Andrew with his saltire cross, and in the loggias above are displayed on special festivals relics of the Passion. Around the dome is a frieze with the Latin text (in letters 2m/6ft high) of the text from St Matthew's Gospel on which the Pope's claim to the headship of the Church is based: "Tu es Petrus . . ." ("Thou art Peter, and upon this rock I will build my church . . . And I will give unto thee the keys of the kingdom of heaven.")

The roof of St Peter's can be reached on foot via a gallery in the inside of the dome and then a flight of very narrow, steep steps (330) to the crown of the lantern. The visitor has a choice between the staircase ascent (entrance on the right near the Baptistery; 142 steps) and a lift (entrance outside near the Gregorian Chapel; fee). From the roof of the Basilica and from the lantern there is a wonderful view across St Peter's Square to the city. At the same time Michelangelo's cupular and the details of his architectural construction can be seen at close quarters.

Under the dome, immediately above Peter's tomb, is the Papal altar, with a bronze baldacchino (canopy) created by Bernini when he was just

Central aisle and Papal altar

Michelangelo's "Pietà"

Statue of St Peter, in bronze

St Peter's throne, by Bernini

25 years old (1624–33) for Pope Urban VIII, using bronze from the portico of the Pantheon. With its twisted columns and fantastic superstructure this is a masterpiece of Baroque sculpture. In front of the altar, on a lower level, is the Confessio, lit by 95 gilded oil lamps, beyond which is the tomb of St Peter; in it is a marble figure of Pope Pius VI (1775–99) kneeling, by Canova. Against the pier with the figure of Longinus is a bronze statue of St Peter enthroned (created by Arnolfo di Cambio in the 13th c., modelled on an ancient sculpture of a philosopher which can be seen in the Sacre Grotte Vaticane), the right foot of which has been worn smooth by the kisses of the faithful.

Apse

In the apse is Bernini's Cathedra Petri, a bronze throne which shows the same Baroque sense of movement as the baldacchino. It is supported by figures of the four Doctors of the Church (Ambrose, Augustine, Athanasius and John Chrysostom). Above the throne is an alabaster window with the symbolic dove of the Holy Ghost.

Flanking the Cathedra Petri are the tombs of Popes Urban VIII Barberini (on right; by Bernini, 1642–47) and Paul III Farnese (on left; by Giacomo della Porta, 1551–75).

Left-hand aisle

In the left-hand aisle are the tombs of other famous Popes by leading artists of their day:

In the passage behind the pier, the monument of Alexander VII (carved under the direction of Bernini, 1672–78).

Diagonally across from the huge sacristy built in 1776–84 in the reign of Pius VI, the monument of Pius VII (by Thorvaldsen, 1823). This is the only work in the church by a Protestant sculptor, and it gave rise to protests at the time it was commissioned.

In front of the Choir Chapel (opposite the Chapel of the Sacrament), a mosaic copy of Raphael's "Transfiguration".

In front of the Cappella della Presentazione, the tomb of Innocent VIII (by Pollaiolo, 1498), on which the Pope is represented twice (enthroned and recumbent). This is the only monument from Old St Peter's which was transferred to the new church. Opposite it is a statue of Pius X.

In the Cappella della Presentazione are a bronze relief commemorating Pope John XXIII (1958–63; on right) and a statue of Benedict XV (1914–22; on left).

Beyond the Cappella della Presentazione are two monuments commemorating the last of the Stuarts: on the right Maria Clementina Sobieska, wife of James the Old Pretender; on the left the Old Pretender, "Bonnie Prince Charlie" and Cardinal Henry of York.

Roof

Adjoining the Stuart monuments near the Baptistery are the stairs (142 steps) and lift leading to the roof of the church, from which visitors can climb to the lantern by way of a gallery inside the drum and further staircases (in places extremely steep). From the roof and the lantern there are magnificent views over St Peter's Square and the city; and from here, too, it is possible to see Michelangelo's dome at close quarters and observe the details of its structure.

Sacre Grotte Vaticane

Opening times
Daily 7am–5pm
(6pm in summer)

The entrance to the "Vatican Grottoes" (Crypt) is at the pillar with the figure of St Andrew. This spacious undercroft was created when Antonio da Sangallo raised the floor level of the church by 3.20m/10½ft to protect it from damp. The tombs of earlier Popes were transferred here from Old St Peter's, and many later Popes have also been buried here, including the last four (Pius XII, John XXIII, Paul VI and John Paul I). A walk around the tombs of the Popes is one of the most impressive experiences of a visit to Rome.

It is also possible, with special permission, to see the excavations (*scavi*) under St Peter's. Here the archaeologists have brought to light the old

Via Appia Antica: a short stretch with ancient paving

cemetery on the Vatican hill, including what is believed to be the tomb of St Peter himself, and the foundations of the original Constantinian basilica.

Via Appia Antica

F/G 9/10

Outside the Porta San Sebastiano in the Aurelian Walls (see Mura Aureliane) is the Via Appia Antica, one of the oldest and most important of the Roman consular highways. It was built about 300 B.C. by the censor Appius Claudius Caecus to link Rome with Capua and was extended to Brindisi about 190 B.C.

Buses
4, 88, 90, 93,
changing to
118 or 218

The road is now metalled for almost its entire length. From the port of Brindisi communications were established across the Mediterranean with the eastern territories of the Empire. Just outside Rome, running parallel with the road, can be seen the ruins of some of the aqueducts which supplied the city with water.

On either side of the road are the remains of tombs belonging to the aristocratic families of Rome – built outside the city since burials were not permitted within its walls. The ruins of these tombs and memorial stones (see Catacombs of San Callisto and San Sebastiano, and Tomba di Cecilia Metella) combine with the lines and cypresses of the Roman Campagna to give the Via Appia Antica its characteristic and picturesque aspect.

Via Condotti

See Piazza di Spagna/Scalinata della Trinità dei Monti

Via dei Fori Imperiali   E 6/7

Buses
85, 87, 88

This six-lane highway, built by Mussolini in 1932, runs from the Capitol (see Campidoglio) to the Colosseum (see Colosseo), passing along one side of the Forum (see Foro Romano).

In 1980 the city council, giving priority to archaeology over traffic, decided to remove the road and thus make it possible to excavate the remains of the great days of the Empire which lie concealed under its 64,000sq.m/76,500sq.yd of asphalt.

Via di San Gregorio   E 7

Underground station
Colosseo (line B)

Buses
11, 15, 27, 81, 85, 87, 88, 90, 118, 673

This broad tree-lined street, in ancient times the Triumphal Way followed by victorious generals, runs south from the Colosseum (see Colosseo) and Arch of Constantine (see Arco di Constantino) between the Palatine (see Palatino) and Caelian Hills, past the church of San Gregorio Magno (see entry), to the south-east end of the Circus Maximus.

Via Veneto (officially the Vittorio Veneto)   E 5

Underground station
Barberini (line A)

Buses
52, 53, 56, 58, 90b, 95, 490, 492, 495

This handsome and fashionable street, which descends in two sweeping curves from the Porta Pinciana to the Piazza Barberini, has been a Mecca for tourists, ever since it was laid out at the beginning of this century. Its elegant fashion shops, lively cafés and exclusive hotels attract those who want to see and be seen. In the 50s the street was associated with the "dolce vita" of the Roman trend-setters as portrayed in Fellini's films.

The macabre Capuchin cemetery is nearby (see Santa Maria della Concezione).

★Villa Borghese   D/E 4/5

Underground stations
Flaminio and Piazza di Spagna (line A)

Buses
3, 52, 53, 490, 495, 510

Trams
19, 19b, 30, 30b

The great families of Papal Rome had their palaces in the city and their villas in the country, which might be just outside the city or even further afield, sometimes as far away as the Alban Hills. It is always necessary in Rome, therefore, to distinguish between the *palazzo* and the *villa* associated with a particular family name.

The Borghese family, which produced Pope Paul V (1605–21), several cardinals and other important figures, had this villa built in an area of vineyards on the outskirts of Rome for Cardinal Scipione Caffarelli Borghese in 1613–16. The villa is complete with extensive grounds, laid out with artificial lakes and garden pavilions, which now combine with the Pincio Gardens (see entry) to form one of the largest parks in Rome. Prince Marc'Antonio Borghese had considerable alterations carried out by an architect of German origin, Unterberger.

Notable features of the gardens are the central artificial lake, with an Aesculapian temple on its peninsula (a copy by Asprucci of a Greek temple 1786); temples to Diana (1789) and to Faustina (1792); the museum of the Italian sculptor Pietro Canonica (1869–1959); a race-track, the Piazza Sena, on which international race meetings are held at the beginning of May, and a number of monuments: to Byron (a copy of the original by Thorvaldsen), to Goethe (1902–04) and to Victor Hugo (1905), both by Gustav Eberlein.

Monument to Byron

The extensive parkland also accommodates the collections of the Galleria Nazionale d'Arte Moderna and the Museo Nazionale Etrusco di Villa Guilia (see entries).

Zoological Garden in the Villa Borghese

Giardino Zoologico

There is a small zoological garden in the park, built in 1911 and modelled on the Hamburg zoo. The enclosures reflect the animals' natural habitat as closely as possible. The zoo is still a popular attraction, even though the enclosures are outdated and in process of renovation. (Admission is free for children and senior citizens; times of opening: daily 8am–6.15pm/5pm in winter. Closed May 1st).

★Museo e Galleria Borghese

At the east end of the gardens is the Casino Borghese (by Giovanni Vasanzio, 1612–15), which now houses the Museo e Galleria Borghese, with the collection of antiquities assembled by Cardinal Scipione Borghese.

The two-story building, with rectangular towers, is only partly open to the public owing to restoration work (1991). The ground floor has a loggia of five arcades, over which is a large open terrace.

The art-loving Cardinal Scipione Borghese, a great collector of antiquities, also commissioned work from contemporary artists. His collection of antiquities was housed in the Casino and formed the basis of the Borghese Museum – though during the Napoleonic period Camillo Borghese was compelled to sell some works to the Louvre. At the beginning of the 20th c. the collection of pictures was formed into the Borghese Gallery.

The five fragments of a mosaic pavement from Torrenuova, contained in the richly decorated entrance hall, date from the 4th c. and show gladiator contests and hunting scenes. The Baroque ceiling frescoes, by Mariano Rossi, represent "Camillus after the parley with Brennus, commander of the Gallic army" and "Allegory of Time".

D/E 4/5

Opening times
Tues.–Sat.
9am–2pm
Sun. 9am–1pm
(Entrance Piazzale Brasile)

While the Villa is undergoing extensive restoration work the picture collection is on show at Galleria San Michelle di Ripa, Via di San Michelle di Ripa (Trastevere).
Open: Tues.–Sat.
9am–2pm,
Sun. 9am–1pm

"David", an early work of Bernini . . .   *. . . and the "Rape of Prosperina"*

Outstanding works of sculpture in the museum include Canova'a figure of Pauline Borghese as Venus (1805); David with his sling (1623–24), commissioned from Bernini by Scipione Borghese; Apollo and Daphne, a masterpiece by Bernini, depicting the transformation of Daphne into a laurel-bush to save her from pursuit by Apollo; the Rape of Prosperina, also by Bernini (1621–22); the Sleeping Hermaphrodite (a Roman copy of a Greek original); Aeneas with his father Anchises, by Gian Lorenzo and Pietro Bernini (also son and father) and Bernini's "Truth revealed by Time".

The picture collection, currently at San Michele di Ripa includes works by Raphael (among them an "Entombment"), Botticelli, Pinturicchio, Perugino, Lucas Cranach the Elder, Sodoma, Dürer, Lotto, Domenichino ("Diana the Huntress"), Caravaggio ("Madonna dei Palafrenieri"), Rubens, Correggio ("Danae"), Bernini, Bassano, Van Dyck, Titian ("Sacred and Profane Love"), Bellini, Paolo Veronese and Antonello da Messina ("Male Portrait").

★Villa Doria Pamphili   A/B 7/8

Situation
Via Aurelia Antica

Buses
31, 42, 144

Adjoining the Janiculum are the extensive grounds of the Villa Doria Pamphili, Rome's largest municipal park, now traversed by the Via Olimpica, a road constructed for the 1960 Olympics. The villa was built by Alessandro Algardi about 1650 for Prince Camillo Pamphili, a nephew of Pope Innocent X.

On a terrace alongside the Via Aurelia Antica is the Casino dei Quattro Venti (country house of the four winds), which is decorated with statues and reliefs.

Villa d'Este

See Tivoli

★★Villa Farnesina

C 6

The Villa Farnesina, which now belongs to the State and houses the National Print Cabinet (Gabinetto Nazionale delle Stampe; viewing by appointment only), was built in the 16th c. with all the lavishness and splendour of the period.

Situation
Lungotevere della Farnesina

Buses
23, 28, 65

This Renaissance palace was designed by Baldassare Peruzzi (1508–22) for the banker Agostino Chigi and decorated by famous artists, including Raphael, Giulio Romano, Sebastiano del Piombo, Peruzzi himself and Sodoma.

Opening times
Mon.–Sat.
9am–1pm
Closed in August
Entrance: Via della Lungara

Here Popes, cardinals, princes, diplomats, artists and men of letters were entertained in princely fashion. Illustrious guests were given silver dishes bearing their own coat-of-arms, which they threw into the nearby Tiber after the banquet (though a net spread in the river enabled them to be recovered afterwards). The palace was acquired by the Farnese family in 1580, and in the 18th c. it passed to the Bourbons of Naples.

On the walls and ceiling on the garden loggia of the Villa are scenes from the myth of Cupid and Psche (after Apuleius), painted by Raphael and his pupils Giulio Romano and Francesco Penni (1517). In a fashion typical of the Renaissance they depict youthful pagan divinities in the setting of Papal Rome, combining Greco-Roman and Christian ideals. The figures in the Spandrels are by Raphael himself.

Garden loggia

In the Sale di Galatea, beside lunette frescoes by Sebastiano del Piombo (scenes from Ovid's Metamorphosis) and Baldassare Perussi's "Starry Sky", is Raphael's magnificent fresco depicting the triumph of the nymph Galatea (1511) who was pursued by the one-eyed Cyclopes Polyphemus. The assumption that Imperia, the beloved of Chigi, was portrayed in this painting is not verified.

Sale di Galatea

Also of interest in the Salone delle Prospettiva on the upper storey are the trompe-l'œil paintings by Balsassare Peruzzi. These were carried out at the beginning of the 16th century and depict a square in ancient Rome in which the colonnades appear to open out to the viewer.

Salone delle Prospettiva

The masterpiece of Sodoma in the bedroom of Agnostino Chigi is "The marriage of Alexander and Roxana" (daughter of the Persian King Darius) painted in 1511–12. The painting shows the bedchamber with the Macedonian commander presenting his betrothed with the crown, symbolising the victory of love; Hymen and the little Erato, with love's arrows, helping to disrobe Roxanne emphasise the erotic nature of the situation. Sodoma also painted "Alexander's pardon of the Persian Family Darius".

Works of Sodoma

Villa Madama

A/B 2/3

On the slopes of Monte Mario, on the side looking towards the city, is the Villa Madama, now used by the Italian government for receptions and

Situation
Via di Villa Madama

Villa Medici

conferences. The villa was designed by Raphael for Cardinal Giulio de'Medici, later Pope Clement VII, and subsequently altered by Antonio da Sangallo the Younger. It passed into the hands of "Madama" Margareta, daughter of the Emperor Charles V, who married Alessandro de'Medici as her first husband and Ottavio Farnese as her second, and in 1735 the property passed to the Bourbons of Naples. The villa fits harmoniously into its natural setting, and offers a magnificent view of the city.

Villa Medici   D 5

Situation
Viale Trinità dei Monti

Underground station
Piazza di Spagna (line A)

To the north of the Trinità dei Monti church, a few paces from the Piazza di Spagna (see entry), is the Villa Medici, a late Renaissance mansion with a severe main front and a richly articulated garden front to the rear, facing the Pincio (see entry).

The villa was built by Annibale Lippe in 1544 for Cardinal Ricci da Montepulciano. It later passed to the Medici and the Grand Dukes of Tuscany, and was finally occupied in Napoleonic times by the French Academy, a foundation (still existing) for French artists.

From 1630–33 Galileo was imprisoned in the villa on the order of the Inquisition.

Villa Torlonia   G 4

Situation
Via Nomentana

The Villa Torlonia park (area 13ha/32½ acres), with the Neo-Classical Palazzo Torlonia (early 19th c.), formerly the property of the Torlonia family, was during the Fascist period the private residence of Mussolini.

It now belongs to the city of Rome, and the park (though not the villa itself) is open to the public.

Buses 36, 37, 60, 62, 63, 136, 137

Zoo

See Villa Borghese, Giardino Zoologico

Practical Information

Telephone numbers in Rome are gradually being changed to eight figure numbers, so it will be advisable to check telephone numbers for 1996 onwards.

Note

Airlines

Via Bissolati 13; tel. 6 56 21
Reservations tel. 6 56 42.

Alitalia

Via Bissolati 54; tel. 47 99 91.

British Airways

Via Barberini 59–67; tel. 47 21.

TWA

Via Barberini 3; tel. 4 88 35 14.

Canadian Airlines
International

Via Barberini 3; tel. 4 82 07 03.

Cathay Pacific

Antiques

In the narrow streets behind the Piazza Navona are the workshops of craftsmen skilled in the restoration of antique furniture and pictures, however badly damaged they may be. In this area visitors will find numerous little shops fiercely competitive with one another, selling antique furniture, silver, jewellery, dolls, pictures, lamps, lace mats and much else besides.

Piazza Navona

"Antique dealers' weeks" take place twice a year, in the second half of May and October in the Via dei Coronari.

Via dei Coronari

The Roman art market is concentrated in the area between the Piazza di Spagna and the Piazza del Popolo. As well as numerous galleries there are also many antique dealers offering rare items (at prices to match!).

Via del Babuino/
Via Giulia

There are numbers of secondhand dealers in the streets known as the "Banchi vecchi" between the Piazza di Campo dei Fiori and the Tiber.

"Banchi vecchi"

A flea-market is held on Sunday mornings at the Porta Portese in Trastevere.

Porta Portese

First impressions of what is on offer and prices can be had by visiting one or more of the following:

Antique dealers

Bilenchi '900 (glass, lamps and objets d'art)
Via della Stelletta 17.

C. E. Rappaport (books, prints and maps)
Via Sistina 23.

Valerio Turchi (marble, especially Greek and Roman)
Via Margutta 91a.

Antichita Davide Sesticvi (Italian and Chinese porcelain, silverware)
Via Margutta 57.

◀ *Galleria Nazionale d'Arte Moderna*

Banks

Opening times Mon.–Fri. 8.30am–1.30 or 2pm; banks are also open for one hour in the afternoon (generally 3–4pm, but each bank fixes its own time).

Eurocheques

Most banks in the city centre will cash Eurocheques. Since each bank may quote a different rate it is worth while making comparisons.

Bureaux de change

Caution is necessary in dealing with small street exchange offices; beware of counterfeit currency.

Bicycle rental

Cycling in Rome itself is hazardous. There are, however, many beautiful parks in the city to tour (see Parks and Open Spaces).

1 Bike Rome
Villa Borghese car park; tel. 3 22 52 40.

Collalti
Via del Pellegrino 82; tel. 68 80 10 84.

Camping sites

Camping Tiber,
km 1·4 on Via Tiberina; tel. 33 61 23 14.
In the north of the city.
On the bank of the Tiber.

Capitol,
Ostia Antica, Via Castelfusano 195; tel. 5 73 44.

Flaminio,
km 8 on Via Flaminia Nuova; tel. 3 33 26 04.

Happy Camping,
Via Prato della Corte 1915; tel. 33 61 38 00.

Roma Camping,
km 8·2 on Via Aurelia; tel. 6 62 30 18.

Salaria Camping,
Via Salaria (km 15·6); tel. 8 88 76 42.

Seven Hills,
Via Cassia 1216 (km 18); tel. 30 31 08 26.

Car rental

Avis

Piazza Esquilino 1/c; tel. 65 01 15 79.
Via Sardegna 38A; tel. 4 82 47 28.

Europcar

Via Lombardia 7; tel. 4 82 57 01.

Hertz

Free telephone number 16 78 80 80 16.

Free telephone number 1 67 86 70 67.

These firms also have desks at the Termini station and at both Ciampino and Fiumicino airports.

Scoot-a-long, Via Cavour 302; tel. 6 78 02 06.

Scooters for Rent,
Via della Purifiazione 66; tel. 46 54 85.

See entry

Catacombs

The catacombs were originally the legally recognised burial places of Christians (and also heathens) and were called by them by the Greek name of Coemetaria (resting places). Until the beginning of the 9th c. the coemetaria and the graves of martyrs enjoyed general veneration, and a great number of remains were transferred as relics to other churches. Then the burial places fell into decay and even the old name was forgotten. The name catacomb comes from Catacumba, one of these burial places which was situated in the area of San Sebastiano. Scientific investigation began at the end of the 16th c. and was treated by the church as a matter of honour. As more recent research has revealed, catacombs served merely as burial places and as places where masses for the dead were said and not as refuges for the Christians or where the usual services were held. The layout is very simple; narrow passages, in the walls of which several long niches were formed for the reception of the corpses. For non-Christians these niches were used for urns containing ashes. The niches were sealed by marble or terracotta tablets. Decoration with painting but little sculpture

General

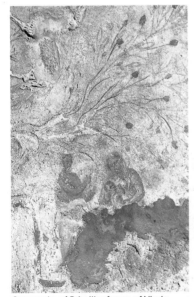 

Catacombs of Priscilla; fresco of Virgin . . .   . . . and Greek chapel

follows the style of the pagan art of the time; according to the contents symbolic representations predominate – the sacrificial lamb, the fish, representing the Greek word "ichthys", the Greek initials of "Jesus Christ, Son of God and Saviour". Early representations of the Last Supper and the Virgin Mary are impressive. The older inscriptions only give the name of the dead person.

Catacombs of Domitilla	Catacombe di Domitilla (see A to Z).
Catacombs of Priscilla	Catacombe di Priscilla (see A to Z).
Catacombs of St Agnes	Catacombe di Sant'Agnese (see A to Z, Sant'Agnese fuori le Mura).
Catacombs of St Calixtus	Catacombe di San Callisto (see A to Z).
Catacombs of St Ciriaca the Basilica	Catacombe di Santa Ciriaca, Via Ciriaca. Visitors wishing to see these catacombs should apply to the sacristy of San Lorenzo (Piazzale del Verano, see A to Z, San Lorenzo fuori le Mura). Interesting painting can be seen in these catacombs.
Catacombs of St Sebastian	Catacombe di San Sebastiano (see A to Z, San Sebastiano).

Chemists (Farmacie)

Opening times	9am–1pm and 3.30–7.30pm.
Farmacia di turno	There is a chemist's shop open 24 hours a day in every district of the city. The names of the chemists on duty are published in the daily papers, or can be found by telephoning 19 21–5.
International pharmacy	Piazza Capranica; tel. 6 79 46 80. Piazza Barberini 49; tel. 4 82 54 56. Open day and night.
Night pharmacy	Via Nazionale 228; tel. 4 88 07 54.

Currency

Currency	The unit of currency is the *lira* (plural *lire*). There are banknotes for 1000, 2000, 5000, 10,000, 50,000 and 100,000 lire and coins in denominations of 10, 20, 50, 100, 200 and 500 lire. There is often a shortage of small change, and telephone tokens (*gettoni*) for 200 lire or postage stamps and "Minicheques" may be used to make up the deficiency.
Lira Nuova	It is probable that in the near future the "new lira" will be introduced. One new lira will be equal to 1000 old lire. Banknotes and coins will be issued in the revised values. For some time both old and new currency will be legal tender.
Import of currency	There are no restrictions on the import of Italian and foreign currency into Italy, but in view of the strict controls on the export of currency it is advisable to declare any currency brought in on the appropriate form (*modulo V2*) at the frontier.

The export of currency is permitted only up to a value of 5,000,000 lire per person except where a large sum has been declared on entry. No more than 1,000,000 lire of Italian currency can be taken out.

It is advisable to take money in the form of travellers' cheques, which are not subject to any restrictions, or to use Eurocheques. Eurocheques may be cashed to a maximum of 300,000 lire per cheque.

Banks, the larger hotels, first-class restaurants and many stores accept most international credit cards. The commonest in Italy are Visa, American Express, Eurocard and Diners Club.

Money can be exchanged at almost all banks and at exchange offices:

Thomas Cook,
Piazza Barberini 21a.

Cambio Roma,
Via Francesco Crispi 15.

Eurocambio,
Via Francesco Crispi 92.

Outside normal business hours and at weekends money (but not Eurocheques) can be exchanged at the following offices:

The Main Station (Stazione Termini).
Leonardo da Vinci Airport (Fiumicino).

Customs regulations

Citizens of countries in the European Union are no longer subject to import restrictions on personal effects and articles for their own personal use. The limits of goods bought "duty free" remain 200 cigarettes or 100 cigarillos or 50 cigars or 300 gr. tobacco; 3 litres wine and 1 litre spirits over 22° Gay-Lussac (38·8° proof) or 2 litres fortified or sparkling wine up to 22° proof; 50 gr. perfume and 0·25 litre toilet water.

Videos, CB radios, car telephones and reserve fuel canisters must be declared. The import of weapons, including imitations, and large hunting knives is prohibited.
    Some of the reduced concessions also apply to visitors from other countries including the United States and Canada.

Personal effects, etc., may be taken out without formality. In addition visitors can take out, without liability to duty, articles they have bought in Italy up to a value of 500 US dollars. For the export of objets d'art and antiques a permit must be obtained from the Chamber of Art.

When bringing large amounts of currency into Italy, it is advisable to complete a declaration on entry (see Currency).

Embassies

Via XX Settembre 80A; tel. 4 82 54 41.

Via Veneto 119A; tel 4 67 41.

Via G. Bastia de Rossi 27; tel. 44 59 81.

Events

Note	Information about day-to-day events can be found in the daily newspapers and in the events list "Roma C'è".
January	Mid December to 6 January: Christmas Market in Piazza Navona. 6 January: Epiphany (children receive presents; fair in Piazza Navona). Alta Moda Italiana (fashion show – spring and summer fashions). Roma Ufficio (Office Equipment Trade Fair, continuing into February).
February	Martedi Grasso (Shrove Tuesday), with street processions in costumes and masks (beginning some weeks previously).
March	9 March: Santa Francesca Romana, Blessing of motor vehicles at Colosseum. 19 March: San Giuseppe (St Joseph). *Zeppole* (cream choux) are sold and consumed in large numbers. Spring Festival in Piazza di Spagna (continuing into April).
March/April	Maundy Thursday: Washing of the Feet in St John Lateran (Papal Mass). Holy Week: services conducted by the Pope on Palm Sunday, Maundy Thursday, Good Friday and Easter Saturday. Good Friday: Stations of the Cross in the Colosseum, with the Pope present. Easter Day: Papal blessing "Urbi et Orbi" (to the City and the World) from the balcony of St Peter's. Second half of April: azaleas in Piazza di Spagna.
May	Second half: Exhibition of antiques in Via dei Coronari. Rose show on the Aventine in the rose garden of Valle Murcia. Fiera di Roma: Exhibition of products from the whole of Italy along the Via Cristoforo Colombo (until June).
June	23–24 June: Midsummer Night (fireworks). Estate Romana ("Roman Summer"): concerts, dramatic performances and exhibitions (mostly in the open air) throughout the summer, continuing to October. Tevere Expo on the banks of the Tiber: Exhibition of products from all parts of Italy (until July).
July	Last week of July: Festa dei Noiantri, a popular festival in Trastevere (fireworks, eating of roasted sucking pigs in the street). Outdoor opera season. Outdoor concert season at Villa Giulia. Roma Musica (until September). Season of drama at Ostia Antica. Alta Mode Italiana (fashion show – autumn and winter fashions).
August	5 August: Festa della Madonna della Neva (Festival of Our Lady of the Snows), with ceremonies in the church of Santa Maria Maggiore. Outdoor opera season. Outdoor concerts at Villa Giulia. Drama at Ostia Antica. Pop concerts and song recitals in the open air.

Children's fashion show.
Tevere Expo Internationale on the banks of the Tiber: Exhibition of products from all over the world.
Antiques Fair (continuing until October).

Furniture and Interior Decoration Show (MOA).
Antique Show in the Via dei Coronari.

8 December: Immacolata Concezione (Immaculate Conception), with ceremony in Piazza Navona.
15 December: Christmas Market in Piazza Navona (until 6 January).
24 December: Solemn Mass in St Peter's.
25 December: Solemn Christmas Mass in St Peter's, followed by the Pope's annual Christmas address from the balcony of St Peter's.
Christmas cribs (Nativity groups) in churches and in the Piazza di Spagna.
Natale Oggi ("Christmas Today") exhibition.

Excursions

Bookings for excursions in the surroundings of Rome and also to Florence, Naples and Pompeii can be made at most travel agents and also at the national tourist agency CIT (Compagnia Italiana Turismo, Piazza della Repubblica 64). Visitors who prefer to travel on their own can reach most of the sights quite easily by using public transport (see A to Z, Ostia Antica, Tivoli) or even more easily by car (see A to Z, Ceverteri, Colli Albani).

Among the most rewarding destinations which are best visited by car is Palestrina, the old Praeneste, 38km (24 miles) SE of Rome; it is reached by taking motorway A2, the Zagarolo exit. The huge complex of the Roman shrine of Fortuna Primigenia (1st and 2nd c. B.C.) in which part of the town has been built, is well worth seeing. Numerous finds from the shrine and from graves in the surroundings are exhibited in the Museo Nazionale Archeologico Prenestino (opening times: Tues.–Sun. 9am to sunset) which is located in the Palazzo Colonna Barberini on the topmost terrace of the shrine.

About 100km (62 miles) N of Rome lies the Etruscan city of Tarquina. It is reached along the motorway in the direction of Fiumicino, the turning to Civitavecchia where the motorway ends, and then along the Via Aurelia (SS 1). In the necropolis of the town can be found the most beautifully decorated graves of the Etruscan culture. Paintings in the burial chambers are, however, not in the best condition, not least because of the large number of visitors, so that altogether only eight chambers (alternately four each day) can be seen. However, finds from the graves are on view in the Museo Nazionale Tarquiniense (opening times: Tues.–Sun. 9am–2pm; in summer also 4–7pm).

From the scenic point of view there is a charming excursion to the coastal town of San Felice 90km (56 miles) SE of Rome. We leave Rome in the direction of Lido di Ostia then turn to the SE along the coastal road and drive via Anzio, Nettuno and Sabaudia to San Felice. About 5km (3 miles) before reaching San Felice rises Monte Circeo where, according to legend, once stood the palace of the sorceress Circe who turned the companions of Odysseus into swine.

From San Felice in clear weather you can see as far as Ischia, Capri, Vesuvius and the Ponza Islands. If you have the energy and can get a permit to cross the military area to Semàforo, 448m (1470ft) high, and from there climb to the highest peak, 541m (1776ft) above sea level, where you will have an even better view and can look back and maybe even discern in the distance the dome of St Peter's in Rome.

First Aid (Pronto soccorso)

Red Cross
First aid, ambulance: tel. 55 10.

Hospitals
See page 182 Medical help.

Food and Drink

Meals
Italian eating habits are different from those in Britain or America. Most hotels provide a continental breakfast, but many Italians are content to drink a cup of coffee (espresso) in a bar, with perhaps a "cornetto" (a roll) to accompany it. Lunch and the evening meal are far more elaborate. A typical lunch or dinner generally consists of a hot or cold "starter" (antipasto), a first course (primo) with noodles (pasta), a second course (secundo) with a meat or fish dish and finally cheese and a dessert (dolce).

Lunch (pranzo or colazione) is generally eaten between 1 and 3pm, dinner between 8 and 10pm. In most restaurants it is difficult to get anything before 12.30pm and in the evening before 7.30pm. A visitor who wants a substantial meal in the evening is recommended to reserve a table, in order to prevent possible disappointment.

Roman cuisine
Roman cuisine does not lay much store on extravagance or sophistication, but has kept its regional character; this is distinguished by the use of good pure ingredients and careful preparation according to simple traditional recipes.

If a restaurant has a notice at its entrance or in the bill of fare stating "cucina romana", this indicates that the dishes served will be prepared according to Roman recipes ("alla romana"). The visitor should not hesitate to try these specialities.

Soups
Zuppa: chicken broth with vegetables, meat dumplings, rice or pasta.

Starters
Broccoli romani: broccoli steamed in white wine.
Canneloni: pasta squares stuffed with meat, calves' brains, spinach, egg and cheese.
Carcioli alla guidà: artichokes fried in oil.
Carcioli alla romana: artichokes seasoned with peppermint and stuffed with anchovies.
Fettucine: ribbon noodles with a sauce of butter, eggs, anchovies and cheese.
Gnocchi alla romana: semolina dumplings.
Gnocchi di polenta: maize flour pasta, either grilled or breaded and fried in fat.
Lumache: snails in tomato sauce, seasoned with ginger.
Panzarottini: small packets of pasta with cheese and butter, often grilled with eggs and anchovies.
Suppli di riso: croquettes of rice and egg with meat ragout.

Fish dishes
Anguilla: eels stewed in white wine.
Calamari fritti: fried rings of squid.
Orate ai ferri: redfish from the grill.

Anitra: stuffed duck with calves' feet.
Cappone: capon with bread stuffing, seasoned with cheese.
Pollo: chicken in tomato sauce with white wine.

Abbacchio: lamb in white wine.
Polenta: polenta slices with lamb stew.
Salsa romana: a brown sweet and sour sauce with raisins, and chestnut and lentil purée (served with game).
Saltimbocca: slices of veal and ham seasoned with sage, steamed in butter and soaked in marsala.
Testerelle di abbacchio: lambs' heads fried in oil, with rosemary.
Trippa: tripe in tomato sauce, with white wine.

Generally wine and water are drunk with meals, but in many restaurants beer can be obtained which, compared with wine, is often considerably more expensive.

The best-known wines of the surroundings of Rome are those of the Castelli Romani, often called Frascati from the principal place of production; from here come strong white wines with a flowery bouquet ("vino bianco"). Other places where wine is produced are grouped around the Largo Albano; Grottaferrata, Marino, Genzano, Velletri (also red wines, "vino rosso" or "vino nero") as well as places in the Colli Lanuvini and the Colli Albani (normally lightly acidic, "asciutto"). From the same district a dry ("secco") table wine can generally be obtained as well as dessert wine ranging from semi-sweet ("abbocato, amabale") to sweet ("dolce").

Table wine ("vino di pasto") is often served in carafes holding a litre, a half litre or a quarter litre ("un litro, un mezzo litro, un quarto") and by the glass ("un bicchiere").

In Rome there are more than five thousand bars, in which the central feature is the Espresso machine. There are few seats; the customer stands at the bar, the furnishing is minimal – therefore the choice of the correct coffee is a science in itself for the Roman citizen. Espresso (a small strong black coffee) is also drunk north of the Alps; in Rome it is simply called "caffè", which in turn is doubled ("doppio"), corrected ("corretto") with grappa, cognac or bitters; cold ("freddo") in summer or weak and stretched ("ristretto"). Another variety is Cappuccino (caffè crowned with frothy milk). It can be had either light or dark ("Chiaro" or "scuro"), at various temperatures and with as much froth as desired. A simple coffee with milk is a "caffelatte" or "macchiato" (spotted); if milk with only a little coffee is preferred it is best to order a "latte macchiato".

Galleries

Galleria Borghese,
See A to Z, Villa Borghese.

Galleria Nazionale d'Arte Antica,
See A to Z, Palazzo Barberini.
See A to Z, Palazzo Corsini.

Galleria Nazionale d'Arte Moderna,
See A to Z.

Galleria Doria Pamphili,
Piazza del Collegio Romano 1a.
Pictures of 15th–17th c.

Van Gogh's "Gardener"

Statue of Bowman, by Bordelle

Galleria Colonna,
See A to Z.

Galleria Spada,
Piazza Capo di Ferro 3.
Open: Tues.–Sat. 9am–7pm, Sun. 9am–1pm.
17th c. works.

Galleria Comunale d'Arte Moderna et Contemporanea,
Via F. Crispi 24.
Open: Tues.–Sat. 10am–5.30pm, Sun. 9am–noon.

Galleria dell'Accademia di San Luca,
Piazza dell'Accademia di San Luca.
Open: Mon., Wed., Fri., last Sun. in month 10am–1pm.
Paintings, etc., by Raphael, Bassano, Rubens, etc.

Getting to Rome

By car

It is a long way from Britain or northern Europe to Rome. Motorists will be well advised, therefore, to use motorways and main trunk roads as far as possible.

Motorways

Tolls are payable on the Italian motorways (*autostrade*). The tickets for each section should be preserved, since they must be given up when leaving the motorways. (For petrol coupons, see Motoring.)

Motorists should carry their driving licence and car registration document. An international insurance certificate ("green card") is not obligatory but is strongly recommended. The car should have a nationality plate, and a warning triangle must be carried.

There is a wide choice of routes from the English Channel to Rome, depending on individual preferences and time available – through France and over one of the Alpine passes into Italy; down to the S coast of France and then on the coastal motorway into Italy; via France or Germany, Switzerland and one of the Alpine passes or tunnels. The journey can be shortened by using one of the motorail services from stations in NW Europe.

There are numerous package tours by coach, either going direct to Rome or including Rome in a longer circuit. For information apply to any travel agent.
   There are also various coach services between Britain or northern Europe and Rome. Euroways run a regular service from London via Milan to Rome; information from Euroways Express Coaches Ltd., 52 Grosvenor Gardens, London W1; tel. (0171) 837 6543, or from a travel agent.

There are daily scheduled flights from London to Rome and weekly flights from Manchester to Rome.
   The Leonardo da Vinci (Fiumicino) Airport is 36km (22 miles) from Rome by the Via del Mare or 26km (16 miles) by motorway.
   There is a train service between Fiumicino and Ostrense station every 20 minutes from about 7am until 10.50pm. A direct link to Termini runs hourly until 9.45pm. A taxi ride to the city will take up to 45 minutes and much longer in the rush-hour.
   There is also Ciampino Airport, mainly used by charter flights.
   Buses between the airport and the terminal at Via Sicilia 52.
   The Urbe airport is for light aircraft only.

See p. 161.

The fastest route from London to Rome takes about 26 hours, leaving London (Victoria) at 10.45am via Calais. Alternatives are to travel via Paris or Brussels, from where there are convenient through trains.

Hotels (Alberghi)

Italian hotels are officially classified in five categories, from luxury (5 stars) to hotels or pensions with modest facilities. The list below follows this classification. After the address and telephone number will be found the number of beds currently available.

Accommodation prices vary considerably according to the season. The prices given below (in lire) are for a single or a double room in the high season. The prices are based on those given by the Rome Tourist Bureau in its hotel list "Alberghi di Roma e Provincia 1995".
Increases due to the rate of inflation are probable.

	Single room	Double room
★★★★★	250,000–450,000	300,000–680,000
★★★★	100,000–400,000	150,000–500,000
★★★	60,000–180,000	100,000–270,000
★★	40,000–130,000	80,000–160,000
★	30,000– 80,000	40,000–110,000

Hassler Villa Medici

Hotel Excelsior

Receipted hotel bills should be kept and shown on demand to government inspectors enquiring into possible tax evasion, otherwise a fine may be levied.

Near Stazione Termini

★★★★★
Le Grand Hotel et de Rome, Via V. Emanuele Orlando 3; tel. 47 09, 328 b.

★★★★
Mediterraneo, Via Cavour 15; tel. 4 88 40 51, 452 b.
Universo, Via Principe Amedeo 5b; tel. 47 68 11, 381 b.
Palatino, Via Cavour 213; tel. 4 81 49 27, 380 b.
Quirinale, Via Nazionale 7; tel. 47 07, 339 b.
Massimo d'Azeglio, Via Cavour 18; tel. 4 88 06 46, 302 b.
President, Via E. Filiberto 173; tel. 77 01 21, 249 b.
San Giorgio, Via G. Amendola 61; tel. 4 82 73 41, 240 b.
Royal Santina, Via Marsala 22; tel. 4 45 52 41, 208 b.
Londra & Cargill, Piazza Sallustio 18; tel. 47 38 71, 198 b.
Genova, Via Cavour 33; tel. 47 69 51, 175 b.
Anglo-Americano, Via 4 Fontane 12; tel. 47 29 41, 165 b.
Napoleon, Piazza Vittorio Emanuele 105; tel. 4 46 72 64, 141 b.
Mondial, Via Torino 127; tel. 47 28 61, 138 b.
Atlantico, Via Cavour 23; tel. 48 59 51, 129 b.
Commodore, Via Torino 1; tel. 48 56 56, 100 b.
Rex, Via Torino 149; tel. 4 82 48 28, 95 b.

★★★
Diana, Via Principe Amedeo 4; tel. 4 82 75 41, 293 b.
Nord-Nuova Roma, Via G. Amendola 3; tel. 4 88 54 41, 250 b.
Siracusa, Via Marsala 50; tel. 4 46 03 96, 197 b.

Archimede, Via dei Mille 19; tel. 4 45 23 78, 196 b.
Madison, Via Marsala 60; tel. 4 45 43 44, 184 b.
Globus, Viale Ippocrate 119; tel. 4 45 70 01, 174 b.
Torino, Via Principe Amedeo 8; tel. 4 81 47 41, 172 b.
Lux Messe, Via Volturno 32; tel. 4 74 17 41, 161 b.
Milani, Via Magenta 12; tel. 4 45 70 51, 150 b.
Villa Franca, Via Villa Franca 9; tel. 4 44 03 64, 125 b.
San Marco, Via Villafranca 1; tel. 49 04 37, 118 b.
Medici, Via Flavia 96; tel. 4 82 73 19, 116 b.
San Remo, Via M. d'Azeglio 36; tel. 4 88 17 41, 113 b.
Aretusa, Via Gaeta 14; tel. 4 44 00 11, 109 b.
Nizza, Via M. d'Azeglio 16; tel. 4 88 10 61, 96 b.
Tirreno, Via S. Martino ai Monti 18; tel. 4 88 07 78, 77 b.
Embassy, Via A. Salandra 6; tel. 4 88 14 02, 62 b.
Valle, Via Cavour 134; tel. 4 81 57 36, 46 b.
Marghera, Via Marghera 29; tel. 4 45 42 37, 36 b.
Villa delle Rose, Via Vicenza 5; tel. 4 45 17 88.

★★

Marconi, Via G. Amendola 97; tel. 4 88 08 64, 94 b.
Igea, Via P. Amedeo 97; tel. 4 46 69 30, 63 b.
Salus, Piazza Indipendenza; tel. 4 44 03 30, 60 b.
Maxim, Via Nazionale 13; tel. 48 68 37, 51 b.
Bruna, Via Marghera 13; tel. 4 55 93 70, 32 b.
Fawlty Towers, Via Magunta 39; tel. 4 45 48 02, 24 b.

★

Reatina, Via San Martino della Battaglia 11; tel. 4 44 14 27, 36 b.
Bergamo, Via Gioberti 30; tel. 4 45 49 96, 22 b.
Tony, Via Principe Amedeo 79d; tel. 4 46 68 75, 13 b.

Holiday Inn, Crowne Plaza Minerva . . .   *. . . Exterior of hotel*

Between the Quirinal and the Villa Borghese

★★★★★
Excelsior, Via V. Veneto 125; tel. 47 08, 658 b.
Bernini Bristol, Piazza Barberini 23; tel. 4 88 30 51, 222 b.
Hassler-Villa Medici, Piazza Trinità dei Monti 6;
    tel. 6 78 26 51, 190 b.

★★★★
Parco dei Principi, Via G. Frescobaldi 5; tel. 8 84 10 71, 366 b.
Jolly, Corso d'Italia 1; tel. 84 95, 346 b.
Ambasciatori Palace, Via V. Veneto 62; tel. 4 74 93, 267 b.
Flora, Via V. Veneto 191; tel. 48 99 29, 264 b.
Regina Hotel Baglioni, Via V. Veneto 72; tel. 47 68 51, 230 b.
Sofitel, Via Lombardia 47; tel. 47 80 21, 221 b.
Savoia, Via Ludovisi 15; tel. 4 74 41 41, 212 b.
Eden, Via Ludovisi 49; tel. 4 74 35 51, 184 b.
Majestic, Via V. Veneto 50; tel. 48 68 41, 182 b.
Imperiale, Via V. Veneto 24; tel. 4 82 63 51, 169 b.
Victoria, Via Campania 41; tel. 47 39 31. 160 b.
Eliseo, Via di Porta Pinciana 30; tel. 4 87 04 56, 97 b.

★★★
King, Via Sistina 131; tel. 4 88 08 78, 122 b.
Alexandra, Via V. Veneto 18; tel. 4 88 19 43, 70 b.
La Residenza, Via Emilia 22; tel. 4 88 07 89, 51 b.

In the Old Town

★★★★★
Holiday Inn Crowne Plaza Minerva, Piazza della Minerva 69;
    tel. 69 94 18 88, 270 b.

★★★★
De la Ville, Via Sistina 69; tel. 6 73 31, 357 b.
Delta, Via Labicana 144; tel. 77 00 21, 290 b.
Plaza, Via del Corso 126, tel. 69 92 11 11, 205 b.
D'Inghilterra, Via Bocca de Leone 14; tel. 6 99 81, 185 b.
Delle Nazioni, Via Poli 7; tel. 6 79 24 41, 176 b.
Colonna Palace, Piazza Montecitorio 12; tel. 6 78 13 41,
    160 b.
Nazionale, Piazza Montecitorio 131; tel. 6 78 92 51, 158 b.
Forum, Via Tor de' Conti 25; tel. 6 79 24 46, 156 b.
Raphael, Largo Febo 2; tel. 68 28 31, 132 b.
Cardinal, Via Guilia 62; tel. 68 80 27 19, 114 b.
Valadier, Via della Fontanella 15; tel. 3 61 19 98, 77 b.
Sole al Pantheon, Via del Pantheon 63; tel. 6 78 04 41, 48 b.

★★★
Santa Chiara, Via Santa Chiara 21; tel. 6 87 29 79, 149 b.
Pace-Elvezia, Via IV Novembre 104; tel. 6 79 51 05, 147 b.
Adriano, Via di Pallacorda 2; tel. 68 80 24 51, 122 b.
Genio, Via G. Zanardelli 28; tel. 6 83 37 81, 99 b.
Cesari, Via di Pietra 89a; tel. 6 79 23 86, 92 b.
Lugano, Via Tritone 132; tel. 4 88 07 33, 70 b.
Due Torri, Vicolo del Leonetto 23; tel. 68 80 69 56, 49 b.
Teatro di Pompeo, Largo del Pallaro 8; tel. 68 30 01 70, 24 b.

★★
Arenula, Via S. Maria dei Calderai 47; tel. 6 87 94 54, 89 b.
Sole, Via Biscione 76; tel. 6 54 08 73, 88 b.
Della Lunetta, Piazza del Paradiso 68; tel. 6 86 10 80, 58 b.
Pornezia, Via dei Chiavar 12; tel. 6 86 13 71, 40 b.
Piccolo, Via dei Chiavari 32; tel. 68 80 25 60, 27 b.
Suisse, Via Gregoriana 56; tel. 6 78 36 49, 22 b.
Brotzky, Via del Corso 509; tel. 3 61 23 39, 20 b.

Northern Districts

★★★★★
Aldrovandi, Via U. Aldrovandi 115; tel. 3 22 39 93, 212 b.
Lord Byron, Via G. de Notaris 5; tel. 3 22 04 04, 73 b.

★★★★
Beverly Hills, Largo B. Marcello 220; tel. 8 54 21 41, 315 b.
Ritz, Via Chellini 41; tel. 80 37 51, 265 b.
Hermitage, Via E. Vayna 12; tel. 8 07 04 54, 185 b.
Claridge, Viale Liegi 62; tel. 8 41 92 12, 166 b.
Borromini, Via Lisbona 7; tel. 8 84 13 21, 147 b.
Rivoli, Via Taramelli 7; tel. 3 22 40 42, 86 b.

★★★
Fleming, Piazza Monteleone di Spoleto 20; tel. 3 33 72 64, 489 b.

Eastern Districts

★★★
Porta Maggiore, Piazza Porta Maggiore 25; tel. 7 02 79 27, 378 b.
San Giusto, Piazza Bologna 58; tel. 44 24 45 98, 97 b.

Southern Districts

★★★★
Sheraton Roma, Viale del Pattinaggio (EUR); tel. 54 53, 1067 b.

★★★
American Palace EUR, Via Laurentina 554; tel. 54 19 71, 258 b.
Dei Congressi, Viale Shakespeare 29 (EUR); tel. 5 92 60 21, 152 b.
Piccadilly, Via Magna Grecia 122, near Porta S. Giovanni;
 tel. 70 47 48 58, 92 b.
EUR Motel, Via Pontina 416; tel. 5 07 41 52, 43 b.

Right bank of Tiber

★★★★★
Cavalieri Hilton, Via Cadiolo 101; tel. 3 50 91, 837 b.

★★★★
Ergife Palace, Via Aurelia 619; tel. 66 44, 1826 b.
Holiday Inn, Via Aurelia Antica 415; tel. 66 42, 645 b.
Holiday Inn EUR, V. le Castello della Magliana 65;
 tel. 6 55 81, 538 b.
Villa Pamphili, Via della Nocetta 105; tel. 56 62, 513 b.
Jolly Leonardo da Vinci, Via dei Gracchi 324; tel. 3 24 99, 501 b.

Visconti Palace, Via F. Cesi 37; tel. 36 84, 489 b.
Cicerone, Via Cicerone 55c; tel. 35 76, 445 b.
Princess, Via A. Ferrara 3; tel. 66 49 31, 412 b.
Michelangelo, Via Stazione di S. Pietro 14; tel. 39 36 68 61, 300 b.
Giulio Cesare, Via degli Scipione 287; tel. 3 21 07 51, 139 b.
Atlante Star, Via Vitelleschi 34; tel. 6 87 32 33, 91 b.
Atlante Garden, Via Crescenzio 78a; tel. 6 87 23 61, 76 b.

★★★
Marc' Aurelio, Via Gregorio XI 135; tel. 6 63 76 30, 220 b.
Clodio, Via S. Lucia 10; tel. 3 72 11 92, 209 b.
Columbus, Via della Concillazione 33; tel. 68 56 54 35, 206 b.
Nova Domus, Via G. Savonarola 38; tel. 39 73 29 55, 185 b.
Nordland, Via A. Alciato 14; tel. 6 63 18 41, 170 b.
Fiamma, Via Gaieta 61; tel. 4 81 84 36, 144 b.
Cristofero Colombo, Via C. Colombo 710; tel. 5 92 13 15, 141 b.
Pacific, Viale Medaglie d'Oro 51; tel. 39 73 20 85, 120 b.
Olympic, Via Properzio 2a; tel. 6 89 66 50, 100 b.
Imperator, Via Aurelia 619; tel. 66 41 80 41, 79 b.

★★
Motel Boomerang, km 10.5 on Via Aurelia; tel. 6 69 03 06, 94 b.
Domus Aurelia, Via Aurelia 218; tel. 63 67 84, 88 b.
Alimandi, Via Tunisi 8; tel. 39 72 39 48, 56 b.
Amalia, Via Germanico 66; tel. 39 72 33 54, 46 b.

★
Foyer Phat Diem, Via Pin Sacchetti 45; tel. 6 63 88 26, 121 b.
La Rovere, Vicolo Sant'Onofrio 5; tel. 68 80 67 39, 40 b.
Manara, Via L. Manara 25; tel. 5 81 47 13, 13 b.
Carmel, Via G. Marneli 11; tel. 5 80 99 21, 10 b.

Day Hotels (Alberghi Diurni)	In the so-called day hotels visitors can have a wash and brush-up, change their clothes, leave their baggage, visit a hairdresser and also rest for a while.

Casa del Passagero, Via Viminale 1; tel. 46 17 95.
Stazione Termini (basement); tel. 4 75 85 82.

Student hostels — See Youth and Student hostels.

Pilgrims' hostels — Various religious orders run pilgrims' hostels which are cheap and well maintained. Information may be obtained from the Catholic church parishes or diocesan authorities in one's own country.

Insurance

Car insurance — It is very desirable to have an international insurance certificate ("green card"), although this is not a legal requirement for citizens of EU countries. It is important to have fully comprehensive cover, and it is desirable to take out short-term insurance against legal costs if these are not already covered. Italian insurance companies tend to be slow in settling claims.

Health insurance — British visitors to Italy, like other EU citizens, are entitled to receive health care on the same basis as Italians (including free medical treatment, etc.);

they should apply to their local social security office, well before their date of departure, for a certificate of entitlement (form E111). Fuller cover can be obtained by taking out insurance against medical expenses; and non-EU citizens will of course be well advised to take out appropriate insurance cover.

In view of the risk of theft it is desirable to have adequate insurance against loss of, or damage to, baggage.

Baggage insurance

Language

English is spoken in the major hotels in Rome. The municipal police wear a badge on the left arm to indicate which foreign language(s) they speak.

Note

The emphasis is usually placed on the second to last syllable of the word or is indicated by an accent on the last vowel (perchè, città), or on the third to last syllable (chilòmetro, sènepa). Accents: é or ó are closed sounds: è or ò are open sounds. Diphthongs are split, e.g. "causa" becomes "ka-usa"; there are no "silent" e's in Italian, but "h" is silent.

Pronunciation

C or cc in front of e or i	"tsch"	Pronunciation table
G or gg in front of e or i	"dsch"	
C and g/ch and gh in front of other vowels	"k" and "g"	
Gn and gl between vowels	"ny" and "ly"	
Qu	"kw"	
S at the beginnings of a word, in front of a vowel is a soft "ss" sound;		
S in front of consonants and between vowels is a harder sound.		
Sc in front of e and i	"sch"	
Z	"ds"	

0	zero	19	diciannove	Cardinal numbers
1	uno, una, un, un'	20	venti	
2	due	21	ventuno	
3	tre	22	ventidue	
4	quattro	30	trenta	
5	chinque	31	trentuno	
6	sei	40	quaranta	
7	sette	50	cinquanta	
8	otto	60	sessanta	
9	nove	70	settanta	
10	dieci	80	ottanta	
11	undici	90	novanta	
12	dodici	100	cento	
13	tredici	101	cento uno	
14	quattordici	153	centocinquantatre	
15	quindici	200	duecento	
16	sedici	1000	mile	
17	diciasette	5000	cinque mila	
18	diciotto	1 mil	un milione	

1	primo (prima)	7	settimo	Ordinal numbers
2	secondo	8	ottavo	
3	terzo	9	nono	
4	quarto	10	decimo	
5	quinto	20	ventesimo/vigesimo	
6	sesto	100	centesimo	

Language

½ un mezzo (mezza)
¼ un quarto
⅒ un decimo

Useful phrases	

Good morning, good day — Buon giorno!
Good evening — Buona sera!
Goodbye — Arrivederci!
Yes, no — Si, no!
Excuse me — Scusi!
Please — Per favore!
Don't mention it/you are welcome — Prego!
Thank you (very much) — (Molte) grazie!
If you will allow me — Con permesso!
Do you speak English? — Parla inglese?
A little, not much — Un poco, non molto
I don't understand — Non capisco
What is that in Italian? — Come si dice in italiano?
What is the name of this church? — Come si chiama questa chiesa?
The cathedral — Il duomo
The square — La piazza
The palace — Il palazzo
The theatre — Il teatro
Where is street X? — Dov'è la via X?
Where is the road (motorway)? — Dov'è la strada (l'autostrada)?
Where to . . . ? — Dov'è per . . . ?
Left, right — A sinistra, a destra
Straight on — Sempre diritto
Above, below — Sopra, sotto
When is it open? — Quando è aperto?
How far? — Quanto è distante?
Today — Oggi
Yesterday — Ieri
The day before yesterday — L'altro ieri
Tomorrow — Domani
Is there a vacant room? — Ci sono camere libere?
I would like . . . — Vorrei avere . . .
A room with bath — Una camera con bagno
A room with shower — Una camera con doccia
Full board — Con pensione completa
How much does it cost? — Qual'è il prezzo? / Quanto costa?
Inclusive? — Tutto compreso?
That is too dear! — E troppo caro!
Waiter, the bill! — Cameriere, il conto!
Where is the . . . toilet? — Dove si trovano i . . . gabinetti? (il servizi, la ritirata)
Wake me up at six — Può svegliarmi alle sei!
Where is there a . . . doctor? dentist? — Dove sta . . . un' médico? un dentista?

At the post office	

Address — Indirizzo
Letter — Lettera
Post box — Buca delle lettere
Stamps — Francobolli
Postman — Postino

Express post	Espresso	
Registered post	Raccomandata	
Airmail	Posta aerea	
Postcard	Cartolina	
Poste restane	Fermo posta	
Telephone	Telefono	
Telegram	Telegramma	
Departure	Partenza	Travelling
Departure (at airport)	Partenza, Decollo	
Arrival	Arrivo	
Stop-over	Sosta	
Station	Stazione	
Platform	Marciapiede	
Ticket	Biglietto	
Timetable	Oriario	
Fare	Brezzo del biglietto, Tariffa	
Flight	Volo	
Airport	Aeroporto	
Aeroplane	Aeroplano	
Luggage	Bagagli	
Porter	Portabagagli, facchino	
Track	Binario	
Stop, station	Fermata	
Non-smoking	Vietato fumare	
Smoking	Fumatori	
Conductor	Conduttore	
Ticket office	Sportello	
To change (trains, etc.)	Cambiare treno	
Waiting room	Salla d'aspetto	
Train driver	Capotreno	
Monday	Lunedi	Days of the Week
Tuesday	Martedi	
Wednesday	Mercoledi	
Thursday	Giovedi	
Friday	Venerdi	
Saturday	Sabato	
Sunday	Domenica	
Day	Giorno	
Weekday	Giorno feriale	
Public holiday	Giorno festivo	
Week	Settimana	
New Year	Capo d'anno	Holidays
Easter	Pasqua	
Whitsuntide	Pentecoste	
Christmas	Natale	
January	Gennaio	Months of the Year
February	Febbraio	
March	Marzo	
April	Aprile	
Mai	Maggio	
June	Guigno	
July	Luglio	
August	Agosto	
September	Settembre	
October	Ottobre	
November	Novembre	
December	Dicembre	
Month	Mese	

Libraries

Road Signs

Road works, resurfacing	Lavori stradali, Acciottolato
Stop!	Alt!
Caution!	Attenzione (attenti)
Beware of trains	al treno
mine works/blasting	alle mine
falling rocks	Caduta sassi (c. massi)
Diversion	Deviazione
No stopping	Divieto di sosta
Crossroad	Incrocio
Road works	Lavori in corso
Level crossing	Passaggio a livello
Reduce speed!	Rallentare
Closed	Sbarrato
No entry	Senso Proibito
One-way street	Senso unico
Dangerous bend	Svolta pericolosa
Keep to the right!	Tenere la destra
No through road	Transito interrotto
Drive slowly!	Veicolo al passo
Maximum speed	Velocità non superiore
15km p.h.!	i 15km/h!
No access	Vietato (proibito) il transito
for heavy vehicles	per tutti i veicoli pesanti

Libraries

Rome has a large number of libraries containing valuable old manuscripts and books as well as modern books and periodicals. Libraries tend not to admit members of the public without an appointment, and in some cases, proof that you have good reason to want access. The following is a brief selection of the more important.

Alessandra Universitaria
Piazza A. Moro; tel. 49 12 09.
Open: Mon.–Fri. 8.30am–10pm; Sat. 8.30am–7.30pm.

Archivo Cenbale Stato
Piazza Archivi 27; tel. 5 41 36 20.
Open: Mon.–Sat. 8.30am–1.30pm.

Biblioteca Angelica
Piazza S. Agostino 8; tel. 6 86 80 41.
Open: Tues., Thurs., Sat. 8.30am–1.30pm; Mon., Wed., Fri. 8.30am–7.30pm (summer until 11.30pm).

Biblioteca Hertziana
Via Gregoriana 28; tel. 6 78 98 57.
Open: Mon.–Fri. 9am–1pm, 4–7pm.
Admission by special permit only.

Biblioteca dell'Istituto Nazionale d'Archeologia e Storia dell'Arte
Piazza Venezia 3; tel. 6 78 99 65.
Open: Mon.–Fri. 9am–8pm; Sat. 9am–1pm.

Biblioteca Vallicelliana
Piazza della Chiesa Nuova 18; tel. 6 54 26 62.
Open: Mon.–Sat. 9am–1pm.

Municipal libraries

Palazzo Borromini, Piazza del Orologio; tel. 6 54 10 40.
Open: Mon.–Fri. 9am–1pm; Tues., Thurs. also 5–7pm.

Via Marmorata 169; tel. 5 74 64 80.
Open: Mon.–Fri. 9am–1pm, 5–7pm.

Roman market

Via Ottavio Assarotti 9B; tel. 3 37 62 42.
Open: Mon.–Fri. 9am–1.30pm; Wed., Fri. also 2.30–7pm.

Via Gela 8; tel. 7 01 76 45.
Open: Mon.–Fri. 9am–1pm, 4–8pm; Sat. 9am–1pm.

Lost property offices (Servizi oggetti rinvenuti)

There are lost property offices at airports and railway stations, usually open continuously.

Airports and railway stations

Via Volturno 65 (near Stazione Termini).
Open: weekdays 10am–noon; tel. 4 69 51.

Municipal transport (ATAC)

Via Bettoni 1, tel 5 81 60 40.
Open: weekdays 9am–noon; tel. 4 69 51.

Municipal lost property office

Markets (Mercati)

Porta Portese (inside streets off Viale Trastevere).
Every Sunday morning.

Flea-market

Maps and prints are sold in the little market in Piazza Fontanella Borghese.
Every morning except Sunday.

Maps and prints

Market in Via Sannio (near St John Lateran).
Every morning except Sunday.

Clothes

Via Trionfale, Tues. 10.30am–1pm.

Flowers

Food

Wholesale market (Mercati Generali),
Via Ostiense, daily from 10am; open to the public.

The "Campo de' Fioro" is the most interesting and characteristic of the daily markets held in the morning all over Rome; also on the Piazza Vittorio and Via Trionfale.

Medical help

Emergency

Emergency telephone number throughout Italy 1 13.

First aid (Pronto Soccorso Autoambulanze)

Red Cross (Croce Rossa);
tel. 55 10.

Medical Emergency Service (visits)

Pronto Soccorso a domicilio;
tel. 4 75 67 41–4.

Hospitals (Ospedali) with emergency admission

San Camillo, Circonvalazione Gianicolese 87;
tel. 5 87 01.

Rome American Hospital, Via E. Longoni 69;
tel. 2 25 51.

San Giovanni, Via Amba Aradam; tel. 7 70 51.

Santo Spirito, Lungotevere in Sassia (near the Vatican); tel. 6 83 51.

San Giacomo, Via Canova 29 (corner of Via del Corso);
tel. 3 62 61.

San Fillipo, Via Martinotti 20; tel. 3 30 61.

San Eugenio, Vialle Umanesimo (EUR); tel. 5 90 41 (day), 5 01 75 71 (night).

Policlinico Umberto I, Vialle del Policlinico (University City);
tel. 4 46 14 81.

Policlinico A. Gemelli, Largo Gemelli 8; tel. 3 01 51.

Detoxication centres (Centri Antiveleni)

Policlinico Umberto I; tel. 49 06 63.

Policlinico A. Gemelli; tel. 3 05 43 43.

Children's clinic

Ospedale del Bambin Gesù, Piazza S. Onofrio 4; tel. 6 85 91.

Medical insurance

As citizens of a country in the EU British visitors have a right to free medical attention while they are in Italy, providing that they have obtained form E111 before leaving home. In emergency, application should be made to the Unità Sanitaria Locale (e.g. Via Ariosto 3; tel. 7 73 01).

Motoring

Note

Rome inner city is sometimes closed to private cars in the morning and afternoon for four and 3½ hours respectively (see local press for details).
The general traffic regulations in Italy differ from those in other European countries. Traffic signs are the normal international ones.

The road system

The main types of road are:
Motorways (*autostrade*), numbered A . . . Tolls are payable.
State highways (*strade statali*), numbered SS . . . Many of them have names (Via Aurelia, Via Emilia, etc.), which are often better known than their numbers.
Provincial highways (*strade di grande comunicazione*), which have no numbers.
Secondary roads (*strade secondarie*), for local traffic.

Within built-up areas the speed limit is 50km p.h. (31 m.p.h.).

Speed limits

Outside built-up areas the limit on ordinary roads is 90km p.h./56 m.p.h. for cars and 80km p.h./50 m.p.h. for cars with trailers.

On motorways, the speed limit for cars with cylinder capacity over 1100 cc is 130km p.h./81 m.p.h. and 100km p.h./62 m.p.h. for cars with trailers. The speed limit for cars under 1100 cc is 110km p.h./68 m.p.h.

Motorcyclists over 21 can ride machines of more than 350 cc. Motorcycles of less than 150 cc and motorcycles and sidecars of less than 250 cc are not allowed on motorways.

Motorcycles

For motorcycles the speed limits vary according to cylinder capacity: on ordinary roads the speed limit for motorcycles up to 99 cc is 80km p.h./50 m.p.h.; and 90km p.h./56 m.p.h. up to 149 cc. The speed limit on motorways is the same as for cars (see above).

The wearing of seat belts is compulsory. Children up to four years of age must travel in a special child's seat.

Seat belts

Traffic on main roads has priority where the road is marked with the priority sign (a square with a corner pointing downwards, coloured white with a red border or yellow with a black and white border).

Priority

At roundabouts traffic on the right has priority.

On mountain roads traffic going up has priority. Vehicles on rails (trams, etc.) always have priority.

Any change of lane (for overtaking or any other purpose) must be signalled with the direction indicator, as must an intention to stop by the roadside.

Change of lane

Outside built-up areas the horn must be sounded before overtaking. It must also be sounded before intersections, side roads, blind bends and other hazards. After dark flashing headlights should be used for the same purpose.

Overtaking

In towns the use of the horn is frequently prohibited, either by an appropriate road sign (a horn with a stroke through it) or by the legend "Zona di silenzio".

Prohibition on use of horn

Dipped headlights are compulsory when passing through tunnels and galleries.

Lights

In the case of a breakdown on the motorway, it is at present prohibited to have cars towed away by unauthorised (i.e. private) vehicles and a fine will be imposed. This rule does not apply to ordinary roads.

Towing

Pedestrians have absolute priority on zebra crossings.

Zebra crossings

The directions of the traffic police (*polizia stradale*) should be exactly complied with. Fines for traffic offences are high.

Traffic police

There are heavy penalties for driving under the influence of drink.

Drink and driving

In case of accident make sure that you have all the necessary particulars and supporting evidence (statements by witnesses, sketches, photographs, etc.). If the accident involves personal injury it must be reported to the police. You should notify your own insurance company as soon as possible, and if you are responsible or partly responsible for the accident you should also inform the Italian insurance company or bureau whose address is given on your green card. This agency will give advice and supply the name of a lawyer should the foreign driver be subject to penal proceedings. If your car is a total write-off the Italian customs authorities must be informed at once, since otherwise you might be required to pay the full import duty on the vehicle.

Accidents

Museums

Petrol coupons	In Italy normal fuel prices (apart from diesel) are considerably above the European average. Tourists are issued with booklets containing petrol coupons and coupons for paying Italian motorway tolls at a reduced price. There are four booklets for the North, South, South and Islands and Central Italy. The booklets are valid for two years and unused coupons may be cashed in for about 90% of the face value. The holder of such a booklet has the right to free assistance by the ACI and free provision of a replacement vehicle. Further information can be obtained from the motoring organisations and from ENIT (see Information).
Automobile clubs	Automobile Club d'Italia (ACI), Via Marsala 8; tel. 4 95 75 67. Automobile Club di Roma (ACR), Via Cristoforo Colombo 261; tel. 5 12 38 92. For information about weather, road conditions, etc., tel. 44 77. Touring Club Italiano (TCI), Via Ovidio 7A; tel. 6 87 44 32.
Breakdown assistance	Tel. 1 16.
Puncture repair	Look for the sign "Riparazione gomme".
Repair garages	Look for "Officina".
Police and ambulance	Anywhere in Italy, dial 1 13.

Museums

Note	Since the opening times of Italian museums frequently alter, it is not possible to be sure that the times given below are in all cases correct. To avoid disappointment visitors should enquire as to the current opening times before going to any particular museum. The University museums are not all very easy to get in. You should write well in advance and may need documentation to prove you have a valid reason for wanting to see them.
Museums	Casa di Keats e Shelley (House of Keats and Shelley), Piazza di Spagna 26. Open: Mon.–Fri. 9am–1pm and 3–6pm. Exhibits and portraits of the English poets, Keats and Shelley, and also of Byron and Hunt. City Antiquarium Via Parco del Celio 22. Open: Tues.–Sat. 10am–4pm; Sun. 10am–1pm. Local archaeological finds. Gabinetto Nazionale delle Stampe (National Print Cabinet), See A to Z, Villa Farnese. Musei Capitolini (Capitoline Museums), See A to Z, Museo Capitolino. See A to Z, Palazzo dei Conservatori. Musei Vaticani (Vatican Museums), See A to Z, Vatican – Vatican Museums.

Porphyry sarcophagus in Museo Pio Clementino in the Vatican

Museo Antiquarium Forense e Palatino
(Forum and Palatine Museums),
Piazza Santa Maria Nuova 53.
Open: Apr.–Oct. Mon.–Sat. 9am–7pm; from Nov.–Mar. daily
    9am–3pm; Sun. 9am–2pm.
Finds from the Roman Forum and from the Palatine. The Palatine Museum
is closed for restoration.

Museo Archeologico di Ostia
(Archaeological Museum of Ostia),
Ostia Antica.
Open: daily 9.30am–1 hour before sunset.

Museo Barracco,
See A to Z.

Museo Burcado,
Via del Sudario 44.
Closed at present (1995)
Theatrical collection.

Museo Capitolino
(Capitoline Museum),
See A to Z, Museo Capitolino.
See A to Z, Palazzo dei Conservatori.

Museo Centrale del Risorgimento,
See A to Z, Monumento Nationale a Vittorio Emanuele II.

Museo dei Gessi dell'Arte Classica
(Museum of Plaster Casts),
Città Universitaria, Facolta di Lettere.
Open: by appointment, tel. 4 99 33 13.
Plaster casts of archaic and Roman sculpture.

Museo del Folclore e dei Poeti Romaneschi
(Museum of Roman Folklore and Poetry),
in the former Sant Egido monastery,
Piazza Sant Egido 1/b.
Open: Tues.–Sun. 9am–1.30pm; also Tues. and Thurs. 5–7.30pm.
Sculptures, sketches of Roman life, memorabilia of Roman poets.

Museo del Istituto Zoologico
(Museum of the Zoological Institute),
Viale dell'Università 32.
Open: by appointment, tel. 4 95 82 54.

Museo della Civiltà Romana
(Museum of Roman Culture),
See A to Z.

Museo dell'Alto Medioevo
(Museum of the Early Medieval Period),
Viale Lincoln 1 (EUR).
Open: Sat. and Sun. 9am–2pm.
Art and culture of late antiquity and the early Middle Ages.

Museo delle Anime del Purgatorio
(Museum of the Souls of the Dead),
Lungotevere Prati 12 ; apply at the sacristy of the Church of Sacro Cuore del
    Suffragio.
Open: daily 6.30am–12.30pm and 5–6.30pm.
Visitors are shown so-called evidence of the presence of the dead.

Museo delle Cere
(Wax Museum),
Piazza Venezia (beside SS. Apostoli 67).
Open: daily 9am–8pm.

Museo delle Mure Romane
(Museum of the Roman City Walls),
Via di Porta San Sebastiano 18.
Open: Tues.–Sat. 9am–1.30pm; also Tues., Thurs. and Sat.
    4–7 pm; Sun. and public holidays 9am–1pm.
Displays illustrating the different building phases.

Museo del Presepio Tipologico Internazionale
(Museum of Cribs),
Via Tor de' Conti 31/a.
Open: Oct.–May: Sat. 6–8pm; 24 Dec.–15 Jan.; Sat.
    4–8pm; Sun. and public holidays 10am–1pm, 3–8pm.

Museo di Etruscologia
(Museum of Etruscan and Italian Antiquity),
Città Universitaria, Facoltà di Lettere.
Can only be visited by special permission.

Museo di Palazzo Venezia. See A to Z.

Museo di Roma,
See A to Z, Museo di Roma in the Palazzo Braschi.

Museo delle Cere (House of Wax) in Piazza Venezia

Museo di Storia della Medecina
(Museum of the History of Medicine),
Viale dell'Università 34A.
Open: by appointment, tel. 49 91 82 03.

Museo e Galleria Borghese. See A to Z, Villa Borghese.

Museo Geologico
(Geological Museum),
Città Universitaria, Istituto di Geologia.
Open: by appointment, tel. 4 99 12 90.

Museo Israelita
(Permanent exhibition of the Jewish community in Rome), Lungotevere
    Cenci (synagogue).
Open: Sun.–Fri. 9.30am–1.30pm and 3–4pm; closed on Jewish holidays.

Museo Mario Praz
Palazzo Primoli, Via Zanardelli 1.
Open: Tues.–Sun. 9am–1pm and 2.30–6.30pm; Mon. 2.30–6.30pm.
The eclectic collections of art and objets d'art of the professor and aesthete
    who died in 1982.

Museo Mineralogico
(Museum of Mineralogy),
Città Universitaria, Facoltà di Scienze Matematiche,
Fisiche e Naturali.
Open: by appointment, tel. 49 91 21 03.
Rocks, marble slabs and fossils.

Museo Napoleonico
(Napoleonic Museum),
Via Zanardelli.
Open: Tues.–Sat. 9am–1.30pm, Thurs. and Sat. also 5–7.30pm; Sun. 9am–12.30pm.
Relics of Napoleon (who was never in Rome!) and of his sisters, Caroline and Paolina.

Museo Nazionale Castel Sant'Angelo. See A to Z.

Museo Nazionale d'Arte Orientale (Museum of Oriental Art).
See A to Z.

Museo Nazionale degli Strumenti Musicali
(Museum of Musical Instruments),
Piazza Santa Croce in Gerusalemme 9/a.
Open: Tues.–Sun. 9am–1.30pm.
Some 3000 exhibits from all over the world illustrating the history of music from antiquity to the end of the 18th c.; the Barberini harp (17th c.) is famous.

Museo Nazionale delle Arti e Tradizione Popolari
(Museum of Folk Arts and Traditions),
See A to Z.

Museo Nazionale della Paste Alimentare (Pasta Museum)
Piazza Skanderbeg
Open: Mon.–Fri. 9.30am–12.30pm and 4–7pm; Sat. 9.30am–12.30pm.
Types of pasta, equipment for producing pasta.

Museo Nazionale Etrusco di Villa Giulia
(Etruscan National Museum in the Villa Giulia),
See A to Z.

Museo Nazionale Romano o delle Terme
(Baths Museum),
See A to Z, Terme di Diocleziano.

Museo Preistoria e Protostoria del Lazio
(Museum of Pre-history and Early History of Latium),
Viale Lincoln 1 (EUR).
Open: Tues.–Sat. 9am–2pm; Sun. 9am–1pm.

Museo Preistorico ed Etnografico "Luigi Pigorini"
(Prehistoric and Ethnographic Museum),
Viale Lincoln 1 (EUR).
Open: Mon.–Sat. 9am–2pm; Sun. and holidays 9am–1pm.
Closed first and third Mon. of each month.

Museo Sacrario delle Bandiere delle Marina
(Flag Museum),
See A to Z, Monumento Nazionale a Vittorio Emanuele II.

Museo Storico dei Bersaglieri
(Historical Museum of the Bersaglieri),
Piazza di Porta Pia.
Open: Tues. and Thurs. 9am–1.30pm.
Exhibits include documents from the War of Liberation, from the African campaign and from the First World War.

Museo Storico dei Carabinieri
(Historical Museum of the Carabinieri),
Piazza Risorgimento 20.
Open: Tues.–Sun. 9am–noon.
Documents and equipment from the wars in which the Carabinieri have taken part; also exhibits which are associated with the corps.

Museo Storico dei Granatieri di Sardegna
(Historical Museum of the Grenadiers of Sardinia),
Piazza Santa Croce in Gerusalemme 7.
Open: Thurs. and Sun. 10am–noon.
Exhibits of the period between 1659 and 1945.

Museo Storico della Lotta di Liberazione di Roma
(Historical Museum of the War of Liberation),
Via Tasso 145.
Open: Tues., Thurs. and Fri. 4–7pm; Sat. and Sun. 9.30am–12.30pm.
(closed in August; admission free).
Documents concerning the persecution of the Jews and Roman resistance in the Second World War.

Museo Storico di Guardia Finanzia
(Historical Museum of the Finance Police),
Piazza Armelini 20.
Open: daily 9am–1pm.

Museo Storico Nazionale dell'Arte Sanitaria
(Historical Museum of Medical Treatment),
Lungotevere in Sassia 3.
Closed for restoration (1995)
Exhibits concerning barbers, surgeons and quack doctors from ancient times to the present day.

Museo Torlonia. See A to Z.

See entry   Galleries

Music

In addition to performances in the Opera House there are open-air presentations in summer.   Opera and ballet

Tickets for the Opera can be bought at the Opera box office, Piazza Beniamino Gigli (open: 10am–1pm and 5–7pm).

Teatro dell'Opera,
Piazza Beniamino Gigli; tel. 36 36 41, 46 17 55.
Season from Dec. to June.

Concerts are given throughout the year in concert halls and churches.   Concerts
Programme details can be found in the daily papers and in "La Settimana in Roma" (*The Week in Rome*), which is published in several languages.

Accademia Filarmonica Romana,   Important Concert
Teatro Olimpico, Piazza gentile da Fabriano 17; tel. 3 20 17 52.   Halls

Night life

Auditoria del Foro Italico,
Piazza L. de Bosis 28.

Auditorio di Santa Cecilia,
Via della Conciliazione 4; tel. 68 80 10 44.

Sala dell'Accademia di Santa Cecilia,
Via dei Greci 8; tel. 3 61 10 64.

Sala Baldini,
Piazza Campi Felli 9; tel. 4 81 48 00.

Sala Pio X,
Via Piemonte 31; tel. 4 74 03 38.

Oratorio del Gonfalone,
Via del Gonfalone 32/a; tel. 67 59 52.

Aula Magna,
Universita La Saprenza,
Piazza Aldo Moro 5; tel. 3 61 00 51.

Church Concerts
San Marcello al Corso,
Piazza San Marcello 5.

San Luigi dei Francesi in Campo Marzio,
Piazza San Luigi dei Francesi 5.

Basilica di San Marco (in the Palazzo Venezia),
Piazza Venezia.

Sant Anselmo all'Aventino,
Piazza Cavalieri di Malta 5
(daily at 7.30pm, Gregorian Chorale at Vespers and every Sunday at the 9.30am Mass).

Night life

Clubs
B-side, Via dei Funari 21.
Café de Paris, Via Veneto 90.
Caffe-Caruso, Via di Monte Testaccio 36.
Club 84, Via Emilia 84.
Heaven, Via di Porta Ardeatina.
Il Castello, Via di Porta Castello 44.
Jackie O', Via Boncompagni 11.
New Open Gate, Via S. Nicola da Tolentino 4.
Radio Londra, Via di Monte Testaccio 67.
Tartarughino, Via della Scrofa 2.

Discothèques
Alten, Via Velletri.
Bella Blu, Via Luciani 21.
Big Mama, Vicolo San Francesco a Ripa 18.
Black Out, Via Saturnia 18.
Carrousel, Via Emilia 55.
Gilda, Via Mario de'Fiori 97.
Il Veleno, Via Sardegna 27.
Le Skelle, Via C. Beccania 22.
Marcello Testa, Via Tirso 32.
Notorius, Via S. Nicola da Tolentino 22.
Piper, Via Tagliamento 9.

Alpheus, Via del Commercio 36.
El Trauco, Via Fonte dell'Olio 5.
Folk Studio, Frangipane 42.
Jazz Caffè, Via Zanardelli 12.
Saint Louis City, Via del Cardello 13a.
Yes Brazil, Via San Francesco a Ripa 103.

Bar della Pace, Piazza della Pace.   Bars
Blue Bar, Via dei Soldati 25.
Derby, Via Collina 38.
Harry's Bar, Via Vittorio Veneto 150.
Hemingways, Piazza delle Coppelle 10.
Il Tartarughino, Via della Scrofa 2.
Limelight, Via dei Maroniti 29.

Opening times

See entry.   Banks

See entry.   Chemists

The larger churches are usually open until noon and for the most part also   Churches
from 4 or 5pm until dusk; some of the major churches are open all day. It is
possible to see the interior of a church during a service if care is taken to
avoid disturbing the worshippers. Visitors should always be suitably
dressed, avoiding sleeveless dresses or blouses, miniskirts, shorts, short-
sleeved shirts, etc. If inappropriately dressed they may be refused admit-
tance; cover-up garments can be hired at the entrance to St Peter's.
   During Lent almost all altarpieces are covered over and not shown to
visitors.

Mon.–Sat. 9am–1pm and 4–8pm; some closed Sat. afternoon in summer.   Shops
Most shops closed Mon. morning. Some shops in centre open continuously from 9.30am–7pm.

Summer: Mon.–Sat. 7.30 or 8am–1.30 or 2pm and 5–7.30 or 8pm; closed   Food shops
   Sat. afternoon (July to September).
Winter: Mon.–Sat. 7.30 or 8am–1.30 or 2pm and 4–7.30 or 8pm; closed
   Thurs. afternoon.

The opening times of museums are given under the relevant heading in the   Museums
A to Z section or in the Practical Information section under "Museums". It
should be noted that most museums are closed on one day a week and also
on public holidays. Since the opening times are frequently changed and
there are often unforeseen closures as a result of staff shortages, strikes,
renovation, etc., it is advisable, before visiting a museum, to check that it
will be open. At the moment there is a move to have continuous opening of
all museums until 7pm. Plans are afoot for this in the main museums in
Rome over the winter 1995–96, but it may not happen.

Petrol stations are usually closed between 12.30 and 3.30pm and from 8pm   Petrol stations
(in winter usually 7pm).

See entry Postal services   Post offices

Parks and Open Spaces

Villa Ada.
Extensive park on the Via Salaria N of the city centre.

Flamingo enclosure in the Giardino Zoologico

Villa Borghese and Giardino Zoologico.
See A to Z, Villa Borghese.

Villa Celimontana.
Between the Coliseum and the Baths of Caracalla.

Villa Corsini, Botanical Garden,
Largo Cristina di Svezia 24.
Open: Mon.–Sat. 9am–6.30pm (in winter 5.30pm).

Villa Dona Pamphili.
See A to Z

Villa Glori.
Small park in a bend of the Tiber, N of city centre.

Villa Sciarra.
Picturesque park in the Trastevere district, with the 18th c. "Teatro delle Stagioni".

Villa Torlonia. See A to Z.

Passeggiata del Gianicolo.
See A to Z.

Pets

A certificate of health, recording inoculations (particularly against rabies) must be presented when bringing in a dog or cat and when taking it out of the country.

Dogs must wear muzzles and be kept on a leash.
In view of their own quarantine regulations, however, English-speaking visitors are unlikely to want to take their pets to Rome with them.

Police (Polizia)

Questura, Office for foreign tourists,
Via San Vitale 15; tel. 46 86.

Police H.Q.

Polizia Stradale,
Via Portuense 185; tel. 5 57 79 05.
(Accidents)

Traffic Police

Vigili Urbani,
Via della Consolazione 4; tel. 6 76 91.

Municipal Police

Viale Romania 45; tel. 8 09 81 (H.Q.); tel. 112 (emergency).

Carabinieri

Tel. 113.

Accident

Postal services

Letters within Italy and to EU countries 750 lire; postcards 650 lire.

Postal rates

Stamps can be bought at post offices, at tobacconists (indicated by a large T above the door) and from stamp machines.

Stamps

The Vatican State has its own stamps and postmarks. There are Vatican City post offices in the colonnades in St Peter's Square, as well as a travelling post office, at which stamps can be bought, in the centre of the square.

Vatican City

Italian Post box

Vatican Post box

Head post office	Piazza San Silvestro. Open: Mon.–Fri. 8.30am–9pm, Sat. 8.30am–noon for Giro transactions and telegraphic money orders. Mon.–Fri. 8.30am–2.30pm, Sat. 8.30am–noon for postal or money orders and cheques. Open day and night for telegrams.
Post offices	Other post offices are open 8.15am–1.50pm, Sat. 8.30–11.50am.

Public holidays

1 January (New Year's Day); 6 January (Epiphany); 25 April (Liberation Day, 1945).

Easter Monday; 1 May (Labour Day); Ascension.

2 June (proclamation of the Republic: celebrations on following Saturday).

15 August (Assumption: a family celebration, the high point of the Italian summer holiday migration).

1 November (All Saints); 4 November (Day of National Unity: celebrations on following Saturday); 8 December (Immaculate Conception).

25 and 26 December (Christmas).

Good Friday, Whit Monday, Corpus Christi, Christmas Eve and New Year's Eve are not public holidays.

Radio

Programmes in English	Information on overseas radio transmissions may be obtained from BBC External Services, P.O. Box 76, Bush House, London WC2B 4PH.

Rail services

Ferrovie dello Stato (FS)	The Italian railway system has a total length of 16,000km (10,000 miles). Most of it is run by the Italian State Railways (Ferrovie dello Stato, FS). (Central Office, Via Marsala 53; tel. 47 03 01.) Information about rail services can be obtained from the Italian State Tourist Office or from Italian State Railways offices abroad.
United Kingdom	50 Conduit Street, London W1; tel. (0171) 434 3844.
United States of America	765 Route 83, Suite 105, Chicago, Ill. 5670 Wilshire Boulevard, Los Angeles, Cal. 668 Fifth Avenue, New York, NY.
Canada	2055 Peel Street, Suite 102, Montreal. 111 Richmond Street West, Suite 419 Toronto.
In Italy	Stazione Termini in Rome; tel. 47 75; and in towns throughout the country.
Tickets	Various special tickets are available, e.g. the tourist ticket which allows the holder unlimited travel over the whole network within a specified period of availability (biglietto turistico di libera circolazione). A network booklet carries a reduction of 10% and allows up to 3000km travel on all ordinary FS trains; surcharges are payable on special trains. Accompanied children up to five years of age not taking a seat may travel free of charge; children up to the age of thirteen pay half fare. The Inter-Rail

tickets (for young people up to the age of 26); the Rail-Europe-Family tickets (for families of at least three) and the Rail-Europe-Senior tickets (with a Senior Citizens' card) entitle the holders to fare reductions in Italy.

Railway stations

The main station: international services and services to all parts to Italy. Information: tel. 47 75.
Lost property office: 47 30. – 66 82.

Stazione Termini

Trains to N and S Italy, motorail.
Tel. 4 95 66 26.

Stazione Tiburtina

Trains to Genoa and Pisa.

Stazione Trastevere

Trains to Viterbo.

Stazione Roma-Nord

Trains to Pescara.

Stazione Prenestina

Trains to Grosseto and Viterbo.

Stazione Tuscolana

Local services.

Stazione San Pietro

Trains to Viterbo and Ostia Lido.

Stazione Porta S. Paolo

Restaurants (selection, not including those in hotels)

Every establishment providing a meal must supply the customer with a receipted bill, which is to be shown on demand to a tax inspector in the vicinity of the restaurant. Failure to produce the bill renders the customer liable to a fine.

Note

In principle visitors should beware of being cheated. This is often tried on with fish dishes. If you are surprised that the amount charged does not tally with the bill of fare, you are often told that you have been served with a particularly large lobster or whatever! If this is not what you had ordered you should not hesitate to complain and if necessary send for the police.

Because à la carte prices tend to be high, the "menu turistico" (usually very good) is to be recommended. In addition to the expensive "ristorante" there are more modest places, called "tavola calda", "rosticceria" or "fiaschetteria", which serve meals of excellent quality. There are many restaurants in Trastevere which offer good value.

Alfredo alla Scrofa, Via della Scrofa 104.
Chez Albert, Vicolo della Vaccarella II (nouvelle cuisine).
El Toulà di Roma, Via della Lupa 29.
Er Faciolaro, Via dei Pastini 13 and 123 (original Roman cuisine, beans a speciality).
Fortunato al Pantheon, Via del Pantheon 55 (frequented mainly by local patrons).
Hostaria dell'Orso, Via dei Soldati 25 (by the Tiber).
Il Bistecchiere, Via dei Gigli d'Oro 2/3/4 (open until 2.30am).
Il Convivio, Via del Orso 44 (modern creative).
La Maiella, Piazza Teatro Pompeo 18.

Restaurants in the triangle Piazza Navona–Piazza Colonna–Mausoleo di Augusto

Restaurants

Café Greco

Trattoria in Via Veneto

Cocktail time in Harry's Bar

Papa Giovanni, Via dei Sediari 4 (near Piazza Navona).
Passetto, Via Zanardelli 14.
La Rosetta, Via della Rosetta 8 (fish and seafood).

★Piperno, Monte dei Cenci 9 (Jewish Roman cuisine).
Al Pompiere, Via de Calderari 38 (Jewish Roman cuisine).
Sora Lela, Via Ponte Quattro Capi 16 (busy, fashionable restaurant on Tiber Island).
Trattoria Evangelista, Via delle Zoccolette 11 (near the Ponte Garibaldi).
Vecchia Roma, Piazza Campitelli 18 (Roman cuisine).

West of Piazza Venezia

Mario's Hostaria, Piazza del Grillo 9 (good Roman cuisine, excellent fish dishes).
Gemma alla Lupa, Via Marghera 39 (typical Roman cuisine, near Stazione Termini).

East of Piazza Venezia

Camponeschi, Piazza Farnese 50 (Italian cuisine).
Il Drappo, Vicolo del Malpasso 9 (Sardinian in peaceful surroundings).
Pier Luigi, Piazza di Ricci (busy, bustling trattoria).

Near Campo dei Fiori

Casina Valadier, Pincio (rendezvous of the famous; good view).
Dal Bolognese, Piazza del Popolo 1–2.
Hassler Villa Medici, Piazza Trinità dei Monti 6 (gastronomic delight with an unforgettable panorama of Rome).
Nino a Via Borgogna, Via Borgognona 11 (well known for Etruscan cuisine).
Ranieri, Via Mario de Fiori 26.

Between Piazza di Spagna and Piazza del Popolo

Andrea, Via Sardegna 26.
Cappricio, Via Liguria 38.
Cesarina, Via Piemonte 109 (mainly N Italian dishes, selected wines).
Eden, Via Ludovisi 49.
La Bruschetta, Via Ancona 35 (near Piazza Pia, quite reasonable).
Relais Le Jardin dell'Hotel Lord Byron, Via Guiseppe de Notaris 5 (elegant interior; Roman and international specialities).
Taverna Flavia, Via Flavia 9/11.
Tullio, Via S. Nicola di Tolentino 26.

Restaurants near Via Veneto

★Alberto Ciarla, Piazza San Cosimato 40 (striking red/black interior, the best Roman fish dishes).
Antica Pesa, Via Garibaldi 18 (good starter buffet, pretty garden).
Capanna del Negro, Via Portuense 45 (Roman cuisine, terrace overlooking the Tiber).
Corsetti, Piazza San Cosimato.
Da Gino in Trastevere, Via della Lungaretta 85.
Da Lucia, Vicolo del Mattonata 2b (popular traditional trattoria).
Galeassi, Piazza Santa Maria in Trastevere 3/3A.
Otello, Piazza San Egidio (excellent pasta dishes).
Ponte Sisto, Via di Ponte Sisto (Piazza Trilussa) (trattoria and pizzeria).
Romolo, Via Porta Settimiani 8 (Roman cuisine, pretty little garden).
Sabatini, Piazza Santa Maria in Trastevere 13.
Taverna Trilussa, Via del Politeama 23 (rendezvous of artists, typical Roman cuisine).

Restaurants in Trastevere

Checchino dal 1887, Via Monte Testaccio 30 (typical Roman cuisine)

Monte Testaccio

Antico Caffè Greco, Via Condotti 86 (opened in the 18th c, it was the meeting-place of many great composers, literary and artistic figures, including Casanova, Baudelaire, Goethe, Schopenhauer, Franz Liszt, Mendelssohn, Wagner and Nietzsche).
Babington, Piazza di Spagna 23 (British-style tea-room).
Bar Marzio, Piazza Santa Maria in Trastevere (wonderful place to watch the world go by).

Cafés, Ice-Cream Parlours, Tea-rooms, bars

Bar Sant'Eustachio, Piazza Sant'Eustachio (possibly the best coffee in Rome).
Caffè Farnese, Via del Baullari 106 (opposite the French embassy).
Canova, Piazza del Popolo 16, 17 (popular meeting-place of artists).
Casina Valadier, Pincio (beautiful, if expensive, view of the city).
Ge. Co., Via dei Baullari 106 (pleasant rendezvous of the intelligentsia, around the corner from the Campo dei Fiori).
Giolitti, Via Uffici del Vicario 14 (Ice-cream parlour in the style of the turn of the century; open to 2am).
Giovanne Fassi, Palazzo del Freddo, Via Principe Eugenio 65/67.
Harry's Bar, Via Vittorio Veneto 150 ("Harry's" famous cocktails).
Rosati, Piaza del Popolo 5 (traditional artists' café).
Tazza d'Oro, Via degli Orfani 86 (near the Pantheon).
Tre Scalini, Piazza Navona 30.

Meals   See Food and Drink.

Shopping

After Paris, Rome is the fashion centre of the world. Every taste is catered for in the shops between the Piazza di Spagna and Via del Corso, in Via Frattina and Via Condotti, whether it be in silk or leather, whether elegant or eccentric, whether shoes or jewellery. One thing, however, all these establishments have in common; if you intend to buy and not merely to look round, you must have ample resources.

Antiques   See entry.

Books   Corner Bookshop, Via de Moro 48.
Economy Book Center (English spoken), Via Torino 136.
Feltrinelle, Largo Argentina.
Herder, Piazza Montecitorio 117.

Ladies' Wear   Degli Effeti, Piazza Capranica 93.
Discount dell'Alta Moda, Via di Gesù e Maria 16.
Emporio Armani, Via del Babuino 140.
Fendi (furs), Via Borgognona 36–39.
Gianfranco Fevrè, Via Borgognona 42c.
Laura Biagiotti, Via Borgognona 43–44.
Luna e l'altra, Via del Governo Vecchio 105 (near Piazza Navona).
Max and Co, Via Nazionale 56.
Mila Schön, Via Condotti 64.
Mission, Piazza di Spagna 77b.
Sorelle Fontana, Via di San Sabastianello 6.
Valentino, Via Gregoriana 24, Via Bocca di Leone 15.

Men's Wear   Babilonia, Via del Corso 185.
Battistoni, Via Condotti 61a.
Cenci, Via Campio Marzo 1–7.
Enzo Ceci, Via della Vite 52.
Testa, Via Frattina 104.
Valentino Uomo, Via Condotti /corner of Via Mario de Fiori.
Versace, Via Borgognona 29.

Departmental Stores/ Supermarkets   Coin, Piazzale Appio 17.
La Rinascente, Piazza Colonna, Piazza Fiume.
Standa, branches in the whole of the city.
Upim, branches in the whole of the city.

Kitchen equipment   Leone Limentani, Via del Portico d'Ottavia 47/48.

Exclusive leather goods in Via Condotti

Elegant Belmonte, Via Emilia 36.
Fendi, Via Borgognona 36–39.
Gucci, Via Condotti 8.
Mandarina Duck, Via di Propaganda 1.
Sirni, Via della Stelletta 33.
Skin, Via dei due Marcelli 59.

Leather goods

See entry.

Markets

Vertecchi, Via della Croce 70.

Paper goods

Discoteca Frattina, Via Frattina 50.

Records

Bozard, Via Bocca di Leone 4.
Buccellati Federico, Via Condotti 31.
Bulgari, Via Condotti 10.
Deletré, Via Fontanella Borghese.
Massoni, Largo C: Goldoni 48.
Petochi, Piazza di Spagna 23.
Tempi Moderni, Via del Governo Vecchio 108.

Jewellery

Campanile, Via Condotti 58.
Cervone, Via del Corso 99.
Fausto Santini, Via Frattina 122.
Raphael Salato, Via Veneto 149.
Salvatore Ferragamo, Via Condotti 73.
Magli, Varese, Zabato, these shops have their branches in the principal
    shopping streets in the city.

Shoes

In addition to the above there are shoe shops on almost every corner and in
almost every shopping street where attractive and reasonably priced shoes
can be bought.

Sightseeing Programme

Toys/Souvenirs	Al Sogno, Piazza Navona 53. Berté, Piazza Navona 107–111.
Fabrics	Bises Novità, Via dei due Marcelli 80. Cesain, Via del Babuino 16.
Wine	Enoteca al Parlamento, Via dei Prefetti 15.

Sightseeing Programme

Note	The recommendations below are intended to help the visitor whose first visit it is to Rome and who has only a short time at his disposal, to plan his stay in the city in the most rewarding way. The names in italic print refer to the A to Z section.
	The visitor who only has a few hours in Rome and nevertheless wishes to see the most important things is advised to join an organised bus tour (see Practical Information, Sightseeing tours).
One day	In order to get a general impression of the historic and cultural influences which have left their mark on Rome a walk through the city from the centre of the ancient town to that of Christian Rome is recommended. The starting point is the Colosseum (*Colosseo*) from where it is only a few steps to the Roman Forum (*Foro Romano*), the most impressive remains of which can be seen on a short walk. Back on the *Via dei Fori Imperiali* we pass the mighty national monument to Victor Emmanuel II (*Monumento Nazionale a Vittorio Emanuele II*) and reach the *Piazza Venezia* which is thronged with traffic; crossing this square can be an adventure in itself! A charming detour leads via the Via del Corso and the Via di Muratte to Rome's largest and most famous fountain, the *Fontana di Trevi*, into which, so it is believed, a coin should be thrown in order to ensure a return to Rome. After crossing the Via del Corso, the more modern and up-to-date face of Rome confronts the visitor in the form of the Italian Parliament building (*Camera dei Deputati*) in the Piazza di Montecitorio. To the south in the Piazza della Rotonda the *Pantheon* attracts attention. From here we go along minor roads with many corners, across the extensive *Piazza Navona* with its magnificent fountains and at length we arrive at the church which is best crossed by the *Ponte Sant'Angelo* to Castel Sant'Angelo. By turning to the left we have a magnificent view of St Peter's (*Vatican – San Pietro in Vaticano*) and the broad open space of St Peter's Square (*Vatican – Piazza San Pietro*). The wide Via della Consiliazione leads directly into the smallest state in the world, the Vatican. A day in Rome can be ended in a very pleasant way by a stroll through lively *Trastevere* which – at least in the opinion of people who live there – is the oldest district of Rome. In the lanes and streets around the church of *Santa Maria in Trastevere* there are many trattorie where you can sample Roman cuisine. The visitor who does not want to do quite so much can leave out the detour to the Fontana di Trevi and to the Parliament building and be content to spend a little more time on the other sights. Otherwise there are many cafés and "bars" for refreshment. A comfortable way of getting to know the city is to take a ride in a horse-drawn carriage (See Practical Information, Sightseeing tours).
Two days	With two days at his disposal in Rome the visitor should try to extend his first fleeting impressions. A highlight, if it has not been covered on the first day, is a visit to St Peter's Basilica (*Vatican – San Pietro in Vaticano*), and if possible also to the Vatican Museums (*Vatican – Musei Vaticani*). It is, of course, personal preferences (and staying power!) which determine how to choose from the many sections, of which the Stanze di Raffaello and the Sistine Chapel (Cappella Sistine) are of prime interest.

Piazza Navona (Fontana del Nettuno)

The visitor who is more interested in worldly things should perhaps spend the afternoon by strolling through the streets around the *Piazza di Spagna* and the *Via Veneto* with their (expensive!) fashion and shoe shops. The hurly burly of the shopping quarter can be avoided by a visit to the park of the *Villa Borghese* behind the Spanish Steps.

In addition to getting to know the most important sights of Rome, a longer stay will give the visitor the chance to make an excursion into the immediate surroundings of the city. Worth-while places to visit, not only from the archaeological but also the scenic point of view, are the *Via Appia Antica*, where can be seen a short stretch of the old Roman road, graves of Roman families and, in the *Catacombe di San Callisto*, one of the largest catacombs; the *Tivoli* with its park and the 16th c. buildings of the Villa d'Este and the Villa Adriana, which dates from Imperial days; *Ostia Antica*, the port of ancient Rome, or the mountainous and lake scenery of the Alban Hills (*Colli Albani*).

Three days

Sightseeing tours

The best way to find out about city tours is to enquire at the Rome Tourist Office EPT (see Information) or at one of the major operators:

City tours

American Express.
Piazza di Spagna 38; tel. 6 76 41.

CIT (Compagnia Italiano Turismo),
Piazza della Republica 64; tel 4 87 00 27.

Univers
Via Marsala 20; tel. 4 45 02 90.

Horse-drawn carriages in Piazza San Pietro

A.T.A.C. (municipal transport authority),
Information office at the Piazza dei Cinquecento, opposite Termini Station;
tel 4 69 51.
Departure point for a bus tour of the city lasting approximately two hours;
in summer daily at 3.30pm, in winter only on Sat. and Sun. at 2.30pm.

On foot

The best way, as well as the quickest, to see the old city is on foot.

**Carrozzelle
(horse-cabs)**

A ride in one of these old-fashioned vehicles, popularly known in Rome as
botticelle ("little barrels"), is a pleasant way of seeing Rome, particularly
recommended for visiting the city's parks, such as the Villa Borghese and
the Janiculum. The journey for up to five people can last from half an hour
up to a whole day. The price should be agreed with the driver before
starting. The question is whether it is better to hire the cab or to pay per
person. They are stationed at the Piazza San Pietro, at the Colosseum, the
Piazza Venezia, the Piazza di Spagna, near the Fontana di Trevi, at the Via
Veneto, the Villa Borghese and the Piazza Navona. A trip lasting an hour
costs about 100,000 lire, after negotiating with the driver!

Authorised guides

For an individual sightseeing tour a guide can be hired through the Sinda-
cato Nazionale Guide Turistiche, Rampa Mignanelli 12; tel. 6 78 98 42.

Art history tours

Art history tours with a guide can be arranged by the following:
Soprintendenza Communale ai Musei e Monumenti, Piazza Caffaeli 3; tel.
67 10 30 69.
Soprintendenza alla Antichità di Roma, Piazza Santa Maria Nova 53; tel.
6 79 01 10.

Stadio dei Marmi of the Foro Italico

Sports facilities

Foro Italico

The large sports complex below Monte Mario, close to the Tiber, was begun for the Fascist Academy of the Farnesina in 1938/39 and finished after the Second World War. It consists of:

Stadio Olimpico (Olympic Stadium)
Football and athletic stadium for 100,000 spectators; this was the venue for the athletic events of the 17th Olympic Games in 1960, of the World Athletic Championships in 1987 and the final of the World Cup on July 8th 1990, for which the stadium was extended. The complex also has tennis courts.

Stadio dei Marmi (Marble Stadium)
The marble stadium was the first sports ground of the Foro Italico; athletic meetings are held in this stadium which accommodates 20,000 spectators.

Stadio del Nuoto (swimming stadium)
This swimming stadium has room for 16,000 spectators; it is not only used for swimming competitions but is also available to private individuals.

Piscina Coperta (covered swimming pool)
The swimming stadium is linked by a stadium to the covered pool; it is decorated with variegated marble and coloured mosaics.

Palazzo dello Sport, in the EUR district
In this gigantic domed building basketball, boxing and tennis matches take place.

Swimming pools

Tre Fontane, in the EUR district
This elaborately laid out sports centre has facilities for hockey, football, rugby, tracks for athletics and rollerskating and a number of sports halls.

Palazzetto dello Sport, near the Piazza Apollodoro
Small sports centre for boxing, roller-skating, wrestling, tennis and fencing.

Stadio Flaminio, on the Viale Tiziano close to the Palazzetto dello Sport
In addition to the football stadium, which holds 45,000 spectators, there is a covered pool, gymnasiums and a fencing hall.

Acqua Acetosa, at the foot of Monte Antenne
Swimming pool, football pitch, pitches for polo and rugby.

Riding	Capannelle Racecourse, 12km on the Via Appia Nuova Flat racing and steeplechasing have taken place here for almost a century.
	Società Ippica Romana (Riding Association of Rome), Via Monti della Farnesina 1.
	Centro Ippico Aurelio (Aurelio Riding Centre), 15km on Via Aurelio.
Golf	Circolo del Golf di Roma, Via Appia Nuova 716/A.
	Olgiata Golf Club, Largo dell'Olgiata 15.
Tennis	See Foro Italico.
Swimming	See Swimming pools.

Swimming pools (Piscine)

Indoor pool	Foro Italico. Open: Nov.–May.
Open-air pools	Stadio del Nuoto, Foro Italico. Open: June–Sept.
	Piscine delle Rose, EUR. Open: June–Sept.
Seaside resorts	The seaside resorts in the neighbourhood of Rome can be reached by the Acotral company's buses.

Taxis

All taxis in Rome are yellow or white. There are plenty of ranks in the inner city.

Fares	When starting a journey be careful to ensure that the meter is switched on and only showing the basic fare. The fare increases every 0·3km.

Supplements are levied for journeys at night (10pm–7am), on Sundays and public holidays, for luggage, for waiting and call-out time, for journeys from the airport in Fiumicino to Rome and from Rome to the airport (which is twice as expensive!). To avoid an unpleasant surprise it is best to establish the fare before beginning the journey.

Tel. 38 75, 49 94, 45 17, 35 70.

Beware of private cars masquerading as taxis – they are many times more expensive and there is no insurance.

Telephone

To the United Kingdom: 00 44.
To the United States or Canada: 001

From the United Kingdom: 00 39 6.
From the United States: 011 39 6.
From Canada: 011 39 6.
    In dialling an international call the initial zero of the local dialling code should be omitted.
    International directory enquiries: 176.
    Intercontinental directory enquiries: 1790.

Most bars have public telephones (indicated by a yellow disc above the entrance to the box) operated by tokens (*gettoni*) or 100, 200 and 500 lire coins.
    More convenient are the phone cards available from tobacconists and post offices for 5,000, 10,000 or 15,000 lire. Most public phone boxes take cards.

There are also public telephones in post offices and in the offices of SIP (the state telephone corporation), in the station and in Via Santa Maria.

Theatres

Rome has numerous theatres, and from time to time new ones are opened and old ones closed. The following is a selection:

Agorà,
Via della Renitenza 33; tel. 68 80 71 07.

Teatro Argentina,
Largo Torre Argentina; tel. 68 80 46 01/2 (mainly Italian classics).

Teatro Colosseo,
Via Capo d'Africa 5; tel. 7 00 49 32.

Teatro del Angelo,
Via Simoni de Saint Bon 17; tel. 3 70 00 93.

Teatro della Cometa,
Via del Teatro Marcello 4; tel. 6 78 43 80.

Teatro delle Arti,
Via Sicilia 59; tel. 4 81 85 98.

Teatro delle Muse,
Via Forli 43; tel. 44 23 13 00.

Teatro Eliseo,
Via Nazionale 183; tel. 4 88 21 14.

Teatro Ghione,
Via delle Fornaci 37; tel. 6 37 22 94.

Teatro Manzoni,
Via Montezebio 14/c; tel. 3 22 36 34.

Teatro Parioli,
Via G. Borsi 20; tel. 8 08 82 99.

Teatro Quirino,
Via M. Minghetti 1; tel. 6 79 45 85.

Teatro Sistina,
Via Sistina 129; tel. 4 75 68 41.

Teatro Valle,
Via del Teatro Valle 23/a; tel. 68 80 37 94.

Teatro Vittoria,
Piazza S. Maria Liberatrice 8; tel. 5 74 05 98.

Box offices
Since the various box offices usually have different opening times it is advisable to ring up and check the time of opening. The most usual hours are 10am–1pm and 4–6.30pm.

Programmes
The programmes of theatres and the Opera House are published in "La Settimana a Roma" (English edition "This Week in Rome") which can be bought at newspaper kiosks.

Opera/ballet
See Music

Time

Italy observes Central European Time (one hour ahead of Greenwich Mean Time; six hours ahead of New York time). From the beginning of April to the end of September summer time (two hours ahead of GMT; seven hours ahead of New York time) is in force.

Tipping (Mancia)

In hotels and restaurants service is inclusive; however, 5 to 10% of the total bill is still expected as a tip. In the "bars" (Italian cafés) service is not inclusive and 12 to 15% is normal.
A good general rule is to give a tip when some special service has been given, but everyone is pleased to have his or her services recognised in this way.

Tourist information

The first place to contact for information when you are planning a trip to Rome is the Italian State Tourist Office. Addresses:

United Kingdom
1 Princes Street, London W1A 7RA; tel. (0171) 408 1254.

500 North Michigan Avenue, Chicago, IL 60611;
   tel. (312) 644 0990–1.
630 Fifth Avenue, Suite 1565, New York, NY 10111;
   tel. (212) 245 4822–4.
360 Post Street, Suite 801, San Francisco, CA 94109;
   tel. (415) 392 6206–7.

United States of America

Store 56, Plaza, 3 Place Ville Marie, Montreal, Quebec;
   tel. (514) 866 7667.

Canada

Ente Nazionale per il Turismo (ENIT),
Via Marghera 2; tel. 4 97 11.
Information bureau; tel. 4 97 12 22, 4 97 12 82, 49 16 46.

In Rome

EPT di Roma, Via Parigi 11; tel. 48 89 91.

Ente Provinciale di Turismo (EPT)

In Stazione Termini; tel. 4 82 40 78, 4 87 12 70.
On Rome–Milan motorway (A1): Area di servizio Saleria Ovest;
   tel. 6 91 99 58.
On Rome–Naples motorway (A2): Area di servizio Frascati Est;
   tel. 9 46 43 41 (open only during the season).
Leonardo da Vinci Airport (Arrivals Hall); tel. 60 12 44 71, 6 01 12 55.

Other tourist information offices

Via Milano 18,
   tel. 46 42 05, 4 74 55 19.

Touristic information of the City of Rome

Ufficio Informazioni Pellegrini e Turisti, on S side of St Peter's Square;
   tel. 69 88 44 66.

Vatican Information Bureau

Compagnia Italiana Turismo (CIT)
(the official Italian travel agency).
Piazza della Repubblica 64; tel. 4 87 00 27.

CIT

In the city centre municipal police can be approached; on their left arm is a little shield indicating which foreign language(s) they speak.

Police

Transport

Eight tram routes and about 300 bus routes ensure an excellent public transport system in Rome; however, the heavy traffic in the inner city means that progress is often very slow.

Buses and Trams

A.T.A.C. (municipal transport system) information bureau at the Piazza dei Cinquecento (opposite Termini Station). Timetables for the buses and trams can be obtained here.

Information

Tickets must be bought in advance either individually or in a pack, before boarding the vehicle, in tobacconists' shops ("tabacchi") or from a newspaper kiosk. A ticket is valid for 75 minutes and can be used for one metro journey and as many bus journeys as you like. There is no conductor in the buses; passengers get on at the back where a red box will be found in which the tickets must be cancelled.
   The day ticket ("BIG") is valid for 24 hours without restriction. For tourists a special weekly ticket is available which is valid for 8 days on all routes and at all times. For a longer stay in Rome a monthly ticket ("tessera intera rete") is recommended. All these multiple tickets can be obtained at the information kiosk in the Piazza dei Cinquecento. Monthly tickets can also be bought in the "tabacchi".

Tickets

Travel documents

Underground (Metropolitana)	Line A: Via Ottaviano (near St Peter's), Flaminio (Piazza del Popolo), Piazza di Spangna, Piazza Barberini, Stazione Termini and from there to Cine-città and Anagnina. Line B: from Stazione Termini via San Paolo fuori le Mura to the EUR district (Via Laurentina).
Local railway (Ferrovia)	Roma–Lido (branch of Metropolitana, line B, from Piramide station to Lido di Ostia). Roma–Nord (from Flaminio station, Metropolitana line A, to Prima Porta).

A ticket for the Metropolitana can be obtained from a tobacconist or from a ticket machine at a Metropolitana station. There is also a monthly season ticket.

Travel documents

Passport	British and US citizens require only a passport (or the simpler British visitor's passport). This also applies to citizens of Canada, Ireland and many other countries. If you lose your passport a substitute document can be issued by the British, US, Canadian, etc., consulate. It is a good idea to photocopy or note down the principal particulars (number, date, etc.) of your passport, so that in case of loss you can give the necessary details to the police.
Driving licence, etc.	British, US and other national driving licences are valid in Italy, but must be accompanied by an Italian translation (obtainable free of charge from the AA). Motorists should also take the registration document of their car and display the national identity disc on their vehicle.
Green card	It is advisable (though not essential for EU nationals) to have an international insurance certificate (green card) if you are driving your own car.
Nationality plate	Foreign cars must display the oval nationality plate.

When to Go

The best times to visit Rome are the months from April to June, when the average temperature lies around 15 °C (59 °F) or September and October, when the average is 20 °C (69 °F).

In July and August life in Rome almost comes to a stop. The Romans curse the often unbearable heat (up to 40 °C/ 105 °F; average temperature 25 °C/77 °F) in the country and on the beaches. In these months half the shops remain closed which leads to protests by those who have remained in the city.

On the other hand the winter is certainly not mild. Even in Rome it can be unpleasantly cold, with average temperatures about 8 °C (46 °F) and heating is often inadequate. The bad weather lasts until well after Easter. Nevertheless the winter months offer an opportunity of seeing the sights of Rome in comfort. At Christmas and Easter, however, Rome is thronged with pilgrims; hotels and pensions are almost completely fully booked. Prospective visitors who do not wish to participate in the ceremonies and who have not booked their accommodation in good time should avoid Rome during these festivals.

Youth and Student hostels (Alberghi per la Gioventù)

Youth hostel	The youth hostels offer young tourists the cheapest form of accommodation; visitors under 30 years of age have priority. When hostels are full, accommodation is limited to maximum three nights in one hostel. In the

main season groups of over five people should book in advance. Visitors are not allowed to use their own sleeping-bags, which are provided by the hostels in the price of an overnight stay. A valid youth hostel association membership card from the visitor's own country is required.

Associazione Italiana Alberghi per la Gioventù
(Italian Youth Hostel Association),
Via Cavour 44 (3rd floor),
00184 Rome,
Italy;
tel. 46 23 42.

Ostello del Foro Italico, Viale delle Olimpiadi 61.

Centro Universitario Femminile,   Student hostels
Piazzale delle Scienze 9.

Centro Universitario Marinum,
Via del Boiardo 30.

Hospitium Gregorianum,
Salita di San Gregorio.

Istituto "Il Rosario",
Via Sant'Agatha dei Goti 10.

YWCA (female students only),
Via Balbo 4.

Useful Telephone Numbers at a Glance

Emergency calls
    General emergency   113
    First Aid (Red Cross)   55 10
    Police in Rome   46 86
    City Police (quick response)   6 76 91
    Carabinieri   112
    Medical emergencies   4 82 67 41
    Breakdown assistance   116
    Automobile Club d'Italia   5 75 67
    Railway Police   4 75 95 61

Information
    Italian State Tourist Office:
        London   (0171) 439 2311
        Chicago   (312) 644 0990–1
        New York   (212) 245 4822–4
        San Francisco   (415) 392 6206–7
        Rome   4 97 11
    EPT (Ente Provinciale di Turismo) di Roma   48 89 91
    Rail services: Roma Termini   47 75
                Roma Tiburtina   4 95 66 26
    Public transport (A.T.A.C.)   4 69 51
    Road conditions   44 77
    Guides   6 78 98 42
    Airport   60 12 36 40

Airlines
    British Airways   47 99 91
    TWA   47 21
    Canadian Airlines   4 88 35 14
    Cathay Pacific   4 82 07 03

Embassies
    United Kingdom   4 82 54 41
    United States   4 67 41
    Canada   44 59 81

Hospitals
    San Giovanni   7 70 51
    Santo Spirito   6 83 51
    Policlinico Umberto   4 46 14 81

Taxis   35 70, 38 75, 49 94

Telephone
    Information: International calls   174/1790
                Internal calls   12
    International calls   15
    Dialling code for the United Kingdom   00 44
    Dialling codes for USA and Canada   001

    Dialling codes for Rome:
    from the United Kingdom   010 39 6
    from the United States or Canada   011 39 6

Index

Warning!

Take good care of your property.

Particularly in built–up areas of towns thefts are a daily occurrence as are handbag snatching; taking of luggage, cameras, binoculars, watches, jewellery and other valuables; thefts in hotels, bars, shops, railway trains, filling stations, on the open road and even while driving (e.g. when slowly approaching a red traffic light). Breaking into and stealing from cars (even from hired cars with Italian number plates), but especially from caravans, mini buses and even large touring buses is commonplace.

Visitors are therefore strongly advised to carry all their valuables (documents, money, cheques, cheque cards and keys) always on their person and to leave absolutely nothing in vehicles which are left out in the open (leave the glove box and the boot empty and do not lock them). At night, if possible, one should keep a car in a locked garage (with insurance protection).

Although the Italian police are always ready to help, in practice they are often powerless against highly organised gangs of thieves. In the event of being robbed the police can normally merely supply a statement, which is necessary for insurance purposes.

If Eurocheques and/or cheque cards are lost one should immediately notify the issuing office so that unauthorised use can be prevented.

Imprint

135 colour photographs
12 plans, 1 coat of arms, 1 large city map

Conception and editorial work
Redaktionsbüro Harenberg, Schwerte
English language edition: Alec Court

Original text: Dr Madeleine Reincke, Dr Heinz Joachim Fisher
Editing and revising: Baedeker-Redaktion (Carmen Galenschovski, Dr Madeleine Reincke)

General direction:
Dr Peter Baumgarten, Baedeker Stuttgart
English translation: James Hogarth
Revising: Barbara Cresswell, Margaret Court

Cartography:
Gert Oberländer, Munich
Hallweg AG, Berne (city map)

Source of illustrations:
Bader (1), dpa (23), Italian State Tourist office (5), Mauritius (1), Prenzel (1), Rogge (7), Uthoff (37)

5th English edition 1995

© Baedeker Stuttgart
Original German edition 1995

© 1995 Jarrold and Sons Ltd
English language edition worldwide

© 1995 The Automobile Association
United Kingdom and Ireland

Published in the United States by:
Macmillan Travel
A Simon & Schuster Macmillan Company
1633 Broadway
New York, NY 10019–6785

Macmillan is a registered trademark of Macmillan, Inc.

Distributed in the United Kingdom by the Publishing Division of the Automobile Association, Fanum House, Basingstoke, Hampshire RG21 2EA

Licensed user: Mairs Geographischer Verlag GmbH & Co., Ostfildern-Kemnat bei Stuttgart

The name *Baedeker* is a registered trademark

A CIP catalogue record of this book is available from the British Library

Printed in Italy by G. Canale & C.S.p.A – Borgaro T.se –Turin

ISBN 0–02–860118–1 US and Canada
      0 7495 1162 1 UK

Notes

Notes